THE THEATRE OF RAFAEL ALBERTI

LOUISE B. POPKIN

THE THEATRE OF
RAFAEL ALBERTI

TAMESIS BOOKS LIMITED

LONDON

Colección Támesis
SERIE A - MONOGRAFIAS, XLVII

Depósito Legal : M. 25.802-1976
I. S. B. N. 84-399-5189-2

Printed in Spain by Artes Gráficas Clavileño, S. A.
Pantoja, 20 - Madrid-2

for

TAMESIS BOOKS LIMITED
LONDON

To my teachers and my students

TABLE OF CONTENTS

PREFACE

Alberti's theatre has been neglected by Spanish scholars and directors alike. Only three of his eight major works have ever been performed in Spain [1]. *Several minor works remain unpublished or can only be obtained in rare editions. The bibliography on Alberti's theatre continues to be meagre. A few literary historians recall the stylistic extravagances of his first works and his eccentric behavior at the time of performance. Two of his plays have caught the attention of critics because they shed light on some of his more difficult poetry* [2]. *Around the time of his sixtieth birthday, there appeared a couple of minor articles on several of the longer works* [3]. *Juan Guerrero Zamora in his* Historia del teatro contemporáneo [4], *Francisco Ruiz Ramón in his* Historia del teatro español siglo XX [5], *and Ricardo Domenech in a recent article* [6] *have each devoted a substantial number of pages to most of the major plays. Domingo Pérez Minik mentions Alberti in a brief discussion of the theatre of the exile* [7]. *Recently one work has been the subject of a more extensive critical study* [8].

1 However, several of these plays have been translated into diverse European languages, including French, German, Swedish, Italian, English, Polish. Some of them have been performed abroad in Argentina, Sweden, France, Germany and the U.S.A. Specific information regarding translations and performances in Spain and elsewhere is contained in Robert Marrast, «Essai de bibliographie de Rafael Alberti», *Bulletin Hispanique*, 57 (1955), 147-77; *ibid.*, 59 (1957), 430-35; Horacio Becco, ed., «Bibliografía de Rafael Alberti», in Rafael Alberti, *Poesías completas* (Buenos Aires: Losada [c 1961]), pp. 1110-27. Performances outside of Spain have been indicated in subsequent footnotes only if they took place in Spanish.

2 See Geoffrey W. Connell, «The Autobiographical Element in *Sobre los ángeles*», *Bulletin of Hispanic Studies*, 40 (July 1963), 160-73; Cyril B. Morris, «Las imágenes claves de *Sobre los ángeles*», *Insula* 18, No. 198 (1963), 12 and 14; and his *Rafael Alberti's «Sobre los ángeles»: Four Major Themes* ([Hull]: University of Hull, 1966).

3 Ventura Doreste, «Sobre el teatro de Alberti», *Papeles de Son Armadans*, 30, 80-90; Fernando Guimarães, «Alguns aspectos do teatro de Rafael Alberti ou o homen sustituido pelos mitos», *Estrada Larga* (Porto), 1962, pp. 679-83.

4 Juan Guerrero Zamora, «Rafael Alberti», in *Historia del teatro contemporáneo* (Barcelona: Juan Flores, 1962), III, 97-112.

5 Francisco Ruiz Ramón, «Alberti», in *Historia del teatro español siglo XX* (Madrid: Alianza [1971]), II, 227-45.

6 Ricardo Domenech, «Introducción al teatro de Rafael Alberti», *Cuadernos Hispanoamericanos*, 259 (January 1972), pp. 95-126. Since we learned of the existence of this article only recently, we have not made use of it in our study.

7 Domingo Pérez Minik, «Cinco españoles fuera de España», in *Teatro europeo contemporáneo* (Madrid: [Guadarrama], 1961), pp. 499-501.

8 Richard A. Cardwell, «Rafael Alberti's, *El hombre deshabitado*», *Iberoromania* (München) 2, 122-33. Like that of R. Domenech, this article came to our attention too late for us to incorporate it into our study.

To date, however, only the French professor and bibliographer Robert
Marrast has taken a special interest in Alberti's plays. In a book and several
articles, he has identified their personal and literary sources. On the basis
of his findings, he characterizes the opus as a whole [9].

In the pages that follow, we take another look at Alberti's dramatic
opus. We describe his plays, trace the evolution of a number of persistent
stylistic traits, draw certain inferences regarding his growth and development
as a playwright, call attention to the importance of his contribution to
twentieth-century theatrical reform. Our first chapter, devoted to a consideration of the author's life and times, is intended to provide background
for the critical discussion that follows. In chapters two through five of our
study we examine each of Alberti's plays in chronological order, analyzing
and evaluating each in terms of its quality and complexity and specifying
its relationship to the other works. Every chapter covers roughly a decade
and what we consider to be a period in the playwright's career. Our
chapter summaries and conclusion represent an attempt to define Alberti's
theatre as a whole and situate him with respect to the traditions of the
Spanish stage. We have chosen to omit from our study any detailed analysis
of the translations of foreign works, adaptations and works of mixed genre
which complete the list of Alberti's activities in the theatre. Clearly each
of these is significant, deserving of attention in itself, and represents
valuable experience for our author; however we believe that a study of the
original works provides an adequate basis for understanding the search
by means of which Alberti became a man of the theatre.

Certain aspects of Professor Marrast's work have been invaluable to us
in carrying out our own research. In dealing with the matter of sources,
we have made extensive use of his documentation and insights. However,
we have had access to four texts which Marrast has not considered; also
we approach Alberti's theatre from a different perspective. Thus for the
most part, our conclusions supplement and complement his. Marrast's
interest in Alberti's theatre is primarily biographical and centers upon the
thematic relationship between the author's life and his work. Whereas the
French critic frequently bases his reading of Alberti's plays on the playwright's experience, we have followed the critical method set forth by
Warren and Wellek in A Theory of Literature [10], seeking meaning only
within the texts themselves. While we agree with Marrast that there is
a relationship between Alberti's life and his work, we believe that vital
factors had their most important effect on the quality rather than the
content of his plays. As we shall attempt to argue, an awareness of certain
of Alberti's experiences enables us to follow him in his long and arduous
journey from apprenticeship to mastery. By viewing these experiences as

---

[9] Professor Marrast first developed his ideas in an unpublished thesis (Uni-
versité de Bordeaux, 1954). He has reiterated and developed them further in
several articles which are cited in subsequent footnotes. An abridged version of his
thesis has appeared in print under the title *Aspects du Théâtre de Rafael Alberti*
(Paris: Société d'Edition d'Enseignement Supérieure, 1967). In citing Professor
Marrast's opinions, we refer to the latter unless otherwise indicated.

[10] René Wellek and Austin Warren, *A Theory of Literature* (N.Y.: Harcourt
Brace [c1956]).

sources of interference, obstacles to be overcome, we can understand how
stylistic diversity and eclectic expertise arose out of the playwright's initial
diffuseness and uncertainty.

Bibliographic citations from Alberti's plays, poetry and memoirs have
been included in the body of the text. For the seven plays currently in
print, we quote from R. Alberti, Teatro, I, 2nd ed. (Buenos Aires: Losada
[c 1959]), II (Buenos Aires: Losada [c 1963]). For the author's personal
recollections we have used R. Alberti, La arboleda perdida: libros I y II
de memorias (Buenos Aires: Fabril, 1959). Unless otherwise specified,
poetic citations are taken from Becco's edition of the Poesías completas [11].
All other sources are identified in footnotes.

We should like to express our sincere gratitude to several people without
whose aid the following study would have been difficult if not impossible.
Our thanks go to Professor Roberto Sánchez, who directed the dissertation
out of which this study grew and taught us virtually all we know about
theatre; to Professor Robert Marrast for his invaluable advice in the initial
stages of our research and for his generosity in making available to us all
of the documentation which he had at his disposal—bibliographic data,
personal letters, newspaper clippings and numerous rare editions; to our
friend and colleague Mathis Szykowski who read the manuscript with a
keen analytical sense and offered numerous suggestions regarding style
and organization; to Victor Berch who made available to us a number of
items from the Spanish Civil War collection of the Brandeis University
library; to our former students Patricia Menges, Lynn Walterick, Ann
Matter and Renée Page who spent many hours typing and transcribing.

---

[11] Hereafter, the two volumes of the *Teatro* are cited as I and II respectively,
La arboleda perdida appears as AP, and the *Poesías completas* as PC.

ABBREVIATIONS USED IN FOOTNOTES

I ... ...   Volume One, Losada edition of the *Teatro*.

II ... ...   Volume Two, Losada edition of the *Teatro*.

AP ... ...   *La arboleda perdida.*

PC ... ...   *Poesías completas,* ed. Becco.

PP ... ...   *La pájara pinta.*

EM ... ...   *El enamorado y la muerte.*

FG ... ...   *Fermín Galán.*

DFR ... ...   *Dos farsas revolucionarias.*

CHAPTER I

THE MAN, THE POET, THE PLAYWRIGHT

Cadiz: 1902-1917

Rafael Alberti was born on December 16, 1902 «en una inespe-
rada noche de tormenta, según alguna vez oí a mi madre, y en uno
de esos blancos puertos que se asoman a la perfecta bahía gaditana: El Puerto de Santa María» (PC, p. 11). His grandparents had
been the wealthy owners of vineyards and wine cellars. They had
been men of influence and purveyors of kings, according to the
faded labels that the youth would come upon years later in the
cracks and hidden crevices of the household. But the author himself was not to know the meaning of affluence. Toward the end
of the century, the family fortunes had taken a turn for the worse :
the Albertis had lost their money and their business. Thus, the
author's father had to work as the travelling representative of
another manufacturer of wines from El Puerto and some of the
memorialist's earliest recollections involve financial hardship.

Alberti evokes certain aspects of his home life during his for-
mative years with a great deal of nostalgia. As he describes his big
white house on Calle de Santo Domingo, its red-tiled patio—the
scene of his childhood games—is inseparably bound up with ten-
der and good-humored recollections of his brothers and sisters. He
recalls with special affection his mother's passion for botany, her
candorous religious faith and her love of tradition :

> Como andaluza criada entre patios de cal y jardines... sabía del
> injerto y la poda de los rosales, conocía las leyendas mil veces
> reinventadas de los narcisos, las pasionarias, las anémonas, las

1 The following account of Alberti's life is based primarily on AP and the
autobiographical introduction to PC. We have also made extensive use of Claude
Couffon, *Rafael Alberti* ([Paris] : Seghers [c1966]) and the memoirs of Alberti's
wife María Teresa León, *Memoria de la melancolía* (Buenos Aires : Losada, [1970]).
Minor bibliographic items which were not of special interest to us have not been
mentioned. References to the many lesser poetic works, prologues, editions of
Spanish authors, translations of foreign works, newspaper articles, unpublished lectures and minor prose works which we have omitted are contained in the biblio-
graphies of Becco and Marrast.

> siemprevivas...; recordaba por centenares los nombres de las flore-
> cillas silvestres, que ella me enseñaba en la práctica cuando los
> domingos salíamos al campo... Era, por todo esto, una mujer rara
> y delicada, que tanto como a sus santos y sus vírgenes amaba las
> plantas y las fuentes, las canciones de Schubert, que tocaba al
> piano, las coplas y romances del sur, que a mí sólo me transmitía
> quizás por ser el único de la casa que le atrayeran sus cultos y
> aficiones.
>
> (AP, p. 22.)

Two servants who were considered part of the Alberti family,
also occupy a preferential place in the author's memoirs. Old
Paca Moy was the children's *nana* and the patient victim of innumerable pranks. Federico is portrayed as «[un] hombre de pueblo,
arrumbador de la antigua bodega de mi padre, lleno de imagina-
ción y muy aficionado al contenido de los barriles que él mismo
trabajaba y pulía» (AP, p. 23). Together with Dona María, these
two servants must have had a decisive influence on Alberti's literary career. Without a doubt, they provided some of the child's
first direct contacts with the world of Andalusian folklore.

It may well have been Federico who first awakened Alberti's
interest in the theatre. The memorialist recalls with relish the
arrumbador's 'dramatic' contribution to the yearly Christmas celebration. Each year there was an excursion to the forest «[en
busca de] el enebro, el pino, y el lentisco que luego habían de ar-
borecer los montes y los valles empapelados por su fantasía» (AP,
p. 23). Then Federico would oversee the construction of a marvelous *Belén:*

> Aquel teatro compuesto de papeles pegados con engrudo a una
> armazón de tablas; encrespado de serranías sobre las que una
> brocha sumida en albayalde hisopaba desde lejos la nieve; aquella
> escena donde unos diminutos personajes de barro representaban el
> misterio de la natividad de Cristo; aquel Belén concebido por Fe-
> derico... surgía, al fin, ante nuestro asombro, como una maravilla
> de gracia.
>
> (AP, p. 25.)

This «delicada y finísima creación del genio popular andaluz» would
serve as a backdrop for comic improvisations. Usually they were
carried out over the loud protestations of Paca Moy:

> Paca Moy le temía [a Federico], porque quitándole el mantón
> y pintándose la cara con un corcho quemado la imitaba, hacién-
> donos reír a todos. Así con bigotes de tizne, sudoroso y siempre
> algo bebido, reinventaba o improvisaba... ante su Belén y al son

de la zambomba bailes y villancicos, con los mismos aciertos y desigualdades que un juglar primitivo.

(AP, p. 25.)

Unlike these beloved figures, the other members of the Alberti household occasioned a good deal of misery for the author. Thus, he often writes of them with a bitter and mordant humor. During his father's business trips to the north of Spain, he was subject to the authority of a group of eccentric and narrow-minded aunts and uncles. Their perpetual spying was a constant source of annoyance :

> En todas partes me los encontraba. Salían, de improviso, de los lugares más inesperados: de detrás de una roca, cuando, por ejemplo, convertía la clase de aritmética en una alegre mañana pescadora entre el castillo de la pólvora y Santa Catalina, frente a Cádiz; o tras una pirámide de sal, la tarde que el latín me hacía coger la orilla de los pinos, en dirección a San Fernando. Tíos y tías por el norte, por el este, por el oeste, por el sur de la ciudad y a cualquier hora: al mediodía, a las tres, bajo la violencia de los soles más duros, al doblar una esquina, fijos en el portal menos imaginado ; a las ocho, de noche, en el banco de piedra de algún paseo solitario, o hablando solos, de rodillas, en el rincón oscuro de la iglesia más apartada.

(AP, p. 15.)

These extravagant beings, whose antics fill the pages of *La arboleda perdida*, would also people Alberti's stage. Years later, the playwright would recreate the repressive atmosphere with which they surrounded him in an autobiographical work entitled *De un momento a otro* (1938). Subsequently he would echo their religious fanaticism in the insanely superstitious ambiance of *El adefesio* (1944).

Alberti received most of his formal education at the Colegio de San Luis Gonzaga. His memories of school are almost totally negative. As a youth he was innately curious and passionately interested in Spanish history and geography ; but he found the Jesuits' traditional approach to education exceedingly boring. During his first year, he made an attempt at being a diligent student. After that he claims to have learned hardly anything at all.

A naturally rebellious spirit, Alberti lost no opportunity to escape to the forbidden liberty of his Andalusia—the Andalusia «llena de transatlánticos y veleros al viento relampagueante de la bahía» that would provide the setting for his earliest poems (AP,

p. 121). Often he would simply lie daydreaming among the dunes
—«mi refugio ardoroso, mi fresca guarida, mientras las duras horas
de las matemáticas y los rosarios del atardecer» (AP, p. 49). At
other times, an adolescent flair for the dramatic led him to act
out his fantasies. The results were frequently embarrassing. On
one occasion, the streets of El Puerto became the setting for an
innocent love affair. The author played the role of romantic hero,
climbing walls and dispatching secret letters. Eventually he was
discovered by one of his aunts and punished with expulsion from
school (AP, p. 81). As a youth he also made numerous excursions
to the pastures of his uncle José Luis de la Cuesta. There he would
rehearse clumsy *pasos de torero* among the cows and calves of
the herd. It was probably during one such outing that he decided
to grow the *coleta* which was to cause a great commotion in school
one day ; mischievously exposed by a classmate, it was promptly
severed from the head of its owner (AP, p. 47).

These adventures which constitute Alberti's only positive recollections of his schooldays were not simply his response to a «dead
and anti-vital world of books» [2]. They were an escape from the
same Catholic and bourgeois pressures to which the child was
subjected at home. Alberti was bothered by the narrow-mindedness
of his teachers, their obsession with chastity and guilt, their hy-
pocrital claims of adherence to Christian doctrine. He also suffered a great deal because of his status as an *alumno externo*.
In the hierarchy of the Colegio, to be an *externo* was to be singled
out as a second-class citizen ; only the pensioners or *internos* were
entitled to wear the school uniform with gilded epaulets. In Alberti's case, the snobbish and unfriendly attitude of the wealthier
boys meant almost total isolation. The other *externos* apparently
considered themselves far too worldly for his youthful games and
daydreams.

According to Alberti's biographers, the author's unhappy experiences at home and at school had a significant effect on his
personality and literary career. The feeling of *déclassé* which
appears in his writing during the 1930s probably had its origin
in the precarious economic situation of his family and his inferior
status at the Colegio. These same factors may have been responsible for the strong anti-bourgeois sentiment that led him to enter
the ranks of the Communist party [3]. Similarly, one can single out
the fanaticism of Alberti's elders as the source of his future attitudes regarding religion : his violent rejection of Catholic doctrine

[2] Geoffrey W. Connell, «A Recurring Theme in the Poetry of Rafael Alberti»,
Renaissance and Modern Studies, 3 (1959), 97.
[3] *Ibid.*, p. 102 ff.

and his furious anti-clericalism probably grew out of the parochial attitudes surrounding his religious training [4].

Madrid: 1917-1927

In 1917, the author's family had to move to Madrid for economic reasons. Their small dark apartment on Calle de Atocha was the source of much anguish for young Alberti. How far he was from the sun-drenched spaces and broad horizons of the Bay of Cadiz! Nevertheless, the youth quickly made his peace with life in the capital. There he found the opportunity to pursue a growing interest in painting.

In reality, Alberti's enthusiasm for the graphic arts was already apparent during his last years in El Puerto. But the possibilities for practice had been limited by academic and family pressures. Now in Madrid, he was free of obligations. He had announced his intentions to quit school, promising to complete the *bachillerato* on his own. After some procrastination, a failing grade in literary theory led him to abandon his formal studies altogether. He resorted to white lies and falsified documents in an effort to appease his parents. Subsequently, he considered himself «on vacation» and thought no more about the matter.

For Alberti, Madrid was a city of museums. Eager to *hacer academias* in accord with then current pedagogical ideas, he headed first for the Museo de Reproducciones. There he spent several months copying the marble figures. Then he moved on to the Prado. The memorialist describes the wonder that he felt during his first direct encounters with the masterpieces of the past. «No sé por qué», he writes, «acostumbrado únicamente en mi pueblo andaluz a las malas reproducciones en colores y a ciertos paisajes de escuela velazqueña vistos en casa de mis abuelos, yo pensaba que la pintura antigua sería toda de sombra, de pardas terrosidades, incapaz de los azules, los rojos, los rosas, los oros, los verdes, y los blancos que se me revelaban de súbito en Velázquez, Tiziano, Tintoretto, Rubens, Zurbarán, Goya...» (AP, pp. 106-7). He goes on to record his surprise at discovering that the walls of the museum were not covered exclusively with «demonios, ángeles, vírgenes, cristos, santos, papas, frailes, y monjas de todas clases...» (AP, p. 107).

One of the great revelations that the Prado held for the youth were the works of Goya, of which he writes the following:

[4] See AP, p. 31.

Las salas de Goya, en las que se colgaban todos sus cartones
para la Real Fábrica de Tapices, me abrían cada mañana los ojos a
una fiesta... alzada en medio de la triste, solemne pintura española
como un chorro de gracia, de refrescante y alegre trasparencia.
Verbena popular de los colores, pregón fino de España. Juego del
aire de la calle, traje de luces de los atardeceres de calesas, cometas
voladoras y estrellas de artificio... Una España... capaz de clari-
dades, de una sonrisa delicada, de un corazón desparramado y casi
estrepitoso en su sana alegría. Mas para cruel contraste, no lejos...
se hallaban los dibujos y parte, si no recuerdo mal, de los feroces
muros de la Quinta del Sordo... como lanzando un rayo de oscuridad mordiente sobre aquel ruedo luminoso, definiendo así lo que
Goya y toda la España que le tocó representar eran realmente: un
inmenso ruedo taurino partido con violencia en dos colores: negro
y blanco. Blanco de sol y lozanía. Negro hondo de sombra, de
negra sangre coagulada.

(AP, pp. 110-11.)

Alberti had discovered in the Aragonese painter a kindred soul,
whose vision encompassed the many faces of a Spain which he
himself knew. The playwright would echo this encounter years
later in a dramatic work entitled *Noche de Guerra en el Museo del
Prado* (1956). Alberti's apprenticeship in these halls that would
one day serve as the setting for his play brought certain immediate
results as well. We know that he exhibited two paintings in the
so-called *Sala del Crimen*—that part of the Salón Nacional de
Otoño where new painters displayed their works. His name figures
significantly in the art-gallery world between 1917 and 1923.

During the time that he was discovering the treasures of the
Prado, Alberti also explored diverse facets of city life. Ultimately,
his desire for live subjects led him to abandon the museum in
favor of the Retiro, the Jardín Botánico, the Moncloa, and the
banks of the Manzanares. «La calle ya más que los museos era mi
escuela», he writes. «Cuando no repetía hasta el infinito escenas
de albañiles tumbados o comiendo bajo los árboles, cuando no di-
bujaba carretas descargando maderas y ladrillos ante las construc-
ciones, paseaba observando la ciudad o recitando versos en las
tardes primaverales con mis amigos...» (AP, p. 131). The streets
of Madrid provided Alberti with schooling in art and in life. As a
result of this experience, he began to feel at home in the capital.
He would always yearn nostalgically for the beaches of Cadiz, and
a longing for the sea was to become a permanent presence in his
writing. Nevertheless, what the memorialist recalls most vividly
about a brief visit to his native city in 1919, is his disappointment
at finding that friends and family had disappeared.

Since Alberti was somewhat sickly by nature, his disordered existence, erratic schedule and characteristic lack of moderation were bound to prove detrimental to his health. Around 1923, he began to suffer fainting spells. One day, a blood-stained handkerchief revealed the presence of a pulmonary lesion. Consequently, the years 1923 and 1924 brought long periods of confinement, in Madrid, in the family's new apartment on Calle de Lagasca, and at a sanatorium in San Rafael, a town in the Sierra de Guadarrama.

Around 1920, the young man had begun to exhibit a marked fondness for poetry. First, encouraged by his friends, he read a great deal; then, there followed his first attempts at writing. In *La arboleda perdida*, Alberti cites 1920 as the date of composition for his first poem. His father's death was the experience which gave rise to his poet's calling:

> Yo me iba de mi casa, en busca de la soledad, por las afueras de mi barrio. La llanura, con sus chopos ensimismados, y el Guadarrama azul en lejanía, fueron mis buenos compañeros de aquellos meses. Me quedaba en el campo hasta muy atardecido. Y—¡oh milagro!—me seguían saliendo los poemas como brotados de una fuente misteriosa que llevara conmigo y no pudiera contener.

(AP, p. 141.)

Now, in the long months of isolation and idleness occasioned by his illness, the author filled his life with books. He read Tolstoy, Dostoyevsky, Chekov, Andreiev—the Russian novelists who only recently had begun to be published in Spain. Leafing through the pages of *Ultra*, he became acquainted with the vanguard tendencies from Europe. He read Machado, Juan Ramón, and the Spanish Renaissance poets: Juan del Encina, Gil Vicente, the *Cancionero de Barbieri*. These voices out of Spain's artistic past would be echoed in his earliest writings. During the years of his exile, they would provide a vicarious link with his beloved homeland.

Slowly, there grew in Alberti the determination to abandon his career as a painter and devote himself entirely to literature. The farewell came in 1923, with an exposition organized by Juan Chabás in the Ateneo de Madrid. Years later he would experience a sudden reawakening of his earlier interest. A keen visual sense, a preponderance of plastic and coloristic images, and a fine sense of spectacle would continue to reflect his training in the graphic arts. However, Alberti would henceforth be a writer by profession. In 1923, after several stays in San Rafael, his *Marinero en tierra* was completed. The following year, that first book of poems would win him the Premio Nacional de Literatura, heralding the arrival on the literary scene of his «maestría alada, aireado vuelo, ingrávido don de musical acierto» [5]. After he had recovered from his long illness, Alberti continued to write verse. His second and third books of poetry were largely the fruit of two trips undertaken between 1924 and 1926. An extensive journey through Castile and the Basque country in 1925 inspired the tome entitled *La amante* (1925). A second long trek took the author through Andalusia —Almería, Málaga and Rute, a small town in Córdoba where one of his married sisters was living. The memorable moments of this trip would be echoed in *El alba del alhelí* (1926) [6].

Alberti's stay in Rute—«aquel dramático pueblo andaluz al pie del Monte de las Cruces... saturado de terror religioso, entrecruzado de viejas supersticiones populares»—, was to have important consequences for his theatre. There, the author encountered the curious case of a mysterious and beautiful maiden, known locally as *la encerrada*. «Allí en el barrio alto», the chronicler recalls, «vivía una hermosa muchacha... a la que solamente podía vérsele, siempre en compañía de alguien, tapado el rostro por un velo, durante la misa de alba» (AP, p. 189). The author goes on to speak of her desperate plight, the sentiments that she and her custodians inspired in the men of the town, her eventual suicide:

> Corrían sobre esta joven las más raras y hasta torpes leyendas... Tanto la madre como las tías que la custodiaban tenían el odio de los hombres, quienes soñaban con la muchacha, deseándola abierta y desvergonzadamente. También mi sueño se llenó de ella, naciendo en mí... un ansia acongojada de arrancarla de aquellas negras sombras vigilantes que así martirizaban su belleza, su pobre juventud entre cuatro paredes. Con el amanecer... me encaminaba ya de prisa hacia la iglesia, ocultándome entre las columnas del atrio, ilusionado con verla llegar... no acompañada sino presa por dos—y hasta por cuatro a veces—de sus tías, espantables rebujos de miradas redondas, desafiantes. Acabada la misa... la veía perderse nuevamente... camino de su cárcel en el barrio alto. Nunca en la calle ni en la iglesia... pude cruzarme con sus ojos... Nunca supe tampoco si tras aquellas rejas y celosías de su casa alguna vez sus ojos se atrevieron... a dirigirse a los míos. Sólo supe más tarde que 'la encerrada'... siguiendo una triste tradición muy an-

[5] Juan Chabás, *Literatura española contemporánea: 1898-1950* (La Habana: Cultural, 1952), p. 429.
[6] There is some question as to the date of this second trip. Alberti recalls having made it in 1926 (PC, p. 12). Arguing that some of the poems of *El alba del alhelí* antedate those of *La amante*, Solita Salinas de Marichal gives 1924 (cf. *El mundo poético de Rafael Alberti* [Madrid: Gredos (c 1968)], pp. 108 ff.).

tigua en su pueblo, se había suicidado. Las causas no me las dijeron nunca. Nunca llegaron hasta mí.

(AP, p. 189-90.)

Alberti concludes his narration by attesting to the impact which this strangely sequestered existence was to have on his career as a writer. It was to provide the inspiration for several of the poems of *El alba del alhelí*. In addition, it would suggest the plot line for one of his plays:

> Con lo que sabía ya de ella y sus terribles guardianas, pude también, pasados casi veinte años tejer mi fábula del amor y las viejas, a la que por todo el horror moral y físico que respira titulé *El adefesio*.

(AP, p. 190.)

Given his natural receptivity and the eclectic attitude which he shared with his contemporaries, Alberti's development as a writer cannot be understood apart from his cultural milieu. His debut as a poet came during the early part of the period known as the *Entreguerra*. The Dictatorship was in full swing and, as life was relatively peaceful, intellectuals had turned their backs on history. Elitism and experimentation were the first order of the day.

For some time, the winds of innovation had been blowing over the Pyrenees, bringing with them the cries of rebellion and new literary vogues of the European vanguard. But almost as soon as the infectious series of *Ismos* made its noisy entrance into Spain there occurred a change. The generation that would profit most from the example of their European counterparts tempered its iconoclasm with a reawakening of interest in tradition. In the pages of *Horizonte* and *Alfar*, and later in the *Gaceta Literaria*, the signatures of the younger writers appear alongside such revered names as Azorín, Unamuno and Juan Ramón Jiménez. Literary research soon replaced the manifesto as a means of defining the vanguard tendencies. The impulse that drove these artists from the heat of combat into the seclusion of their studies was symptomatic of their conciliatory and receptive attitude. According to Alberti, this would distinguish «[la] nueva y verdadera vanguardia [que] íbamos a ser nosotros» (AP, p. 168).

An important testing ground for the new theories were several centers of artistic ferment, including the famed Residencia de Estudiantes—point of convergence of many of the stellar members of the Generation of '27. While Alberti never lived at the Residencia, he was a familiar presence in its rooms and gardens. He maintained close professional and personal ties with its inhabi-

tants. Sharing the enthusiasm of his contemporaries, and their simultaneous orientation toward past and future, he participated
actively in their tireless questioning and endless debates. He also
took part in the numerous public events which followed in the
wake of their discussions. One of these was the famed *Homenaje
a Góngora* held on the 300th anniversary of the Cordoban poet's
death. This experience led directly to the composition of *Cal y Can
to* (1927), Alberti's fourth book of poetry.

Notwithstanding the seriousness of purpose and artistic integrity of its inhabitants and *habitués*, life at the Residencia was far
from lacking in humor. As Moreno Villa tells us, «[allí] todo tenía
un aire de juego» [7]. The numerous anecdotes with which he and
Alberti fill their memoirs indicate that these artists were capable
of imparting a comic and irreverent dimension to the most solemn
of events. A high-spirited playfulness—typical of the vanguard as
a whole—appears to have taken a somewhat original form for Alberti and his contemporaries; *nanas* and children's rhymes
enjoyed a widespread popularity among the poets of '27. According
to certain critics, this was the Spaniards' characteristically traditional version of the more extravagant literary games of their
European counterparts [8].

As a result of this renewed interest in children's literature,
Alberti wrote his earliest extant play. The brief work entitled *La
pájara pinta* was composed in 1925 and presented around 1930 in
the gardens of the Instituto Escuela [9]. *La pájara pinta* is a nonsense play for puppets, full of the winged and playful echoes of
children's rhymes. Clearly it is a joyful recreation of elements out
of the author's past. At the same time it is an important indication
of his sensitivity to contemporary vogues. From the beginning of
his career, Alberti has existed in symbiotic relation to his surroundings. His own interests have helped to determine the literary
trends of the day, and external circumstances have provided a
natural outlet for his artistic and vital needs. Though there is
evidence that the playwright initiated several other projects during
the 1920s, we know very little about these since we do not have
the texts. What we do know however, suggests that they are to

---

[7] José Moreno Villa, *Vida en claro* (México: Colegio de México [1944]), p. 146.
[8] See Carmen Bravo Villasante, *Historia de la literatura infantil española*
([Madrid]: Doncel, 1963), I, 152-54; Cyril B. Morris, *A Generation of Spanish
Poets: 1920-1936* (London: Cambridge University Press, 1969), chs. 1 and 2.
[9] According to Sra. Bravo *(op. cit.,* p. 154), this performance took place in
1935. Marrast gives the date as 1931 (cf. «Prólogo», in Rafael Alberti, «*Lope de
Vega y la poesía contemporánea*» seguido de «*La Pájara Pinta*» [Paris: Centre de
Recherches de l'Institut d'Etudes Hispaniques (c 1964)], p. xi). Marrast also informs
us that Oscar Esplá and Federico Elizalde collaborated on a musical version of
Alberti's play, performed in 1932 at the Salle Gaveau in Paris

be regarded along with *La pájara pinta*, as constituting a first stage in his career as a dramatist.

Given the openly conventional and stylized nature of Alberti's own works, what we know of his early preferences as a theatregoer does not surprise us. He frequently attended the opera and the ballet. To paraphrase the memorialist himself, he was repulsed by «tenores cursis de cara empalagosa» (AP, p. 129). He took a special interest in details of production and staging. What impressed him most about Diaghilev's production of Manuel de Falla's *Three Cornered Hat* were Picasso's sets, which he perceived in intimate relationship to the choreography:

> ¡Aquel maravilloso telón añil sobre aquel sugerido puentecillo de ojos negros, aquella cal hirviente de los muros y el pozo, toda aquella simple y cálida geometría que se abrazaba fusionándose al quiebro colorido de los bailarines!

Alberti further asserts that the Russian Ballet offered «el más nuevo lenguaje, la más audaz expresión del nuevo ritmo corporal, musical y pictórico que inauguraba el siglo veinte» (AP, p. 130). These comments are suggestive of the future playwright's extreme fondness for visual rhythmic effects. Equally foreseeable was his early interest in cinema as a potential source of technical innovation; Alberti saw in the movies «una nueva visión, un nuevo sentimiento que a la larga arrumbaría de una vez al viejo mundo desmoronado ya entre las ruinas de la guerra europea» (AP, p. 239). In these words, we can sense the presence of the future scenographer. His images would often succeed one another with cinematographic velocity and fluidity.

At the crossroads: 1928-1932

1. *Years of crisis (1928-1931)*

The years 1928 to 1931 were a time of great spiritual ferment for Alberti, a moment of crisis that would have a decisive influence on his future work. In *La arboleda perdida* the author cites 1928 as the terrible moment when he suddenly found himself plunged into darkness:

> ¿Qué espadazo de sombra me separó casi insensiblemente de la luz, de la forma marmórea de mis poemas inmediatos, del canto aún no lejano de las fuentes populares, de mis barcos, esteros y salinas, para arrojarme en aquel pozo de tinieblas, aquel agujero

de oscuridad, en el que bracearía casi en estado agónico, pero violentamente, por encontrar una salida a las superficies habitadas, al puro aire de la vida?... Yo no podía dormir, me dolían las raíces del pelo y de las uñas, derramándome en bilis amarilla, mordiendo de punzantes dolores la almohada.

(AP, p. 268) [10].

Among the multiple causes to which the author attributes his suffering are an unhappy love affair with its attendant feelings of betrayal and jealousy, the suicide of a friend, economic difficulties, dissatisfaction with his work. A prominent position is also accorded the scars left by his repressive Catholic upbringing: «la familia, indiferente o silenciosa ante esta tremenda batalla que asomaba a mi rostro... los miedos infantiles, invadiéndome en ráfagas que me traían aún remordimientos, dudas, temores del infierno, ecos umbríos de aquel colegio jesuita que amé y sufrí en mi bahía gaditana» (AP, p. 268-269).

«¿Qué hacer?», Alberti goes on to ask. «¿Cómo hablar, cómo gritar, cómo dar forma a esa maraña en que me debatía, cómo erguirme de nuevo de aquella sima de catástrofes en que estaba sumido? Sumergiéndome, enterrándome cada vez más en mis propias ruinas, tapándome con mis escombros, con las entrañas rotas, astillados los huesos» (AP, p. 269). Having answered his own anguished question in this manner, the memorialist confirms something critics had suspected:

> Y se me revelaron entonces los ángeles, no como los cristianos, corpóreos, de los bellos cuadros o estampas, sino como irresistibles fuerzas del espíritu, moldeables a los estados más turbios y secretos de mi naturaleza. Y los solté en bandadas por el mundo, ciegas reencarnaciones de todo lo cruento, lo desolado, lo agónico, lo terrible y a veces bueno que había en mí y me cercaba.

(AP, p. 269.)

---

[10] This crisis and Alberti's ensuing adhesion to the Communist party provide Marrast with the basis for his principal assertion. According to the French critic, our author's rejection of God and the Catholic church, his conversion to a Marxist philosophy and the commitment of his energies to the liberation of man is repeatedly echoed in his dramatic works. «Le thème fondamental de toute l'oeuvre de Rafael Alberti», he writes, «est l'illustration de la rébellion de l'homme, qui doit refuser toute force arbitraire imposée en vertu de principes imposés. Que cette force soit le rachât du péché originel, ou un certain orden établi, ou la composante d'autres forces secrètes, il démeure toujours cette volonté de montrer la nécessité de la révolte. Le sens de l'engagement politique d'Alberti est clair, même dans ses pièces les moins demonstratives et les plus poétiques». («Théâtres nationaux: l'Espagne. Les grands dramaturges de la république», in *Histoire des spectacles* [(Paris): (Gallimard) (c 1956)], p. 1258.

Sobre los ángeles (1929), one of the most difficult and hermetic of Alberti's works, was a response to his vital dilemma. In an attempt to vanquish the dark forces that assailed him from without and from within, the poet plumbed the depths of his despair. He created a world of devastated plains and crumbling cities under siege by hosts of rebellious and fallen angels. The battle waged in this desolate landscape was personally symbolic. It represents Alberti's break with the past, a repudiation of his religious training. Toward the end, it expresses his yearning after a lost innocence [11].

While he was composing *Sobre los ángeles*, Alberti appears also to have begun work on his first full-length play, an «auto sacramental sin sacramento» entitled *El hombre deshabitado*. Subsequently he abandoned this proyect, returning to it in 1929. He finally completed it in 1931 for a performance by the troupe of the Mexican actress María Teresa Montoya. He tells us that he wrote the last act «en poco más de una semana, mientras se ensayaba con los carteles ya en la calle» (AP, pp. 287, 308-9). Much of the figurative language of *Sobre los ángeles* recurs in *El hombre deshabitado*—images of sterility, material desintegration and paralysis. This play can therefore be regarded as another outgrowth of Alberti's spiritual condition. Like the poet, the playwright attempted to free himself from despair by exteriorizing it, casting it out, naming it and converting it into an artistic object.

The memorialist describes a feeling of hollow emptiness following his intense visionary experience and burst of creative energy. «Los ángeles ya se me habían ido», he writes, «quedándome desventurado de ellos, permaneciendo sólo en mí la oquedad dolorosa de la herida. Mas no era tiempo de llorar», he concludes. «El momento predicho turbiamente en uno de mis poemas no se acercaba. Allí estaba presente, incitándome» (AP, p. 281). As a participant in the student riots of 1929 and 1930 against the Primo de Rivera regime, Alberti found a badly needed emotional outlet. Thus he set out on the path that was to lead to his affiliation with the Communist Party. The distraught young man who had broken with church and family would find in this political commitment a new solidarity and a *credo* of human dimensions to replace that which he had lost.

On December 12, 1930 there occurred an event which was much

---

[11] On the autobiographical origin of *Sobre los ángeles*, see Connell, «The Autobiographical Element». However, we have based our comments regarding the meaning of this work on the 'paradise lost' readings developed in Morris, «Las imágenes claves»; R. Ter Horst, «The Angelic Prehistory of *Sobre los ángeles*», *Modern Language Notes*, 81 (1966), 174-94; C. M. Bowra, «Rafael Alberti, *Sobre los ángeles*», in *The Creative Experiment* (London: Macmillan, 1949), pp. 220-53.

publicized during the turbulent moments just prior to the fall of
the Monarchy and the establishment of the Second Republic. Two
army captains named Fermín Galán and Angel García Hernández
led an abortive coup in the garrison at Jaca. The memorialist
characterizes the incident as a rallying point for the Republican
cause :

> Aquel grito que zigzagueaba potente pero sigiloso, fue a agol-
> parse de súbito, apretado de valor y heroísmo, en la garganta de
> los Pirineos, estallando al fin un amanecer en las nieves de Jaca.
> ¡ Viva la República! Es Fermín Galán, un joven militar, quien lo
> ha gritado, Fermín Galán, a quien el fervor popular naciente va
> a incorporarlo al cancionero de la calle. El pueblo adivina, ilusio-
> nado, un segundo respiro. Las cenizas ensangrentadas de Galán y
> García Hernández van a desenterrar, del panteón donde yaciera
> cincuenta y siete años, el cuerpo de la Libertad, sólo adormecido,
> ondeándolo, vivo, en sus banderas. Era un golpe de sangre quien
> había dado la señal, aunque no había llegado la hora.

(AP, p. 307.)

While on vacation in 1931 following the opening of *El hombre
deshabitado*, Alberti composed a *romancero* in commemoration of
the two heroes (AP, p. 312). Shortly thereafter, with the promise of
a new production by Margarita's Xirgu's company, he turned these
ballads into a political play entitled *Fermín Galán* (AP, pp. 318-
319).

In or around 1930, Alberti appears to have composed at least
two other works for the stage—*El enamorado y la muerte* [12] and
Santa Casilda [13]. On one occasion when the author read the latter
work to a group of friends, he met María Teresa León, whom he
married shortly thereafter. The poet recalls their meeting and the
role that it played in the resolution of his crisis :

> Cuando tú apareciste,
> penaba yo en la entraña más profunda
> de una cueva sin aire y sin salida.
> Braceaba en lo oscuro, agonizando,

---

[12] Performed Madrid, Teatro Español, 20 July 1936 by Misiones Pedagógicas.
Text contained in Manuel Bayo (ed.), «Una obra escénica inédita de Rafael Alberti», *Revista de Occidente*, 128 (Nov. 1973), 151-58. According to Bayo *(ibid.*, p. 151)
this work was also performed at the Instituto Francés and on several occasions
by experimental groups.

[13] Act One performed Paris, Institut d'Etudes Hispaniques, 1931. The text
of this work remains unpublished. We assume that Bayo refers to a recently
discovered manuscript copy when he states that *Santa Casilda* «ha permanecido
perdida hasta hace muy poco» *(idem)*. We were unable to consult this copy prior
to press time.

oyendo un estertor que aleteaba
como el latir de un ave imperceptible.
Sobre mí derramaste tus cabellos
y ascendí al sol...

(PC, p. 931) [14].

María Teresa's presence was also to have important consequences
for Alberti's theatre. Like her husband, she is passionately interested in drama. As a young woman she studied with Tairov. She
also had a good deal of practical experience as an actress and
director. Throughout the playwright's career María Teresa was
to provide companionship, support and valuable assistance. She
would collaborate with Alberti on a number of projects.

Alberti's account of his role in the opposition to the Dictatorship suggests that his debut as a political activist had little
to do with conviction. It appears instead to have been the result
of a fortuitous coincidence between the national crisis and his
own :

> El grito y la protesta que de manera oscura me mordían rebo-
> tando en mis propias paredes, encontraban por fin una puerta de
> escape, precipitándose, encendidos, en las calles enfebrecidas de
> estudiantes, en las barricadas de los paseos, frente a los caballos
> de la guardia civil y los disparos de sus mausers. Nadie me había
> llamado. Mi ciego impulso me guiaba. La mayor parte de aquellos
> muchachos poco sabía de mí, pero ya todos eran mis amigos. ¿Qué
> hacer? ¿Cómo darles ayuda para no parecer únicamente un insti-
> gador?
>
> (AP, p. 282.)

The memorialist goes on to speak of «palabras que antes no había
escuchado o nada me dijeron: como república, fascismo, libertad...», claiming that at the time of these interventions he was «a
sabiendas, un poeta en la calle» (AP, p. 282). Nevertheless his
own words indicate that what he had discovered was a chance to
vent his spleen and find momentary relief from his confused and
anguished condition. Alberti's initial ascent from the depths to
the proletarian warmth of the street was only a first step toward
commitment. The year 1931 finds him at a midpoint between his
first stance as an artist and the one that would be more characteristic of his work during the 1930s. The «ángel superviviente» of

---

14 From *Retornos de lo vivo lejano*, cited in AP, p. 304. See also León, *op. cit.*,
pp. 30-34.

Sobre los ángeles had yet to discover a substitute for his lost paradise.

According to G. W. Connell, the existence of this intermediate stage in the poet's spiritual development sheds light on the complex character of much of what Alberti wrote between 1929 and 1931 [15]. The incoherent poems of *Yo era un tonto y lo que he visto me ha hecho dos tontos* [16] and *Sermones y moradas*—all of them written in 1929—must be regarded not merely as a surrealistic game, as other critics have claimed, but as a sign of the author's confusion. The «Elegía cívica» (1929), Alberti's first attempt at political and social composition, is similarly equivocal. Connell characterizes this long and difficult poem as «rather an outpouring of the 'mal humor'—the envy, the 'antitodo' feeling that motivates the poet—than any political conviction» [17]. Alberti's as yet amorphous commitment is reflected in a somewhat different manner in the four plays which he probably wrote during these years. *El enamorado y la muerte* is the stage version of a well-known *romance viejo*, similar in spirit and conception to his earliest attempts at dramatic composition. *Santa Casilda*, later repudiated by the fully committed author [18], was apparently a lyric evocation of legendary figures. *El hombre deshabitado* bespeaks its author's extreme involvement with the artistic traditions of the *auto sacramental*. *Fermín Galán*, subtitled «romance de ciego en diez cuadros y un prólogo», is a somewhat self-conscious artistic experiment as well as a political play. None of these works would be likely to figure among the writings of a true political zealot, especially if he were also a fervent youth. However, if we assume that at the time he wrote them the author only aspired to the role of «poeta en la calle», their existence poses no problem.

The effects of Alberti's crisis and unripe commitment are also visible in another major work, the autobiographical *De un momento a otro* (1938). The author has described this play as «[una] obra dramática de guerra... y a la vez testimonio de mi propia crisis interior» [19]. It reflects Alberti's circumstances at two

[15] Geoffrey W. Connell, «The End of a Quest: Alberti's *Sermones y moradas* and Three Uncollected Poems», *Hispanic Review*, 33 (July 1965), 290-309.

[16] The bibliography of the *tonto* poems is especially complex. Originally published in diverse issues of the *Gaceta Literaria*, they found their way into successive editions of Alberti's *Poesías*. Some still remain uncollected. See Marrast's bibliography; Connell, *ibid.*; Carlos A. Pérez, «Rafael Alberti: Sobre los tontos», *Revista Hispánica Moderna*, 32 (1966), 206-16.

[17] Connell, «The End of a Quest», p. 292.

[18] In a newspaper interview which took place in 1933. See Marrast, p. 41 and our p. 21.

[19] Letter from the author to Marrast (May 2, 1954).

moments in his life—the first months of his exile, and these years in which his most painful childhood recollections returned to haunt him. Although our interest in the author's development as a playwright obliges us to study his works in strict chronological order, it is important to note the relationship between *De un momento a otro* and Alberti's writing in 1930. As we shall see, *De un momento a otro* incorporates much of the anti-clerical, anti-bourgeois content of the «Elegía cívica» and *Sermones y moradas*. It is linked to *El hombre deshabitado* by the image of a house crumbling into ruin [20].

In 1930 there existed a movement for theatrical reform which had been steadily gaining momentum since the turn of the century. Among the members of Ortega's generation were a number of prominent critics who had profited from the experiments of the Generation of '98—Ramón Pérez de Ayala, Melchor Fernández Almagro, Enrique Diez-Canedo, Enrique de Mesa. By about 1918, their efforts had resulted in the creation of a sophisticated audience which refused to be satisfied with a deplorably decadent Spanish stage. This audience helped sustain an experimental theatre which would persist alongside the more staid and less interesting *teatro de bulevar*. The years that followed were a time of profuse activity. The *Revista de Occidente* published numerous translations of foreign plays. Between 1917 and 1925, Gregorio Martínez Sierra undertook daring scenographic experiments in the Teatro Eslava. Cipriano Rivas Cherif initiated a whole series of activities on behalf of a renovated theatre, including his famous project for the Teatro Escuela de Arte. The decade of the 1920s also brought with it the arrival of Margarita Xirgu to usher in the second great period of the Teatro Español, the proliferation of small experimental theatre companies such as Rivas Cherif's *El Caracol* and Pura Ucelay's *Anfistora*, Lorca's and Casona's activities with *La Barraca* and the troupe of Misiones Pedagógicas.

The efforts of so many critics, actors, directors and theatre technicians must have generated extraordinary pressures. Probably they were an encouragement and a challenge to aspiring young artists like Alberti [21]. This helps to explain our author's persistent

[20] Morris, *A Generation of Spanish Poets*, p. 212.
[21] The following comments, with which A. de Obregón Chorot heralded the publication of the magazine *Nuevo Escenario* are suggestive of the mood that prevailed during the 1920's:

> Lo cierto es que el teatro está herido de cuidado. El cínema y el ballet son sus presuntos enemigos y él se deja anular por su afición por no definirse. Es preciso que recobre su juventud de arte primitivo e inmutable... Al teatro sólo puede salvarlo un público «snob»... «Nuevo Escenario» nos ratifica del alarma evidente.

and aggressive experimentation with style and form during his
years of extreme self-involvement and growing commitment. His
overt statements regarding the theatre and what we know of his
activities at the time make it clear that he concurred with the
opinion of his contemporaries. Like them he desired to find a
remedy for the 'sclerosis' from which Spanish theatre had long
been suffering. «Nuestra escena, invadida aún... por Benavente,
los Quintero, Arniches, Muñoz Seca... nada podía darme», he says
in his memoirs (AP, p. 285). Then he mentions among the few
specific titles that he deems noteworthy, precisely those which
literary historians have designated as experimental : Ignacio Sánchez Mejías' *Sinrazón*, Claudio de la Torre's *Tic-Tac*, Azorin's
Brandy, mucho Brandy and Gómez de la Serna's *Los medios seres*.
The poems of *Yo era un tonto*, dedicated to the great stars of
silent films, betoken Alberti's continuing interest in what he considered a more innovative form of spectacle [22]. Above all, the two
works which gained him legitimacy as a playwright attest to his
status as a champion of reform.

On February 26, 1931, *El hombre deshabitado* opened at the
Teatro de la Zarzuela. Judging by the incidents surrounding the
première, it was a milestone in the annals of Madrid theatre for
1931 [23]. Following the performance, Alberti appeared on stage to
greet his audience with a categorical and triumphant «¡ Viva el
exterminio ! ¡ Muera la podredumbre de la actual escena española !».
These words seem to have produced the desired effect ; the memorialist describes what ensued as a second *bataille d'Hernani* :

> El teatro, de arriba abajo, se dividió en dos bandos. Podridos
> y no podridos se insultaban amenazándose. Estudiantes y jóvenes

> Nos ayuda a ponernos en guardia.
> Es decir, en vanguardia...

(«[Review of] *Nuevo Escenario*», in *La Gaceta Literaria*, 15 Aug. 1928, p. 5). For
a description of the theatrical scene of this period, see Enrique Diez-Canedo,
«Panorama del teatro español desde 1914 hasta 1936», in *El teatro español de 1914
a 1936: artículos de crítica teatral*, I (México: Mortiz [1968]), 13-67. (This now
classic article was originally published in *Hora de España* 16 [1938], 13-52.) See
also Vol. IV, «Elementos de renovación».

[22] Alberti's enthusiasm was characteristic of the times. From accounts
of the activities of the *Cine Club de Madrid* which appeared in the *Gaceta Literaria*, it is clear that the new art form had become an object of deep curiosity
by 1927. Several poets of Alberti's generation, including Lorca and Salinas, were
inspired by the *tontos* of the cinema.

[23] For a more detailed account, see AP, p. 309 ; León, *op. cit.*, pp. 97-99 ;
Marrast, pp. 44-48. However we disagree with Marrast's claim that Alberti's play
placed new values before the audience of Benavente and the Quintero brothers for
the first time. We fail to see how the audience of Feb. 26, 1931, differed from
the one that frequented the Eslava between 1917 and 1925 and saw *Mariana Pineda*
at the Español in 1927. Thus for us, Alberti's attempt at reform was one among
many, rather than *the* theatrical event Madrid had been waiting for.

escritores, subidos en las sillas, armaban la gran batahola, viéndose
a Benavente y los Quintero abandonar la sala, en medio de una
larga rechifla.

(AP, p. 309.)

Subsequently a polemic of several days duration held the attention
of Madrid's theatre enthusiasts. The critics wrote passionately for
and against the *auto* and its author's extravagant behavior. A
theatrical organiaztion called *Cancela Abierta* declared itself
Alberti's ally and decided to end all its sessions with «el grito
Alberti» as a sign of solidarity [24]. A mere three months later there
was a second scandal when *Fermín Galán* opened at the Español.
Judging by Alberti's own account however, this time the motive
was more political than literary:

> Esa noche, como era de esperar, acudieron los republicanos,
> pero también nutridos grupos de monárquicos, esparcidos por todas
> partes, dispuestos a armar bronca. El primer acto pasó bien, pero
> cuando en el segundo apareció el cuadro en el que tuve la pere-
> grina idea de sacar a la Virgen con fusil y bayoneta calada acu-
> diendo en socorro de los maltrechos sublevados y pidiendo a gritos
> la cabeza del rey y del general Berenguer, el teatro entero protestó
> violentamente: los republicanos ateos porque nada querían con la
> Virgen, y los monárquicos por parecerles espantosos tan criminales
> sentimientos en aquella Madre de Dios que yo me había inventado.
> Pero lo peor faltaba todavía: el cuadro del cardenal —Monseñor
> Segura—, borracho y soltando latinajos molierescos en medio de
> una fiesta en el palacio de los duques. Ante esto, los enemigos ya
> no pudieron contenerse. Bajaron de todas partes, y en francas
> oleadas, entre garrotazos y gritos, avanzaron hacia el escenario...

[24] «La cancela abierta», *Ahora*, 3 March 1931, p. 6. The critical judgement
of many of Alberti's contemporaries was noticeably affected by their own beliefs,
and by their reactions to the playwright's unorthodox handling of theme and
supposed lack of refinement. In fact, Alberti's morality and orthodoxy were
more the object of discussion than were the qualities of his play. E.g., in one
review he was accused of writing a tiresome and repetitious work, «irrespetuosa
[e] inmoral por la pintura franca de la pasión». The author of this opinion further
states that in *El hombre deshabitado*, «el empaque de irreverencia es de una
visible pedantería porque... nada heterodoxo se dice; que el condenado odia a
Dios y lo increpa es de fe...» Jorge de la Cueva, «[Review of] *El hombre deshabitado*», *El Debate*, 27 Feb. 1931). As we shall see, this is an obvious misrepresen-
tation of the *auto*. Several more perceptive critics however, did recognize the
author's seriousness of purpose, as well as his limited success. For the best
contemporary evaluations of *El hombre deshabitado* see M. Fernández Almagro,
«Estreno de *El Hombre deshabitado*, en la Zarzuela», *La Voz*, 27 Feb. 1931;
A. Hernández-Catá, «El chaleco de Gautier y el 'jersey' de Alberti», *Ahora*,
6 March 1931, p. 10; E. Diez-Canedo, «[Review of] *El hombre deshabitado* por
Rafael Alberti», *El Sol*, 27 Feb. 1931; L. E. Palacios, «Anotaciones a *El hombre
deshabitado*», *La Gaceta Literaria*, 15 March 1931, p. 5; Felipe Sassone, «La
opinión de... ¿un podrido?», *ABC*, 12 March 1931, pp. 23-24.

A pesar de esto... Margarita, una Agustina de Aragón aquella noche, tuvo todavía el coraje de representar el epílogo, siendo coro-
nada, al final, con toda clase de denuestos, pero también de
aplausos por su extraordinario valor y ganado prestigio.

(AP, p. 320) [25].

In this instance, the author's seriousness of purpose seems to have
been lost in the shuffle. Even the critical appraisals which followed
the performance repeatedly sidestep the artistic issues in favor of
partisan considerations [26]. Thus, the text of *Fermín Galán* will
have to serve as our principal index of the significance of the
theatrical event.

2. *The trip of 1932*

In 1931, Alberti and María Teresa left Spain for Paris, where
they would spend several months in the company of other Spanish
intellectuals. The couple spent the following year studying contemporary trends in European theatre under a grant from the Junta
para la Ampliación de los Estudios. In the course of their travels
they visited Germany, Holland, Belgium, Scandinavia and the
Soviet Union. Since Volume two of *La arboleda perdida* concludes
in 1931, and María Teresa alludes to the trip only in passing, we
will have to rely on rather sparse documentation and inference in
attempting to retrace their steps [27].

In conversations with Alberti, Marrast has learned something
about the professional aspects of this trip. Our author observed

[25] See also León, *op. cit.*, pp. 259-60.
[26] The few critics who reviewed *Fermín Galán* with the esthetic qualities of
the work in mind judged it to be less successful than *El hombre deshabitado*.
Three explanations were proposed to account for the failure of Alberti's experiment.
One was poor taste. Another was the proximity of the historical events which
he treats (i.e., lack of perspective and the audience's consequent reluctance
to accept departures from established fact). A third was the notion that bourgeois
spectators could not accept the ingenuous theatre poetry of *Fermín Galán*, and
that the work would have been better suited to performance in a public square
before a popular audience. For further elaboration of these views see José de la
Cueva, «En el Español: *Fermín Galán*», *Informaciones*, 2 June 1931; A. Espina,
«[Review of] *Fermín Galán*», *Crisol*, 4 June 1931, p. 5; M. Fernández Almagro,
«*Fermín Galán*, en el teatro Español», *La Voz*, 2 June 1931.
[27] Certain of our assertions regarding the 1932 trip are borne out by a series
of newspaper articles written by Alberti during his travels and unedited until 1969.
See Robert Marrast, ed., *Prosas encontradas: 1924-1932* ([Madrid]: Ed. Ayuso
[1970]). The articles in question and others that appear in the same volume were
published earlier in R. Marrast, «Rafael Alberti, proses retrouvées», *Bulletin
Hispanique*, 70, 486-509; and his «Rafael Alberti, un réportage inédit sur son
voyage en U. R. S. S.», *ibid.*, 71, 335-53.

at close range the revolutionary work of several writers and directors who were attempting to deliver the European stage from the
onus of Realism. The experiments that appear to have impressed
him most were : (1) Piscator's functional use of schematic sets
and movie projections, and his political reinterpretation of classic
authors ; (2) the didactic techniques of Berthold Brecht as exemplified in the *Lehrstücke* ; (3) the extravaganzas of Max Reinhart ;
(4) the constructivist sets of Meyerhold and Tairov [28]. Alberti had
already anticipated some of what he saw in his own work. The
decor of *El hombre deshabitado* resembles the sets of Meyerhold
and Tairov ; *Fermín Galán* exhibits many of the characteristics of
Epic Theatre. Thus these encounters probably had a reinforcing
effect on his career. In at least one instance there would be a direct
influence as well ; in his *Noche de guerra en el Museo del Prado*
the author would make a conscious attempt to apply the theories
of Piscator and Brecht.

The object of much attention in 1932 was a series of
ongoing theoretical debates between the so-called Formalists
—advocates of formal renovation—and the Realists—those
writers who held theme to be of primary importance and argued
for a de-emphasis of the *mise en scène*. These discussions concerning
the civic functions of art focused principally on the theatre because
of its peculiarly collective nature. Moreover, they were especially
heated around April 23, 1932 ; on that day, the Communist Party
issued a series of edicts designed to dispose administratively of the
'counterrevolutionary' tendencies of the Formalists. Undoubtedly,
Alberti followed all of this with interest in his passage through
the literary circles of Communist Europe [29].

The ideas of the Realists seem to have had an immediate effect
on the playwright. Evident in his public statements in 1933 is a
radical change in attitude. In the April 23 issue of *El Imparcial*,
there appeared the text of an interview between Alberti and J.
Pérez Domenech [30]. Only two years earlier, our author had shouted

---

[28] See Marrast thesis, pp. vii-viii, for additional details. In her memoirs, Maria
Teresa records the couple's contacts with these major figures of contemporary
theatre.

[29] A useful brief treatment of this topic is Nina Gourfinkel, «La politique
théâtrale russe et le réalisme», in *Le théâtre moderne: hommes et tendances*, ed.
Jean Jacquot, 2nd ed. (Paris : C. N. R. S., 1956), pp. 193-210.

[30] «Rafael Alberti dice que la burguesía tiene el teatro que se merece», *El
Imparcial*, 23 April 1933. N.B. that Alberti's direct contact with the Soviet
theoreticians seems here to have been the factor which determined a change in
his behavior. Whereas Brecht's plays—by which Alberti would later be influenced—
remained virtually unknown in Spain in 1931, the debates between the Formalists
and the Realists had received extensive coverage in the *Gaceta Literaria* and
other Spanish publications. Thus Alberti had probably given some thought to
the relationship between art and society prior to his departure.

his challenge from the proscenium of the Zarzuela. Now he categorically denies the value of formal experimentation and openly
advocates a theatre for the masses:

> Todo lo que hoy no se haga buceando en el espíritu popular, en
> los anhelos de las grandes masas, no ofrece interés según mi crite-
> rio. La crisis teatral de que tanto se habla encuentra su justifica-
> ción lógica en ese «desaire» de los problemas que hoy afectan
> hondamente a las multitudes... No creo en eso que llaman teatro
> experimental y de minorías. Desde mi particular punto de vista,
> no veo otra [solución] más que la de organizar tropas o grupos de
> agitación, para crear el teatro de masas... Deberán estar integrados
> por estudiantes, obreros e intelectuales en general. Para que la
> tarea responda a sus propósitos, las obras resumirán las preocupa-
> ciones actuales de los obreros; sus luchas por las reivindicaciones,
> sus protestas contra la guerra imperialista y contra el fascismo, etc.
> El teatro, aunque se crea lo contrario, tiene que ser tendencioso
> y volver a su fuente natural: el pueblo.

The content and manifesto-like quality of these declarations leave
little doubt as to their origin. The playwright was to echo them
in his own work during the remainder of the 1930s.

For countless Europeans in 1932, the artist's role in society
was an issue of deep personal concern. Following World War One,
a general fatigue with the realities of war had led many artists to
seek refuge in the detached attitude of the esthete; the 1920s
were a haven for the vanguard and a time of furious experimentation. Now with the rise of Hitler to power and the emergence of
National Socialism in Germany, these same artists were faced with
the threat of a new holocaust. Many of them felt that their own
retreat from reality and responsibility had helped to produce this
state of affairs. Thus they were experiencing a severe crisis of
conscience.

The most lasting effects of Alberti's trip seem to have grown
out of his presence in the mainstream of developing intellectual
and artistic currents at just this moment. At the time of his arrival
on the European literary scene, such prominent figures as Louis
Aragon, Paul Eluard, Stephen Spender and W. H. Auden were
embarking on a journey similar to his own. We know that Alberti
was in contact with many of these writers. As he searched for a
way to give new direction to his life and work, he must have been
affected by their mood. Surely the human encounter brought a
measure of depth which would not have been possible through his
more academic experiences. Probably it was decisive in determining

the specific direction which his commitment would take. Our author himself has stated that when he returned to Spain in 1933, he was truly a «poeta en la calle», a writer for whom literary composition had become a form of social activism as well as a creative act:

> Regresaba otro: nuevo concepto de todo, y como era natural, del poeta y de la poesía. Con mi mujer fundé la revista *Octubre*, la primera española que dio el alerta en el campo de la cultura y que agrupó a una serie de jóvenes escritores, cuyo sentido del pueblo cada vez se fue haciendo menos vago, menos folklórico, es decir, más directo, real y profundo [31].

His experience abroad had taught him a more conscious and programmatic way of living out his commitment. For the young Alberti, this meant the final resolution of his crisis.

Spain and Europe: 1932-1940

At the moment when the rise of National Socialism began to threaten the seclusion of a generation of artists abroad, the political situation in Spain also necessitated a crisis of conscience. Just prior to Alberti's departure in 1931, there was a growing tendency toward commitment. The memorialist tells us that even those intellectuals who had most steadfastly avoided involvement in national affairs found themselves affected:

> El escritor, por primera vez en esos años, va a unirse al escritor por afinidades políticas y no profesionales. Todos a una comprendieron que tenían si no bancarias, serias cuentas que arreglar con la Casa del Rey... Unamuno, Azaña, Ortega, Valle-Inclán, Pérez de Ayala, Marañón, Machado, Baeza, Bergamín, Espina, Díaz Fernández... se agitan y trabajan ahora ya abiertamente 'al servicio de la República'.
>
> (AP, p. 307.)

As the problems of the government grew more critical by the hour, politics increasingly took precedence over art. According to Alberti, literary *tertulias* became political meetings; café tables were converted into tribunals. By March 1931, such a fever pitch of tension had been reached that politics was virtually the sole topic of discussion. Every bar was the potential setting for a

[31] Rafael Alberti, *Primera imagen de...* *(1940-44)* (Buenos Aires: Losada [c 1945]), p. 51.

secret meeting. The most innocent joke gave rise to heated partisan
debates. Any artistic performance was liable to turn into a noisy
demonstration [32].

This description of the mood of Madrid's citizens is somewhat
novelesque. As should be clear from our previous discussion,
intellectual life was not exclusively political. Nevertheless, it is
important to note that the situation in Spain in 1932 mirrored
conditions abroad. By the end of the year, commitment had become
a vital reality for many Spanish intellectuals. Thus, the Spain to
which Alberti returned as «poeta en la calle» proved fertile ground
for his new esthetic stance. Almost everything he was to do during
the 1930s would be justifiable in the name of political and social
action. Immediate circumstances would determine the two most
prominent characteristics of his art: its tendentious quality and
its precipitous mode of composition.

For Alberti and his wife, the years 1933 to 1936 meant incessant
activity on behalf of the Republican cause. Our author gave endless
recitals of poetry «en los actos políticos, en las bibliotecas obre-
ras y en las plazas públicas» [33]. In 1934 after founding the revolutionary magazine *Octubre*, he and María Teresa attended the First
Congress of Soviet Writers in Moscow. There he found further
support for his ideas in Gorki and Jdanov's declarations defining
Social Realism [34]. In Moscow, the couple learned of the repressed
uprising of the Asturian miners. Desirous of aiding the victims, they
undertook a trip to America. In America despite the many difficulties which he encountered because of his political views, Alberti gave poetry readings and lectures for over a year. Following a
stay of several months duration in Mexico, he stopped in New
York, Havana, Venezuela, and Trinidad. In 1936, he returned to
Spain to take part in the campaign on behalf of the Popular Front.

In the midst of all this, Alberti continued writing—mainly
circumstantial poetry. The repression of the Asturias uprising

---

[32] The final performance of Alberti's *auto* on March 5, 1931 was such an
occasion. A farewell tribute had been planned for María Teresa Montoya, and many
illustrious personages were present—Salinas, Lorca, Marañón, Pérez de Ayala,
Salvador Bacarisse, Cipriano Rivas Cherif. At first the proceedings were artistic
in nature. There were songs by Oscar Esplá; José Bergamín praised Alberti's
work. Then, in the course of some comments about Soviet theatre, Alvarez del
Vayo turned the audience's attention to the national situation. José María Alfaro,
a republican at the time, mentioned the names of several imprisoned leaders whose
support had been carefully obtained—Alcalá Zamora, Fernando de los Ríos, Largo
Caballero. To quote the author himself, the excitement reached a climax when a
telegram from Unamuno «hizo poner de pie a la sala, volcándola, luego, enarde-
cida, en las calles. Cuando acudió la policía ya era tarde. El teatro estaba vacío»
(AP, p. 309-10).

[33] Alberti, in PC, p. 13.

[34] Gourfinkel, *op. cit.*, p. 209. For further details see León, *op. cit.*, pp. 46-47.

inspired the verses of *El burro explosivo*. He gathered other poems
in several small collections : *Consignas*, *Un fantasma recorre Europa*, *El poeta en la calle* (1931-35), and *De un momento a otro* (1934-
39). *Verte y no verte* (1934), Alberti's elegy to Ignacio Sánchez
Mejías, dates from this period as does the first edition of his *Poesías* (1924-30), published in 1935. His bibliography for these years
also encompasses several minor prose works : lectures on Spanish
poetry, a few newspaper articles and a semi-narrative piece entitled
«Una historia de Ibiza» [35]. In 1934, he published his *Dos farsas
revolucionarias*, two brief dramatic texts entitled *Bazar de la
Providencia* and *Farsa de los Reyes Magos*. Openly didactic, rabidly
anti-clerical and pro-Marxist, these works are clearly a result of
his experience in the Soviet Union.

Notwithstanding the tendentious character of his published
works, the pressure brought to bear by historical circumstances,
and the strength of his commitment, at this time Alberti still
retained something of his first esthetic attitude. José Luis Cano
knows of an unpublished adaptation of Tirso's *La venganza de Tamar* [36], written in 1934. The author went to Ibiza in 1936 with the
intention of beginning work on a new play, which he hoped to
enter in the competition for the Premio Lope de Vega. *Costa sur
de la muerte*, as this work was to be called, seems not to have
been conceived as an ideological work ; rather it was apparently
a first version of *El trébol florido* (1940), the first of three neo-
popular plays written in exile [37].

The July 18th insurrection surprised Alberti and María Teresa
on Ibiza. They hid out in a cave for almost a month to avoid
capture by the Franquist forces. Upon returning to the Peninsula,
they again placed their lives and pens at the service of the Republican cause. They worked mainly from the ranks of the Alianza
de Intelectuales Antifascistas, an organization which they had
helped to found in February 1936. Alberti was secretary of the
Alianza. He was also one of the co-founders and directors of *El
Mono Azul*, the newspaper that was distributed on the Republican
front between 1936 and 1938. He compiled a *Romancero de la
guerra civil*, containing a large part of the circumstantial poetry
originally published in the columns of that newspaper. Continuing
his activities as a member of the Communist Party, he attended

---

[35]   Contained in AP, I, 1st ed. (México : Ed. Seneca [1942]).
[36]   See Marrast bibliography, p. 431.
[37]   Marrast, pp. 92-93. However, we have not succeeded in finding a source for
Marrast's assertion. Both *Costa sur de la muerte* and *El trébol florido* appear in a list
of works contained in the 1942 ed. of AP. Thus, there remains some uncertainty
on this point.

the Second Congress of International Writers in Paris in 1937. He
also helped to organize the Segundo Congreso de Escritores Antifascistas para la Defensa de la Cultura, which met in Valencia,
Madrid and Barcelona in August of that year. In 1937, he became
a soldier in the Arma de Aviación. Along with his other responsi-
bilities, he found time to direct the Museo Romántico.

During the Civil War, there existed on the Republican side
numerous theatre groups and organizations. These were an echo of
the *agitprop* groups of the Revolution of 1917 [38]. They were also
a continuation of the touring activities which had occurred in
Spain during the early 1930s. The Alberti's were extremely active
in several of these organizations. They were the guiding lights of
Nueva Escena, the theatrical section of the Alianza which was
housed in the Teatro Español. In 1937 María Teresa was named
directress of *Teatro de Arte y Propaganda* a Communist organization which was created during the congress in Valencia and
lodged in the Teatro de la Zarzuela. That same year the Consejo
Nacional de Teatro was created to coordinate and direct the
theatrical efforts of the liberal factions ; Alberti and his wife were
nominated to the *junta directiva*. These responsabilities kept the
couple in Madrid most of the time. However, they also traveled up
and down the Republican front with the *Guerrillas del Teatro*, a
sub-organization of *Teatro de Arte y Propaganda* [39]. Recalling
the dedication of her companions and colleagues in these undertakings, María Teresa describes the atmosphere of euphoria mingled
with tragedy in which they worked :

> ¡ Ah, horas sin retorno !... Era muy dulce atravesar la España
> que aún nos pertenecía. A veces la aviación nos obligaba a tirarnos
> al suelo. Tenían la costumbre de tirotear las carreteras que sobre-
> volaban... Encontramos una vez un carro que llevaba sentado,
> muerto, al carretero, y las mulas seguían, seguían hacia la casa sin

[38] The term *agitprop* (agitation and propaganda) was in widespread use in
the U. S. during the 1930s to refer to the work of several highly class-conscious
itinerant theatre groups which patterned themselves after Russian and German
models and staged largely improvised performances aimed primarily at propa-
gandizing the public. It has since been used to refer to works similar to the
ones performed by these groups. *Agitprop* plays usually involve sparse sets and
symbolic costumes «deliberately calculated for mobility and adaptability to the
playing environment.» Their scripts are «crude in plot and characterization and
full of revolutionary... clichés» (Mordecai Gorelik, *New Theatres for Old* [NY :
Dutton (c 1962)], pp. 401-2).
[39] For a more complete discussion of the theatrical activities of the Republicans,
see Ignacio Soldevila Durante, «Sobre el teatro español de los últimos veinticinco
años», *Cuadernos Americanos*, 22, No. 126 (1963), 256-89 ; Robert Marrast, «Le
théâtre à Madrid pendant la Guerre Civile», in *Le théâtre moderne : hommes et
tendances*, pp. 257-74.

equivocarse, con todas las campanillas cantando... Nuestros guerri-
lleros eran soldados... Teníamos nuestra ración de pan... Y cantá-
bamos. ¡Cuánto hemos cantado durante aquellos años!... Cantába-
mos para sacudirnos el miedo... Y nos queríamos. Cuánto amor a
los otros hombres da el destino común de la muerte [40].

Alberti's original and theoretical contributions to theatrical life
on the Republican side were as important as his participation as
an organizer. In the pages of *El Mono Azul* and the *Boletín de
Orientación Teatral*, he and María Teresa called for the creation
of a «teatro de urgencia». This was to be a repertoire of plays
suited to the vicissitudes of combat and adaptable to the limited
critical capacities of a popular audience. In the February 15, 1938
issue of the *Boletín*, Alberti published his formula for these works:

> Hacen falta... obritas rápidas, intensas —dramáticas, satíricas,
> didácticas...— que se adapten técnicamente a la composición espe-
> cífica de los grupos teatrales. Una pieza de este tipo no puede
> plantear dificultades de montaje ni exigir gran número de actores.
> Su duración no debe sobrepasar la media hora. En 20 minutos es-
> casos, si el tema está bien planteado y resuelto, se puede producir
> en los espectadores el efecto de un fulminante [41].

The two plays which Alberti wrote in 1936 and 1937 were an ex-
tension of his campaign on behalf of a revolutionary theatre;
in them he applied his dramatic formula. *Los salvadores
de España* (1936) remained unpublished and has been lost. Originally based on a ballad like *Fermín Galán*, *Radio Sevilla* (1937)
appeared in the May 1938 issue of *El Mono Azul* [42]. Both of these
works probably figured in the repertoire of *Nueva Escena* [43],

---

[40] León, *op. cit.*, pp. 40-41. See also her autobiographical novel *Juego Limpio*
(Buenos Aires: Goyanarte [1959]).
[41] R. Alberti, «Teatro de urgencia», *Boletín de Orientación Teatral*, 15 Feb.
1938, p. 5. This publication was the principal organ of the Consejo.
[42] Pp. 6-8. Alberti published the ballad on which *Radio Sevilla* is based in
El Mono Azul, 1 Oct. 1936. The play also appeared in an anthology entitled *Teatro
de urgencia* (Madrid, 1938) along with four works by other authors.
[43] *Los salvadores de España* was part of the first program presented by
Nueva Escena, once on Oct. 20, 1936 and again on Oct. 25, 1936. Apparently
there were also several other performances of this play, including some on the
front (Marrast thesis, pp. 58-59). There is only indirect evidence of performances
of *Radio Sevilla*. A note which appears at the end of *Teatro de urgencia* mentions
performances of the other four works contained therein. Since those plays were
presented, it is likely that Alberti's play was also seen by theatre audiences.
However, *Radio Sevilla* has to have been put on somewhat later than its companion
pieces—i.e., at some time after the publication of the aforementioned anthology
in the summer of 1938 *(ibid.*, p. 65).

along with Alberti's *Bazar de la Providencia*, correctly designated by Marrast as «théâtre d'urgence avant la lettre» [44].

A full account of Alberti's theatrical activities during the Civil War must include two additional projects. A dramatic poem entitled *Cantata de los héroes y la confraternidad de los pueblos* was presented by the Alianza in 1938, on the eve of the departure of the International Brigades [45]. Alberti also composed a *versión libre* of Cervantes' *Numancia*. This work is known to have been performed on several occasions beginning around December 15, 1937 [46]. We do not intend to study either of these two works in detail, since the former is not really a play and the latter is not an original composition. Nevertheless, we note their significance as theatrical events. The adaptation of *Numancia* in particular attests to the seriousness of Alberti and his co-workers in the theatre. They sought an effective instrument of propaganda and a means of returning to the *pueblo* an important part of its artistic heritage. By modernizing Cervantes' text, Alberti placed one of the great classical masterpieces within reach of people of little culture. By actualizing it as well, dressing the soldiers as Civil Guard and labelling the Romans Fascists, he imparted a new relevance to past events. Judging by María Teresa's recollection of its performance, for those who witnessed the play within earshot of enemy fire, the historical example was a source of great inspiration :

> Había un heroísmo en la sala tan atenta que correspondía a los personajes. Era todo un grito, un combate, una razón de vida heroica lo que se escuchaba, lo que se veía. Nunca hubo mayor correspondencia entre una sala y un escenario. Allí los numantinos, aquí los madrileños. Cervantes nos resultó el mejor sostenedor de nuestra causa... Luego, llegaban los aplausos... Saludábamos los vivos y los muertos al pueblo de Madrid que teníamos delante. Se abrían de par en par las puertas del Teatro de la Zarzuela y todos un instante escuchábamos los duelos de la artillería, el bombardeo de la aviación... y salíamos hacia las calles de Madrid... [47].

[44] Marrast, «Le théâtre à Madrid», p. 266.

[45] R. Alberti, *De un momento a otro; cantata de los héroes y la confraternidad de los pueblos; Vida bilingüe de un refugiado español en Francia* (Buenos Aires: Bajel, 1942). Performed Madrid, Teatro Auditorium, 20 Dec. 1938.

[46] Miguel de Cervantes, *Numancia*, ad. Rafael Alberti (Madrid: Signo, 1937). Presented Madrid, Teatro de la Zarzuela, Dec. 1937 (see Marrast thesis, p. 59). See also León, *Memoria*, pp. 52-54.

[47] León, *loc. cit.* For critical discussion of this adaptation see Robert Marrast, «L'esthétique théâtrale de Rafael Alberti», in *La mise en scène des oeuvres du passé*, ed. Jean Jacquot and André Veinstein (Paris: C.N.R.S., 1957), pp. 53-80; his thesis, pp. 59-64; and his *Miguel de Cervantès: dramaturge* ([Paris]: L'Arche [c 1957]).

Alberti's wartime experiences were also to leave a mark on one of his later works. The members of the Alianza took upon themselves the task of safeguarding the national art treasures from destruction at the hands of the Franquist forces. On several occasions, Alberti and María Teresa took great personal risks in order to salvage endangered masterpieces. In November 1936, as enemy bombs fell on Madrid, they were charged with transferring to Valencia the collection housed in the Prado. In her memoirs, María Teresa recalls the night on which they carried out their mission :

> Una linterna iluminó nuestros pasos... Entramos en un sotanillo, pasamos silenciosos entre cuadros vueltos del revés, unos sobre otros, bajados de las salas altas a un precario refugio. Arriba todo el Museo estaba en pie de guerra. Las ventanas habían sido protegidas por maderas y sacos terreros, la larga sala central era como una calle después de una batalla, la huella de los cuadros manchaba de recuerdos melancólicos las paredes desnudas, hasta la luz que bajaba de las cristaleras rotas era funeralmente triste. Seguramente habían temblado de frío y de miedo los cuadros ilustres. Bombas, bombas sobre el Museo del Prado... Poco tiempo bastó para que las obras elegidas, en primer lugar las de escuela española, estuviesen dispuestas a partir hacia Valencia... Soldados del V Regimiento y de la Motorizada rodeaban los camiones, esperando la orden de marchar... Hombres crédulos y magníficos que a pesar de no haber pisado jamás las salas de un museo... no vacilaron en salvar para los inteligentes y los cultos del mundo la maravillosa pinacoteca de Madrid [48].

Years after the conclusion of the hostilities, this incident would provide a stimulus for the playwright's imagination. It would be the dramatic nucleus around which he would construct his *Noche de guerra en el Museo del Prado* (1956).

In early March 1939, on the eve of the defeat of Negrín's government, Alberti and his wife left Spain for good. They headed first for Oran and then for Paris, where they received by Pablo Neruda and his wife. There they earned their living for several months as announcers and translators for Radio Paris-Mondial. In Paris, Alberti initiated his career as an exiled writer. His first compositions were the long play *De un momento a otro* (1937-38) and an autobiographical poem entitled *Vida bilingüe de un refugiado español en Francia* (1939-40, pub. 1941) [49]. The broad dimensions of these works reflect a momentary restoration

---

[48] León, *op. cit.*, pp. 202-4. See also her *Juego limpio*, pp. 136-38.
[49] Date of publication is indicated where it differs from the last date of composition.

of exterior calm. Their confused outpourings, vitriolic tones and bitter denunciations give expression to what must have been the exiled writer's first state of mind. At the same time, certain more consoling lines began to flow from his pen—the nostalgic evocations of the first volume of *La arboleda perdida* and some of the poems of *Entre el clavel y la espada* (1939, pub. 1942).

The outbreak of World War Two brought new disruptions and new spiritual anguish for the Albertis, who found themselves in danger of persecution because of their political views. On the night of February 10, 1940, they fled from the Pétain government and headed for America. Upon arriving in Buenos Aires, they were welcomed by numerous artists and writers ; immediately, they were accorded a place in the intellectual world of the Argentine capital. With the generous assistance of the editor Gonzalo Losada, they were able to set up housekeeping. Buenos Aires was to be their home for the next two and a half decades.

Years of exile: 1940 to the present

Alberti has not written about his life following his departure from Spain. To date, nobody has undertaken a systematic search through the libraries and newspaper files of Latin America for source material concerning his professional activities. María Teresa's memoirs for the years in exile consist principally of personal evocations of Buenos Aires and anecdotes about the many prominent literary and intellectual figures whom she and Alberti have known over the years. This means that our account of the playwright's years in the New World must be based almost exclusively on a list of publications and performances and a consideration of his work in relation to his situation as an exiled writer.

One of the first things that the author's arrival in America brought was a measure of external tranquility such as he had not known for at least a decade. Suddenly there was time for non-political pursuits. During the years that followed, Alberti would give numerous lectures and recitals of poetry throughout Latin America. In the 1940s, he travelled through Argentina, Uruguay and Chile. In 1960, he spent time in Venezuela, Colombia, Chile and Peru. In 1945 he also experienced a resurgence of his former vocation ; this led to several new exhibitions of drawings and paintings in addition to his literary activities. Despite a schedule full of more academic commitments, the author has continued to devote a large part of his energies to furthering the cause of International Communism. The first time he returned to Europe in

1950, it was to attend the World Congress for Peace in Warsaw. At some point prior to 1956 [50], he, María Teresa, and their daughter Aitana (b. 1941) made another long trip to Eastern Europe—Warsaw, the U.S.S.R., Rumania, Czechoslovakia, East Germany. In 1957, they traveled to Communist China, revisiting the U.S.S.R. and Rumania on the way home.

The most tangible result of Alberti's more stable situation is a substantial bibliography. In addition to the circumstantial pieces grouped in the *Poesías completas* under the titles *Signos del día* (1945-55), *Poemas diversos* (1945-59), *Poemas de Punta del Este* (1945-56) and *Primavera de los pueblos* (1955-57), the author published nine major collections of poetry between 1942 and 1964 : *Entre el clavel y la espada* (1939-40), *Pleamar* (1942-44), *A la pintura* (1945-52), *Retornos de lo vivo lejano* (1948-52), *Coplas de Juan Panadero* (1949-53), *Ora marítima* (1953), *Baladas y canciones del Paraná* (1953-54), *Poemas escénicos: 1.ª serie* (1961-63), *Abierto a todas horas* (1962-63, pub. 1964). His three most significant prose works were written largely during the first years of his exile. Volume One of *La arboleda perdida* and another autobiographical text entitled «El poeta en la España de 1931» [51] were published in 1942 ; they were followed in 1945 by a collection of essays entitled *Primera imagen de... (1940-44)* [52]. In 1959 Volume Two of *La arboleda perdida* appeared.

The works which the playwright composed during his years in America are just as varied and rich in expressive forms as those of the poet and memorialist. Between 1940 and 1946, Alberti wrote a neo-popular trilogy which includes *El trébol florido* (1940), *El adefesio* (1944) and *La Gallarda* (1944-45) [53]. In 1956 there followed *Noche de guerra en el Museo del Prado*, a tendentious work which reflects the author's continuing commitment and his renewed interest in painting [54]. In 1963, he publised his most recent play, *La lozana andaluza*. In addition

[50] See our note 54 below.

[51] R. Alberti, *El poeta en la España de 1931 seguido del Romancero de Fermín Galán y los sublevados de Jaca* (Buenos Aires: P.H.A.C. [1942]). Subsequently incorporated into AP, II.

[52] These are largely evocations of major literary figures.

[53] The Losada edition of Alberti's *Teatro* gives 1942 as the date of composition of *El trébol florido*. Alberti has corrected this in a letter to Marrast (2 May 1954). Only two of these three plays have been performed in Spanish—*El adefesio* (Buenos Aires, Teatro Avenida, 8 June 1944 by Margarita Xirgu's troupe ; Bordeaux, Teatro del Instituto de Estudios Ibéricos, 1959 by an experimental group from Barcelona ; Barcelona, Teatro Capsa, 20 November, 1969) and *El trébol florido* (Buenos Aires, Plaza San Martín, 1 March 1966 directed by Francisco Silva). Projects for a production of *La Gallarda* by Margarita Xirgu's troupe were never realized (cf. *Correo Literario* [Buenos Aires], 1 May 1945, p. 1).

[54] 1956 is the date of publication. The work may have been completed earlier. In Jan. 1956, when the Albertis met with Bertholt Brecht in Berlin, the composition

32   LOUISE B. POPKIN

to these works, Alberti's theatrical production includes several
lesser projects: a translation from the French of the anonymous medieval work entitled *Farsa del Licenciado Pathelin* [55], a
translation of Jules Supervielle's *El ladrón de niños* [56]; the sce-
nario for a movie version of Calderón's *La dama duende* [57]; a
second version of *Numancia* [58], this time modified in accord with
exclusively esthetic considerations; a long dramatic poem entitled
Cantata de la paz y la alegría de los pueblos [59]; a translation of
Molière's *Las picardías de Scapin* [60]; a benefit performance of
Lorca's *Mariana Pineda* [61].

Alberti's circumstances in exile have affected the quality of
his literary production as well as its volume. Far from the turmoil
that had driven the troubadour of *Marinero en tierra* out of his
ivory tower, there existed renewed possibilities for artistic detachment. Thus in 1939, the author reclaims the treasures of his
imagination with renewed urgency:

> Vuelva a mí la palabra precisa
> virgen el verbo exacto con el justo adjetivo...

Nevertheless, as a writer who would continue to think of himself as «poeta en la calle», he is quick to acknowledge his social
responsibility. The poet reaffirms his commitment:

> Si yo no viniera de donde vengo... si mi nombre no fuera un
> compromiso, una palabra dada, un expuesto cuello constante, tú,
> libro que ahora vas a abrirte, lo harías solamente bajo un signo de
> flor, lejos de él la fija espada que lo alerta.

of *Noche de guerra* was at least well underway. At that meeting, the author
agreed to deliver the completed manuscript to Brecht by May (presumably
translated) so that the German playwright could begin rehearsals for a performance
by the Berliner Ensemble, scheduled to take place in November. Owing to Brecht's
death, the project was never realized (León, *Memoria*, p. 269). Recently a
revised version of *Noche de guerra* directed by Ricardo Salvat was performed
twice in Mexico (May 1974 at the annual Festival Cervantino in Guanajuato and
in Mexico City, Teatro Jiménez Rueda).

[55] Published in *Sur* 10 (March, April, May 1941) and also in Buenos Aires
by the Centro Editor de América Latina [c 1970]. Presented Buenos Aires, Teatro
Presidente Alvear, 27 Nov. 1944.

[56] Unpublished. Presented Montevideo, Estudio Auditorium del S.O.D.R.E.,
16 Oct. 1943.

[57] 1944, in collaboration with María Teresa León. Directed by Luis Saslavsky.

[58] Miguel de Cervantes, *Numancia*, ed. R. Alberti (Buenos Aires: Losada,
1943). Presented Montevideo, Estudios Auditorium del S.O.D.R.E., 6 Aug. 1943.
For a study of this work see Marrast, «L'esthétique théâtrale», pp. 64-65.

[59] Written in 1944 with music by Salvador Bacarisse. Published in R. Alberti,
El poeta en la calle (Paris: Ed. de la Librairie du Globe, 1966).

[60] Unpublished. Presented Buenos Aires, Teatro Caminito al aire libre de la
Boca, 25 Dec. 1958.

[61] León, *op. cit.*, pp. 270-71. Evidently performed in 1946.

With these words from the prologue of *Entre el clavel y la espada,*
Alberti expressed a new poetic *credo.* Following his recent experience, he was more aware than evei of the ambivalent nature
of human experience. His work—like the rest of his existence—
would henceforth encompass two realities : «de un lado un seco
olor a sangre pisoteada, de otro un aroma a jardines» (PC, p. 445).

In general, Alberti's new attitude has enhanced the many
facets of his literary production. As earlier in his career, the
proletarian writer sometimes dissipates his energies in incon-
sequential epigrams and hollow rhetoric. But from 1940 on, he has
shown a greater concern for esthetic matters and tended toward
a simpler, more direct, and more moving form of expression.
Similarly, the forger of beautiful images has sought to avoid the
merely anecdotal and picturesque. He has attemnted to transcend
the occasionally facile lyricism of his earlier works. The playwright's
newly discerning critical attitude is most apparent in the unprecedented craftsmanship and truly dramatic properties of his three
masterpieces. In the neo-popular trilogy, the ideological content
of the 1930s disappears ; Alberti is first and foremost a man of
the theatre. This shift in emphasis marks the beginning of a third
stage in his career. The author's continuing preoccupation with
form would later determine a fourth phase, which encompasses
Noche de guerra and *La lozana andaluza.* In both of those works,
Alberti's own esthetic vision is shaped in a curious and original
manner by that of other artists.

While Alberti's arrival in Argentina meant material tranquility,
it also brought the pain of separation. «Nos desenraizaron de dis-
tinta manera», writes María Teresa, «y todos comprendimos, de
pronto, que hay una soledad compartida que se llama destierro» [62]. Throughout the years of his exile, our author has continued
to consider himself a Spaniard. He has continued to feel a strong
bond with his native land. As several of his biographers and critics have observed, Alberti's literary talents have provided him
with an important means of overcoming his vital dilemma. Much
of what he has written since leaving Spain is best interpreted as a
vicarious return. The author draws nearer the traditions, land-
scapes and relationships that he left behind by recreating them in
his art [63].

Alberti's exile is never absent from his plays or his poetry.
For the poet, there has resulted a synthesis. He has found a purer,
more concentrated and more effective way of expressing commit-

[62] *Ibid.,* p. 302.
[63] See Biruté Cipliauskaité, «La soledad en el destierro», in *La soledad y la
poesía española contemporánea* (Madrid : Insula, 1962), pp. 187-231.

4

ment. He has achieved a more tempered lyricism than was con
tained in the carefree metaphoric world of his early poetry or the
hermetic verses of his critical years. The mature Alberti has replaced the crude denunciations of his first social poetry with personal testimony. He has made of his uprootedness a new and
universal sign of combat ; he has brought Spain to the fore in a
manner more congruent with his naturally elegiac tendencies—as
nostalgic evocation, melancholy, *saudade*. Apparently understanding that the subjective elegiac musing of the lyric poet is ill-
suited to the dramatic process, the playwright has found a different means of sublimating life in art. With his increased capacity
for esthetic contemplation, he deliberately detaches himself from
his dramatic work. Nevertheless, in the neo-populaɪ plays, he has
created a «mundo cuajado de España» ; in it he returns to his
personal, historical and artistic past—to the world of his earliest
writings, of his childhood, of Andalusian folklore.

In 1964, the Alberti family moved to Rome and established
themselves in the old Spanish quarter which had provided the
setting for *La lozana andaluza*. We know little about the author's
activities there, except that he has had several exhibitions of
painting and drawing, written three new volumes of poetry and
published some of his early and previously unpublished work [64].

---

[64] See J. P. González Martín, «Alberti y la pintura», *Insula*, 28, No. 305
(1972), pp. 1, 12, and 13. In *Poesías anteriores a «Marinero en tierra»* Alberti has
collected his very earliest work. *El poeta en la calle* (1966) contains much of the
civic poetry written between 1931 and 1965. Recent new volumes of poetry are
Roma, peligro para caminantes (1968), *Los ocho nombres de Picasso y no digo
más que lo que no digo* (1970), *Canciones del Alto Valle del Aniene* (1972).

CHAPTER II

THE THEATRE AS LYRICISM : THE 1920s

Unpublished and lost texts

In order to give a complete account of Alberti's theatre, we must go back to the beginnings of his literary career. Unfortunately, the material we have at our disposal barely attests to the author's early interest in dramatic composition. It is impossible to ascertain exactly what his first works were like. In some cases we cannot be certain how much of a projected work was actually written. Moreover Marrast, who has spoken with Alberti, indicates that even the author has only vague recollections of his early attempts at playwriting. Therefore we will have to rely chiefly on inference in discussing this first period, and our conclusions will be tentative. Nevertheless, it seems possible to affirm (1) that the young playwright of the 1920s leaned heavily on popular and folkloric elements [1] and ; (2) that he composed pieces of a fundamentally lyric, or otherwise non-dramatic, nature.

Excluding *El hombre deshabitado* which we discuss in our next chapter, there are indications that between 1925 and 1930 Alberti conceived of eight plays. All but two of them remained incomplete. Six have never been published and five have probably been lost [2]. Two titles, *Ardiente-y-Fría* and *La novia del marinero, appear* in a list of works in preparation contained in the first edition of *Marinero en tierra* (1925). A third play called *Santa Casilda* is known to have been completed and read in public several times during 1930 and 1931. In a letter to Marrast [3], Alberti speaks of two farces entitled *Lepe, Lepijo y su hijo,* and *La hija de la gran puta.* He recalls having written a few scenes of these works during the dictatorship of Primo de Rivera ; the titles subsequently appeared in lists of works in preparation for 1932 and 1934. Another title,

---

1 We infer this largely on the basis of Marrast's discussion of sources. Unless otherwise indicated, what follows is drawn from Marrast, pp. 10-12 and 19-25. In some cases further conclusions are drawn.
2 Regarding the status of *Santa Casilda* see our note 13, p. 14.
3 Dated 23 Nov. 1952.

El colorín colorete, is mentioned by the author in *La arboleda perdida.*
(1) According to Marrast, the source of *Ardiente-y-Fría* was a brief composition of identical title which appears in *Marinero en tierra:*

MADRIGAL DRAMÁTICO DE ARDIENTE-Y-FRÍA

Ardiente-y-fría—clavel
herido de mediodía—,
desnuda, en la sastrería.

El niño, aprendiz de sastre,
¡cómo la deshojaría!

Ardiente-y-fría un corpiño
de ondas calientes y frías
quisiera para sus senos
—algas flotantes del mar
blanco y quieto del espejo—.

El niño, aprendiz de sastre,
le ofrece una begonía.

Ardiente-y-fría una falda
de lunas en agonía
quisiera para su cuerpo
—delfín moreno del mar
verde y quieto del espejo—.

El niño, aprendiz de sastre,
le ofrece una peonía.

Ardiente-y-fría una cofia
de luz hirviente y sombría
quisiera para su sueño.

El niño, aprendiz de sastre,
le da una manzana, muerto.

(PC, p. 47.)

As the French critic observes, the exchanges of fruit and flowers for articles of clothing are the figurative expression of a youthful love affair. The maiden searches for caresses which an inexperienced young man does not succeed in supplying:

Le symbolisme... est assez transparent: Ardiente-y-Fría est la jeune fille qui ressent les premières atteintes de l'amour; son coeur est brûlant d'une fièvre inconnue, et son corps frais réclame du Niño des caresses qui calmeraient cette fièvre, et que le poète désigne par les différentes parties du vêtement énumérées ici: corsage, jupe, résille. Le tailleur, jeune apprenti, ne connaît pas encore l'art de vêtir—c'est-à-dire d'aimer—et lui offre successivement les fleurs et le fruit qui ne pourront remplacer les parures —c'est-à-dire les caresses—que réclame Ardiente-y-Fría. Le désespoir tue le jeune garçon [4].

The maiden's encounter with the tailor's apprentice ends sadly. The sharply contrasting images of heat and cold, light and darkness imply a certain intensity of feeling. Nevertheless, Alberti's poem is not dramatic. The poet has written a variant of the playful «What will you give me? This shall I give thee...» dialogue which recurs frequently in European folklore. Through association with that popular tradition, he eludes the tragic possibilities of his subject matter and imparts to his poem a fundamentally lyric quality. The maiden's unfulfilled desire does not convey any real sense of frustration. Since the plot line of the play probably followed that of the poetic text, we imagine the former to have been equally devoid of dramatic conflict.

(2)   The title which appeared along with *Ardiente-y-Fría* was probably also related to the neo-popular poems of *Marinero en tierra*. Possible sources for *La novia del marinero* might be any of several compositions in which Alberti takes up the traditional theme of the *novia ausente*. This work may have been a remote ancestor of *El trébol florido*.

(3)   What we know of *Santa Casilda* (misterio en tres actos y un prólogo) comes from three brief descriptions of the play. Regarding this third of Alberti's lost texts María Teresa León has written the following:

> Tenía *Santa Casilda*, escrita en toda clase de metros y ritmos, un encanto extraordinario. Era la vida y glorificación de una santita hija de un rey moro de Toledo que se enamora de un conde cautivo y se fuga con él hacia Castilla, llegando hasta Briviesca en Burgos, donde el conde muere. Ella funda un monasterio. El monasterio y la fuente—se arroja un guijarro y se consigue novio— existen todavía [5].

In her memoirs, María Teresa refers to one additional element which figures in Alberti's plot. While bringing bread to her father's Christian captives one day, CASILDA is apprehended by the king:

---

[4]   Marrast, p. 11.
[5]   Letter from María Teresa León to Marrast (4 Aug. 1952).

«Su padre el rey la [sic] preguntó: 'Hija, ¿qué llevas en ese delantal?'. Y la muchacha contestó, asustada: 'Flores, padre'» [6].

Marrast cites as the source for this work the hagiographic legend which inspired Lope's *Santa Casilda* and Tirso de Molina's *Los lagos de San Vicente*. In the most widely accepted version, Casilda flees because she has incurred her father's wrath by mercifully bringing food to his prisoners. She founds the monastery of Briviesca after receiving the miraculous aid of God and Saint Vincent [7]. Casilda's flight with the Captive Count does not appear in the original. While Alberti apparently followed the general outlines of the Santa Casilda legend, his play must have differed markedly from the more traditional versions of the classical authors. Both Lope and Tirso wrote clearly hagiographic works focusing on Satan's attempt to bring about Casilda's perdition. By inventing the figure of the Captive Count, our author made possible a sweeping reinterpretation of the material. Virtually disgregarding the religious emphasis of the Christian legend, he apparently preferred to have his protagonist act out of purely sentimental motives [8]. Alberti's CASILDA undertakes her trip for love of the Count; she converts and takes the veil when he dies.

An anonymous critic who attended a public reading of *Santa Casilda* has provided us with some idea of its formal characteristics. His description highlights the primitive and evocative qualities of the work:

> *Santa Casilda* está destinada al teatro y es perfectamente repre-
> sentable, aunque habrá de vencer, quizá, en la escena, aquello con
> que suele chocar en la realidad toda producción de elevado lirismo.
> Su autor ha escrito tres actos con los elementos sencillos, primiti-
> vos, claros, del romancero [en los que]... las estampas se preceden
> con la sugestión de los tonos de oro de los retablos del siglo xv...,
> suenan... letras de canciones ingenuas y otras, transmitidas por
> labios infantiles de generación en generación... [y se nota] el
> perfume de viejos pergaminos, el color de pinturas desvaídas, halla-
> das al azar en algún viejo y apartado templo [9].

All available evidence suggests a generally lyric handling of the legendary material. Alberti seems to have avoided any potentially dramatic elements in favor of a smooth unfolding of events. There appears to have been no revelation of truth in his *Santa Casilda*, no spiritual struggle between the law of Mohammed and that of

---

[6] León, *Memoria*, p. 31.
[7] For a more complete description of the traditional material see Marrast, p. 20.
[8] Marrast, p. 20.
[9] «La *Santa Casilda* de Rafael Alberti», *ABC*, 27 Jan. 1931, p. 36.

Christ, no pitting of the protagonist against a powerful adversary. Probably there was no amorous conflict either, since CASILDA's conversion follows immediately upon the Count's death. Alberti's protagonist seems to have been bound to her lover by a tenderness devoid of passion. His play was probably above all a charming and ingenuous piece of theatre poetry.

(4, 5) We know little about *Lepe, Lepijo y su hijo* and *La hija de la gran puta*. Since both titles originate in popular speech, we can assume that these works incorporated numerous folkloric elements. Probably they were brief political satires written in a grotesque comic vein. The latter conclusion is suggested by the crudeness of the second title and the chronology which Marrast has succeeded in establishing for the two plays [10]. The few scenes which were actually written date from some moment prior to the fall of the Primo de Rivera regime (January 30, 1930). However these titles appear in lists of works in preparation in 1932 and 1934, indicating that Alberti still intended to complete them at that time. This makes them more or less contemporary with *Fermín Galán* (1930) and the *Dos farsas revolucionarias* (1934). That is, the playwright's intention corresponds to a moment when the tendentious use of caricature plays an important role in his work.

(6) When Alberti returned to the composition of *El hombre deshabitado* in 1929, he had evidently completed still another lost work. «Entonces... intenté hacer libretos musicales, como aquel de *La pájara pinta*», he tells us. «Con un nuevo libreto—'El colorín colorete'—me fui a ver a Adolfo Salazar, proponiéndole se lo enviase a un músico francés: a Darius Milhaud, por ejemplo.» Alberti adds that he had written *El colorín colorete* «en un lenguaje inventado, que hacía innecesaria su traducción» (AP, pp. 286-87). Since Marrast makes no reference to this text, all we know about it is what the memorialist tells us in these few lines. Probably it resembled in language and content the work to which we now turn our attention [11].

---

[10] Marrast, pp. 22-25.

[11] Another unidentified title which appears in AP corresponds to a moment just following the *première* of *El hombre deshabitado*. Writing about his activities in 1931, the memorialist tells us that «animado por mi reciente éxito teatral, [planeé] una nueva obra: 'Las horas muertas', que comencé a escribir...» (AP, p. 312). We do not know to what this title corresponds and therefore only mention it here. *Las horas muertas* may be another lost text, or it may be an early title of a work which was later completed.

«La pájara pinta»

The nonsense play entitled *La pájara pinta* (1925) [12] is the
earliest extant example of Alberti's first attempts at dramatic
composition. This brief text confirms our suspicions regarding the
essentially non-dramatic character of the early plays. Originally
Alberti conceived *La pájara pinta* as a prologue and three acts.
Only the prologue and a first act were written. The action consists
of a series of loosely related episodes involving numerous characters.
The latter are drawn either from the world of children's rhymes
—LA PÁJARA PINTA, LA CARBONERITA, ANTÓN PERULERO, LA VIUDI-
TA, EL CONDE DE CABRA—or from the *refranero*—DON DIEGO CON-
TRERAS, JUAN DE LAS VIÑAS, LA TÍA PIYAYA, BIGOTES. There is no
plot line, properly speaking; a few meaningful details lend coherence to the work. LA PÁJARA PINTA is accorded a position of central
importance with respect to the other characters, distributed in
pairs or couples. She presides over them as a sort of CELESTINA, and
they bring her gifts on her saint's day.

In 1935, Alberti gave a lecture entitled «Lope de Vega y la
poesía contemporánea». He concluded with the reading of these
fragments —as he put it, «unas escenas teatrales, que a Lope segu-
ramente divertirían» [13]. Thus, he recognized his debt to popular
tradition. Alberti's utilization of the language of children's rhymes
is extensive and faithful to the spirit of the originals. In fact, *La
pájara pinta* can almost be regarded as an anthology of that
popular poetic genre. On numerous occasions the author simply
transposes traditional material:

> LA VIUDITA *(cantando)*.
> Yo soy la viudita
> del Conde Laurel
> que quiere casarse
> y no encuentra con quién.
> CORRO.
> La viudita, la viudita,
> la viudita se quiere casar
> con el Conde, Conde de Cabra.
> Conde de Cabra se le dará.

---

[12] Textual citations are taken from R. Alberti, *«Lope de Vega...» seguido de
«La Pájara Pinta».* Hereafter cited as PP.
[13] PP, p. 36. Delivered in Havana, April 1935.

LA VIUDITA *(a* LA PÁJARA*)*.
Yo no quiero al Conde de Cabra.
Conde de Cabra, sino a ti.

(PP, p. 83) [14].

At other times Alberti glosses the original :

CORRO DE LOS INVITADOS.
Ochavito a la Pájara Pinta
pinta, pinta en el verde limón.
Con el pico picaba la hoja,
con la hoja picaba la flor
¡ ay !
¿cuándo vendrá mi amor?
¡ ay !
¿cuándo lo veré yo?
TODOS.
Me arrodillo a los pies
de mi amante
fiel y constante.
Dame una mano,
dame la otra ;
toma un besito
para tu boca.
CORRO.
Daremos la media vuelta,
daremos la vuelta entera.
Daremos un paso atrás...
pero no, pero no, pero no...
pero no, que me da vergüenza ;

[14] Cf. the texts of two popular sources, cited in Marrast, p 17 :

(1) La rueda.
La viudita, la viudita,
la viudita se quiere casar
con el Conde, Conde de Cabra,
Conde de Cabra se le dará.
La Viuda.
Yo no quiero al Conde de Cabra,
Conde de Cabra, ¡triste de mí!
Yo no quiero al Conde de Cabra,
Conde de Cabra, si no es a ti.
(2)
Yo soy la viudita
del Conde Laurel
que quiere casarse
y no encuentra con quién.

pero sí, pero sí, pero sí...
(Empieza a bajar el telón...)

(PP, pp. 80-81) [15].

Verses which are pure invention are elaborated within a traditional framework. The following example recurs with slight variants in *Marinero en tierra* (PC, p. 42):

LA CARBONERITA *(llevando el ritmo con la regadera).*
Don Diego no tiene don.
LA PÁJARA.
¡ Don!
LA CARBONERITA.
Don Diego,
de nieve y de fuego,
don din don,
que no tenéis lon.
LA PÁJARA.
Abrete de noche,
ciérrate de día,
cuida no te corte...

(PP, pp. 47-48.)

Sometimes Alberti abandons all pretense of coherence. He simply improvises «con alegre locura, interminables retahilas sin sentido y estribillos ilógicos, absurdos y disparatados, cuajados de bellas imágenes» [16]:

---

[15] The traditional *rima* is as follows:

Estaba la pájara pinta
sentadita en el verde limón.
Con el pico recoge la hoja,
con el pico recoge la flor.
¡ ay, mi amor!
M'arrodillo a los pies de María,
M'arrodillo porqu'es madre mía.
M'arrodillo a los pies de mi hermana,
M'arrodillo porque me da gana.
Dé usté la media vuelta.
Dé usté la vuelta entera.
Pero nó, pero nó, pero nó,
Pero nó, que me da vergüenza.
Pero sí, pero sí, pero sí,
Amiguita te quiero a tí.

(Francisco Rodríguez Marín, *Cantos populares españoles*, I [Seville: F. Alvarez, 1882], 95-96, cited in Marrast, p. 14).
[16] Bravo Villasante, *op. cit.*, p. 154.

¡ Rabidola lillo,
cólbida dindirindillo!
¡ Colbilí, colbilirí!
¡ Kikirikiií!
¡ Faralay direlo,
mórabel dindirindelo!
¡ Farolí, farolerí!
¡ Kikirikiií!

(PP, p. 43.)

Here again he echoes the many children's rhymes in which sonority takes precedence over meaning. The entire prologue, of which we have quoted a section, is made up of nonsensical onomatopoeic effects, recited by a certain PIPIRIGALLO «—gran cresta de campanillas—, puntero en la mano, dispuesto a explicar el argumento de la obra»[17]. These enable the author to achieve a good part of the musicality which he seems to have envisioned when he subtitled the work «guirigay lírico-bufo-bailable»[18].

La pájara pinta was conceived as a puppet play. The lack of subtlety and great formal economy normally associated with guiñolesque farce are immediately apparent in the text. For example, in the following brief sequence, ANTÓN confronts his rival suitor DON DIEGO:

> DON DIEGO (persiguiendo a ANTÓN con unas enormes tijeras de sastre).
> > Tus narí, tus narí,
> > tus narí-narices,
> > Peru-Perulero,
> > por mal caballero,
> > don Diego, don Diego,
> > don Diego Contreras
> > con sus sus tijeras
> > ti-ti-ti-tijeras
> > te te cortará,
> > y en un pu-puchero
> > las las hervirá.
> ANTÓN.
> > ¡ Pajarriquita Pintita!

[17] We find this notion preferable to Marrast's suggestion (p. 18) that these passages echo the entremeses of Quiñones de Benavente.
[18] Regarding the meaning of this subtitle, Marrast says the following: Que signifie exactement ce mot 'guirigay'? Son sens courant est: charabia, langue incompréhensible. Mais 'guirigay' est aussi une seconde ortographe de l'ancienne danse nommée 'guiriguirigay'... Puisque La pájara pinta est un guirigay à la fois «lírico, bufo» et «bailable», c'est qu'Alberti a joué sur le double sens du mot (pp. 13-14).

que pierdo mis naricitas.
Don Diego *(le atrapa)*.
    Primero, primero,
    primero al puchero.
Antón.
    ¡Carbonerita bonita,
    perdí el corazón y mis naricitas!
Don Diego *(va a cortarle las narices con las tijeras)*.
    Luego... luego, luego,
    al pato
    y al gato,
    de-de-don-don Diego.
Antón *(se defiende, y sacando un cuchillo va a atacar a* Don Diego).
    Ahora verás, don Diego,
    por mal sastre y barrigón.

                                        (PP, pp. 58-59.)

In this episode the comic effect derives from two standard slapstick devices. Don Diego's allegedly dangerous weapon poses an unlikely threat to Antón's anatomy. The aggressor is a chronic stutterer.

The sparse, broad brushstrokes and mock seriousness of this highly stylized art form were to leave their mark on a major part of Alberti's theatre. We cannot fully appreciate the extent of that influence at this time. We wish however to call attention to the continuing importance of guiñolesque elements. Just as the preceding scene will recur in later plays, we shall also be able to identify elements present in the following sequence. Here, as Antón attempts to deal with the coquetry of La carbonerita, the stereotyped situations, rudimentary characterization and elemental staging are once more distinctly characteristic of puppet theatre:

(Antón Perulero *da media vuelta y ve de pronto a* La carbonerita *que continúa regando las flores. Se va hacia ella contando las zancadas)*.

Antón.
    Una, dos y tres
    a la cuarta... a tus pies.
(Se arrodilla ante La carbonerita *y ésta le rocía con la regadera.)*
    Agüita que viene
    de mi Carbonera,
    agüita
    que quita
    la sed a cualquiera

¡Carbonerita, te quiero!

LA CARBONERITA.
Tiempo perdido, señor Perulero.

ANTÓN.
Carbonerita, me muero.

LA CARBONERITA.
Puede morirse, señor Perulero.

ANTÓN.
Carbonerita, ¡mírame!

LA CARBONERITA.
Señor Perulero, ¡levántese!

ANTÓN.
Carbonerita, ¡ ¡quiéreme! !

LA CARBONERITA.
Señor Perulero, váyase.

ANTÓN.
¿Acaso no valgo
más que el Carbonero?
Don Diego, Contreras
es mi compañero,
y en cuantito muera
don Diego Contreras,
seré yo el primero.

LA CARBONERITA.
¡Te quiero, te quiero
mi Antón Perulero!

ANTÓN.
¡Viva mi amor,
que ya floreció!

(Saca ANTÓN *un gran corazón florido.)*

LA CARBONERITA.
¡Viva el amor mío!
que ya ha florecido.

(Coge LA CARBONERITA *el corazón.)*

LA CARBONERITA Y ANTÓN *(danzan cogidos del* talle).
Vuela, corre y vuela,
de prisa, canela...
diré diré dirreví,
de prisa, perejil...

*(*LA CARBONERITA, *al terminar la danza, le* tira el corazón a ANTÓN.)*

ANTÓN.
¡ ¡ ¡Aaaaaaaay! ! !
¡Lagarta lagartijilla!
lagartija,
lagartona.

Cara de mica y andares de mona.
(Reacciona Antón *saliendo en persecución de*
La carbonerita, *en un entretejido de danza.)*
La carbonerita.
    Lagarto, lagartijillo,
    lagartijo,
    lagartón.
    Cara de mico, cabeza de melón.
Antón.
    Date prisa prisa,
    ¡ligero, ligero!
La carbonerita.
    ¡Aire! que me prisa
    mi Antón Perulero.
Antón.
    Aire, ligereza,
    corre que te corto,
    mi amor, la cabeza.
La carbonerita.
    ¡Pajarita Pinta!
    pronto, ¡que me muero!

                                    (PP, pp. 50-54.)

In this example familiar scenographic and histrionic devices serve to express conventional sentiments. Among these are: (1) the extravagant literary posturing of Antón, the desperate lover and swaggering braggart who counts his strides in childlike fashion; (2) the sudden comic reversals of La carbonerita, whose disdain readily gives way to amorous yielding; and (3) a number of explicitly allegorical elements—the dance that turns into a chase, the flower pot, the sprinkler, the huge paper heart which is literally tossed back and forth in keeping with the changing inclinations of the fickle woman.

La pájara pinta is a delightful work which must have been especially charming as spectacle. The author's use of popular elements, his concern with musicality, the absolute conventionality of his theatrical space, prefigure his mature theatre. Nevertheless, the virtues of *La pájara pinta* are more poetic than dramatic. This early work is a graceful and playful *divertimento* whose author—as Carmen Bravo Villasante puts it—, «sentíase a la vez juglar, marioneta y muñeco de guiñol» [19].

---

[19] Bravo Villasante, *loc. cit.*

El enamorado y la muerte

The brief play entitled *El enamorado y la muerte* [20] may have been written after *El hombre deshabitado*. However in spirit and theme it is closest to *La pájara pinta* and what we imagine most of the lost works to have been like. Therefore we include it in our discussion of the playwright's first period. In this instance, Alberti's principal source was a well-known *romance viejo* on the theme of the *emplazado* [21]:

> Un sueño soñaba anoche,
> soñito del alma mía,
> soñaba con mis amores
> que en mis brazos los tenía.
> Vi entrar señora tan blanca
> muy más que la nieve fría.
> —¿Por dónde has entrado, amor?
> ¿Cómo has entrado, mi vida?
> Las puertas están cerradas,
> ventanas y celosías.
> —No soy el amor, amante:
> la Muerte que Dios te envía.
> —¡Ay, Muerte tan rigurosa,
> Déjame vivir un día!
> —Un día no puede ser,
> una hora tienes de vida.
> Muy de prisa se calzaba,
> más de prisa se vestía;
> ya se va para la calle,
> en donde su amor vivía.
> —¡Abreme la puerta, blanca,
> ábreme la puerta, niña!
> —¿Cómo te podré yo abrir
> si la ocasión no es venida?
> Mi padre no fue al palacio,
> mi madre no está dormida.
> —Si no me abres esta noche,
> ya no me abrirás, querida;
> la Muerte me está buscando,
> junto a ti vida sería.

[20] Textual citations are taken from Manuel Bayo, *op. cit.*, hereafter referred to as EM. In our critical discussion we corroborate and expand upon some of the points made in Bayo's introduction.

[21] Text taken from Ramón Menéndez Pidal, *Flor nueva de romances viejos* (Madrid: Espasa Calpe, 1959), pp. 78-79. The source is not, as both Marrast and Bayo have claimed, another ballad by Juan del Encina from which the one we cite is derived (Yo me estaba reposando / durmiendo como solía, etc.).

                    —Vete bajo la ventana
                    donde labraba y cosía
                    te echaré cordón de seda
                    para que subas arriba,
                    y si el cordón no alcanzare
                    mis trenzas añadiría.
                    La fina seda se rompe;
                    la Muerte que allí venía:
                    —Vamos, el enamorado,
                    que la hora ya está cumplida.

Alberti's plot follows that of the traditional version. As a young
man—EL ENAMORADO—dreams about his beloved—LA ENAMORA-
DA—, there appears at his bedside a female figure—LA DONCELLA,
later LA MUERTE—whom he at first confuses with the object of his
affections. He soon discovers that his visitor is Death who has
come to carry him off. Death grants him but an hour in which to
see his beloved for one last time, and he rushes off to her house.
Roused by his cries, LA ENAMORADA lowers a silken cord from an
upstairs window so that her lover may gain entrance. As he
attempts to scale the wall, however, time runs out; Death reappears, severs the cord and carries off her victim. In a final scene,
she deposits him on his deathbed and kneels at his feet.

    As the subtitle «escenificación de un viejo romance» suggests,
Alberti intended for his work to resemble its source in structure
and language as well as in plot. Thus, the play is not entirely in
dialogue. While the dramatic passages of the ballad have been
distributed among the three characters just mentioned, narrative
parts have been assigned to a LECTOR who does not intervene in
the action. When not identical with that of the ballad, the
language taken from it presents only slight variants. We cite as
an example the exchange which occurs right after EL ENAMORADO
discovers the identity of his visitor:

            EL ENAMORADO.
                ¡Ay muerte, si eres mi muerte,
                déjame vivir un día!
            LA MUERTE.
                Un día no puede ser,
                una hora tienes de vida.
                Pasada una hora, amante,
                tu vida será cumplida.
            EL LECTOR.
                Ya salta el enamorado
                del lecho donde yacía.
                Si de prisa se calzaba,

más de prisa se vestía.
Ya se va para la calle
en donde su amor vivía.

(EM, p. 156.)

Minor additions to the traditional text, such as the ones contained here, sometimes appear when there is a change of speaker. They serve to avoid the choppines that would have resulted, if verses meant to be sung or recited by a single balladeer had been assigned without modification to several performers.

While Alberti has adhered closely to the traditional text, he has also expanded it so as to add to its dramatic and theatrical qualities. The mysterious visitor of the *romance viejo* identifies herself immediately upon appearing at the lover's bedside ; Alberti's DONCELLA on the other hand, offers only hints as to who she is :

> *(Se abren las cortinas del fondo de la alcoba*
> *y entra, sigilosa, la careta y el traje blancos,*
> LA DONCELLA. *Va girando, despacio, alrededor*
> *del lecho.)*
> EL ENAMORADO *(Como sonámbulo).*
> ¿Por dónde has entrado, amor?
> ¿Cómo has podido, mi vida?
> Las puertas están cerradas,
> ventanas y celosías.
> LA DONCELLA.
> Yo entro sin abrir las puertas,
> ventanas y celosías.

(EM, pp. 153-54.)

Death's movements, her pale demeanor, the suggestion that she possesses supernatural powers all render her ominous without revealing her identity unequivocally. Taking advantage of the darkness which assures her victim's continued innocence, she repeatedly beckons and evades him :

> EL ENAMORADO.
> Ven que te abrace, mi amor,
> y duerma en tu compañía...
> LA DONCELLA.
> A tientas te busco, amante :
> la alcoba no está encendida.
> EL ENAMORADO.
> También a tientas mis manos
> te buscan a ti, mi vida.

EL LECTOR.
Mientras sus manos la buscan,
ella sus manos esquiva.
Al borde de la almohada
una vela le encendía...
EL ENAMORADO.
¡Oh, qué blanco estás amor,
a la luz de la bujía!
(Intenta tocarla. Ella se aleja.)

(EM, p. 154.)

Throughout this sequence of pursuit and flight, all of which is
Alberti's invention, visual and sound effects enhance the poetic
material. In a symbolic play on notions of light and darkness, the
stage directions call for four candles to progressively illumine the
set; this suggests the lover's growing awareness of Death's
presence. As the scene culminates, the elusive woman reveals her
identity. Her highly theatrical gesture is accompanied by the tolling
of bells and the entoning of the *Dies Irae*:

(Al encender[se] la cuarta vela, EL ENAMORA-
DO se tiende en el lecho y LA DONCELLA, de rodi-
llas, canturrea sordamente la melodía funeral del
«Dies Irae». Dentro, débiles, doblan las campanas.
Silencio.)

EL ENAMORADO.
Di, ¿qué me cantas, amor,
que la sangre se me enfría?
LA DONCELLA. *(De pie, quitándose la careta y*
abriéndose la túnica, muestra la calavera y el es-
quema de LA MUERTE.)
No soy tu amor, soy la muerte,
la muerte que Dios te envía.

(EM, pp. 155-56.)

In the scene which follows this revelation, EL ENAMORADO
attempts feverishly to fulfil his desire within the hour alotted him.
Here, Alberti expands the ballad version by developing elements
already contained therein. Implicit in the *romance viejo* is an
ironic contrast between the omnipotence of Death and the impotence of her victim. While Death violates the intimacy of the
lover's bedchamber at will—even though doors and windows are
closed—, a closed door stands as an obstacle between the lover
and amorous fulfillment; later the silken cord which is his sole
alternative means of access proves useless. As can be seen from a

passage already cited [22], from the outset Alberti insists more than does his source on the presence of doors and windows. Now, as the youth arrives at his lady's house, the narrator states: «las puertas están cerradas, / ventanas y celosías. / La muerte, sólo la muerte / es su sola compañía» (EM, p. 156). This affirmation is followed by a moment of dramatic irony ; unseen by her victim, Death appears before the audience. As she enters, the ominous barking of dogs and the hissing of bats foreshadow what is about to take place. The lover knocks on the door and incites his lady to let him in ; in Alberti's version, he has to call not once but twice before he is heard. The exchange which then occurs centers upon the matter of access to the house (EM, p. 157). Taken directly from the source, its ironic effect is considerably greater in the stage version. In both of the examples just discussed, the young playwright demonstrates an intuitive grasp of the nature of his task. The musical, plastic, and histrionic qualities present in his stage version of El enamorado y la muerte are only possibilities in the romance viejo. The disembodied voices of the ballad have materialized in a richly sensorial spectacle. Carefully integrated with the dialogue, stage effects become a means of dramatic gradation. The drama contained in the original is further heightened through the addition of elements of suspense, augury and dramatic irony.

As Bayo has observed [23], certain features which link El ena- morado y la muerte to other works roughly contemporary with it also afford a glimpse of what Alberti's mature theatre would be. Like others of his generation, our author would continue to draw his inspiration from popular traditions. Extremely attentive to details of costuming, lighting, sound effects, stage movement, he would repeatedly strive for total spectacle. Incipient elements of allegory join El enamorado y la muerte to El hombre deshabitado. The exclusive use of ballad meter parallels a similar usage in Fermín Galán. The presence of a narrator points to that work and beyond it to later plays in which commentator-characters figure importantly—De un momento a otro, La Gallarda, Noche de gue- rra en el Museo del Prado. Nevertheless in a global consideration of Alberti's theatre, the stage version of El enamorado y la muer- te must be placed alongside La pájara pinta as an example of his earliest efforts. A total absence of ideological content differentiates this work from those which precede and follow. Being a fairly direct transposition of the ballad, it is fundamentally theatre poetry as distinguished from true drama. Moreover in assessing its author's

22 See our page 49.
23 Op. cit., p. 152.

technical expertise at the time of its composition, we should bear
in mind that *El enamorado y la muerte* is a work of limited
dimensions. As we shall see, a similarly literal use of the conventions of balladry was to have less fortunate results in *Fermín
Galán* [24]. Used to excess in that more ambitious play, the kind of
repetition which here surrounds the matter of doors and windows
would prove anti-dramatic. While visual irony is successfully
employed in *El enamorado y la muerte*, the longer and more
complex *El hombre deshabitado* suffers precisely because possibilities for visual irony are overlooked. Thus, although the virtues of
this brief work are many, their importance should not be exaggerated. At the most, they offer us a hint of the excellent craftsmanship which would characterize the playwright's best work.

* * *

On the basis of fragmentary evidence, we conclude that Alberti's first plays were a prolongation of his poetic works. In them
the author seems to have followed his natural inclination as poet,
musician and anthologist. At this moment in his career, Alberti
probably regarded the stage as a vehicle, a means rather than an
end. His chief esthetic concern appears to have been the recreation
in plastic theatrical form of a series of popular and frequently
lyric elements.

[24] See our pages 67-68.

CHAPTER III

THE THEATRE AS IDEOLOGY: THE 1930s

El hombre deshabitado

El hombre deshabitado (1929), Alberti's first full-length work, represents a major step forward, a radical change of direction and an extremely ambitious undertaking. In attempting a modern version of the traditional *auto sacramental*, the author was subject to the danger of banality which threatens any didactic author. In addition, he had to seek great originality if he was to avoid the clichés of an otherwise outmoded form.

The play consists of prologue, act (the traditional *aucto)* and epilogue. Its protagonist is a character designated as EL HOMBRE, representative of the human condition. In the course of the action, this character prepares to venture forth into the world (prologue), embarks upon his earthly journey *(acto)*, and finally returns to his point of departure (epilogue). Although he is one individual, his development encompasses three visions of humanity, presented in dialectic relation to one another; from two images which contrast in the prologue, there emerges a third which partakes of the attributes of the other two, yet is unlike either.

In his first manifestation, the protagonist of the play is an «hombre del subsuelo» (I, 12)—the inhabitant of a barren landscape and one among many «trajes huecos que no desean nada, movidos tan sólo por un aburrimiento sin rumbo» (I, 11). He has no god, no concept of freedom, aspires to nothing and is characterized above all by spiritual emptiness. With the arrival of the VIGILANTE NOCTURNO—a magician-like deity who works sleight-of-hand miracles with the aid of a magic lantern—this spiritless creature is transformed and given a soul. Stripped of the diver's suit in which he first appeared, he becomes a young *caballero* whose attributes are a childish innocence and five senses—«five balconies» that open onto the world, offering a promise of happiness if he uses them well, or a threat of perdition if he acts foolishly. It is this hopeful young man who embarks upon an earthly journey, there to undergo a second transformation. His fall before the forces that seek his destruction represents the negation of his freedom and the frustration of his hopes.

For the duration of the act, the protagonist inhabits a terrestrial paradise along with his wife and five allegorical characters that symbolize his five senses. But here his similarity to the biblical Adam ends. Whereas Adam might have been saved had he maintained his innocence intact and refused the knowledge of good and evil, EL HOMBRE can only succumb to temptation. His innocence prevents him from recognizing evil ; thus he cannot exercise his will [1]. Temptation penetrates Alberti's Eden not as a serpent, but as a swooning woman whose sickly aspect inspires feelings of pity. Upon seeing her, LA MUJER exclaims prophetically, «Está helada y llena de arañazos...» ; immediately she adds, «¡ Pobre ! ¡ Tiene los pies heridos !» (I, 29). Like EL HOMBRE, she is blind to the danger that lurks behind the appearance of a pious act ; her innocence is ignorance rather than purity. Because they insist compassionately that Temptation remain in their house, the couple is left defenseless. By the time EL HOMBRE discovers her identity and perceives the threat to his innocence, he is already lost. Though repulsed by the demands of his seductress, he can only offer up a weak resistance. He yields gradually to a desire to possess her, permitting himself to be led through a series of vilifications that culminates in the murder of his wife. This act costs him his happiness. When as last he finds himself in the arms of Temptation, his victim appears as a ghostly configuration of his remorse and shoots him dead.

In the epilogue we find the protagonist back in the barren landscape from which he emerged. But now he is neither the resigned inhabitant of the depths, nor the ambitious *caballero* of the *acto*. Instead he is a rebel who aspires to an impossible happiness, fully aware that it will be denied him. Realizing that the promises of his creator were false, he accuses the VIGILANTE NOCTURNO of having deceived him :

> EL HOMBRE. — ¡ Un asesino, sí ! Porque tú, señor, puesto que ya lo sabías todo, lo manejabas todo, conocías todos los resortes y secretos nublados de mi alma en el mundo, bien pudiste evitar estas catástrofes, mandándome una luz, un aviso celeste, o habiéndome creado de otro modo. Yo no tengo la culpa, yo... fui derrotado porque quisiste..., porque tú así lo habías dispuesto desde

---

[1] Ventura Doreste appears to have noted this when he wrote, «En el auto de Alberti el Hombre carece de claridad espiritual y, por consiguiente, de albedrío» (*op. cit.*, p. 83).

mil siglos antes de concederme la vida. Y hubiera sido inútil toda
súplica, todo llanto, toda llamada a ti...

(I, 46-47.)

Desirous of understanding the reasons for his dilemma, EL HOMBRE
demands an explanation. But all he can wrest from his deity is a
final, enigmatic statement: «Mis juicios son un abismo profundo»
(I, 49).

The essential difference between the protagonist of the epilogue and the hopeful *caballero* of the prologue is the former's
anguished consciousness of his dilemma. Throughout the play, EL
HOMBRE seeks knowledge and understanding. He questions the
nature of his desires and attempts to discover the identity of his
supposed benefactor. But unlike his innocent queries in the prologue, his questions in the epilogue are urgent and painful:

> EL HOMBRE. — ¿Por qué lo permitiste tú, Señor, por qué lo
> permitiste? ¡Tú, tan bueno, que me creaste solamente para la
> felicidad y la alegría! Dímelo, antes de que esta boca se cierre,
> devorándome a la luz de los astros. ¡Que no me hunda en esta cue-
> va sin saberlo!
>
> (I, 48.)

What has occurred here is a change in the way the protagonist
perceives his own nature. While his questioning is as constant as
the attitude of his creator is implacable, EL HOMBRE has discovered
that no answers will be forthcoming. In addition, he has experienced the crippling effects of guilt.

The protagonist's battle with Temptation is portrayed as a
gradual awakening of consciousness to anguish. In his weak
attempts to resist the demands of his seductress, EL HOMBRE repeatedly protests his incomprehension. «Es que no te comprendo...
ni sé quién eres», he exclaims (I, 27-28), and later, «No puedo
más... No sé ya quién soy» (I, 32). At the same time, he exhibits
an ever-growing awareness of his plight. Before he confronts
Temptation, he never acknowledges the allegorical presence of his
Senses. Now he addresses them directly, pleading for the numbness
that would permit him to avert his eyes from his unbearable
situation:

> EL HOMBRE. — ¡Dejadme, por favor! ¡No os conozco! No sé
> quiénes sois. Nunca os he visto. Me espantan vuestras voces, vues-
> tras máscaras horribles y monstruosas. Quiero dormir... [a EL
> TACTO]. Si te conozco, no quiero conocerte. Anestésiame el cuer-
> po. Déjamelo más insensible que el de un perro atacado de pará-

lisis. Descuájame los brazos de raíz, los labios, la lengua, todo mi
ser. Que mis manos se queden sin memoria.

(I, 32-33.)

Realizing that he is incapable of renouncing that which he has
once acquired, he demonstrates yet a deeper understanding of his
own nature:

> EL HOMBRE. — ¡ No, no ! ¡ No me dejes ahora ! ¿ Qué sería yo
> sin ti ? Un río sin agua, una vena sin sangre, un cuerpo sin cuerpo.

(I, 33.)

Because of his newly gained awareness, the protagonist will
signal his defeat with a weary gesture of self-knowledge. This is
his recognition of the foreordained failure to which his so-called
innocence—really his blindness—has led him:

> EL HOMBRE. — Sé muy bien lo que digo... Sé que estáis cons-
> pirando contra mí para perderme y matar la inocencia de un ar-
> cángel.

(I, 33.)

Thus, while the overt manifestations of his bewilderment do not
change even at the very end, the exhausted sentence which precedes his final capitulation is an affirmative statement—a characterization of Man's condition rather than simply a sign of confusion:

> EL HOMBRE. — *No sé ya quién soy en medio de las tinieblas...*
> Haced de mí lo que queráis. Me abandono a vosotros. Tendrá que
> ser así. No puedo más (our italics).

(I, 34.)

EL HOMBRE now knows that he is spiritually deformed, that his
very innocence has cost him his happiness. What he does not understand is *why* it should be so. As he discovers in the epilogue, this
understanding will forever be denied him. In the traditional *auto*,
Man is accompanied by the allegorical figure of Reason, who serves
as a possible defense against Temptation and Sensuality ; here
there is no such character. In the face of his frustrated dreams of
happiness and spiritual clarity, Alberti's protagonist has nothing
but a bitter consciousness of his own desperate impotence. That
consciousness of what he would have liked to be defines him in
the end. «El hombre deshabitado»—the Spanish is ambiguous—

is no longer simply a hollow creature ; he is a creature disposses-
sed as well, deprived of his illusions and stripped of his hopes.
The allegorical language of *El hombre deshabitado* owes a great
deal to that of the traditional *auto sacramental* [2]. Such phrases
as «traje hueco», «salida a un paraíso terrestre» or «volver al subsuelo» are immediately interpreted as 'spiritual emptiness',
'earthly sojourn', 'condemnation'. This constant movement from
concrete to abstract was a standard feature of the classical genre.
Alberti also follows the classical authors in his heavy emphasis on
visual and plastic symbols. Costumes and concrete objects play an
important part in our perceptions. In the prologue, the diver's
suit worn by the protagonist immediately establishes his identity
as an inhabitant of the depths. The Five Senses are distinguished
by the suits they wear :

> LA VISTA *es un monstruo todo lleno de ojos;* EL OÍDO, *todo
> lleno de orejas;* EL OLFATO, *de narices;* EL GUSTO, *de bocas, y* EL
> TACTO, *de manos.*
>
> (I, 14.)

The VIGILANTE NOCTURNO works his miracles by manipulating stage
props. He awakens the senses of the protagonist with the aid of
a star, the night wind, a rose, an orange, a beautiful woman. With
his magic lantern, he conjures up images of a humanity grown
weary of its frivolity :

> EL VIGILANTE NOCTURNO *(Prolonga una luz de su linterna...
> [y] aparece la esquina de una calle cualquiera.. Sin pisar, pasan
> pendientes de un alambre, trajes vacíos, fláccidos, de señoras, de
> caballeros, militares, curas, jóvenes, niños, colgados de caretas ho-
> rribles, pintadas, con ojos y sin ellos. Carrusel triste, silencioso,
> sin orden).* — Humanidad hastiada, viviendas vacías repintadas
> por fuera para disimular el abandono y oscuridad en que viven
> por dentro.
>
> (I, 11.)

---

[2] Regarding the specific sources of Alberti's *auto*, Marrast (pp. 29-31) mentions
Gil Vicente, with whom the author himself claimed kinship (AP, p. 309), Calderón's
El gran teatro del mundo and, principally, some of the works that appear in the
sixteenth-century «Códice de autos viejos» (see Leo Rouanet, ed., *Colección de
autos, farsas y coloquios del siglo XVI*, 4 vols. [Barcelona, 1901]). For a discussion
of Alberti's use of traditional conventions, see Marrast, «L'esthétique théâtrale»,
pp. 56-57. See also Cyril B. Morris, «Parallel Imagery in Quevedo and Alberti»,
Bulletin of Hispanic Studies 36, 135-45. Morris has noted that Alberti follows the
classic and baroque authors, especially Quevedo, in referring to the body and soul
figuratively as 'habitations'. However, he implies wrongly in our estimation that
the two authors' theological outlooks are similar.

In several instances Alberti has borrowed specific allegorical
devices from the classical *auto;* the example just cited can be
regarded as a modern Dance of Death. In a lyric interlude the Five
Senses play catch with a huge red fish ; their sequential behavior
is a standard convention of the traditional genre :

> EL OÍDO.
> Escucho en sus ojos y oigo en sus escamas
> el barco, la vela, la brisa y el agua...
> Toma, vivo te doy el pez...
> EL OLFATO.
> Yo huelo en sus alas y huelo en su cola
> la estrella marina, las algas, las rosas...
> Toma, vivo te doy el pez...
> LA VISTA.
> Veo en sus agallas y veo en sus ojos
> las velas partidas y los barcos rotos...
> Toma, vivo te doy el pez...
> EL GUSTO.
> Yo gusto en las púas finas de sus dientes,
> ni miel ni salitre sino sangre y muerte.
> *(Lo aprieta, ahogándolo.) (a* EL TACTO*)*
> Muerto te devuelvo el pez...

(I, 25.)

Another familiar allegorical procedure in Alberti's *auto* is the
symbolic compartmentalization of the stage. The sewer cover from
beneath which the diver makes his initial entrance suggests a
subterranean hell. In the decor of the *acto,* a lush garden and a
dark granary are separated by a low wall of crumbling bricks.
This transitional zone between the beautiful and the ugly is
bounded on one side by sea and sky and on the other by brimstone
and broken tiles. EL HOMBRE and LA MUJER inhabit the garden.
The protagonist will make love to Temptation in the granary,
under the shadow of a huge spider web.

Notwithstanding Alberti's frequent use of traditional elements,
El hombre deshabitado is a highly unorthodox *auto* and a tho-
roughly modern work. The action of the prologue takes place in
an Expressionistic landscape of twisted metals, lime and coal,
rusty cans and rotting wood :

> (Decoración): *En el centro de la escena, y en primer término,
> la gran boca cerrada de una alcantarilla. A su derecha, y al borde,
> clavados en la tierra, tres hierros retorcidos, unidos por un cordel.
> (El más próximo a la alcantarilla tendrá atado en la punta un tra-
> pajo blanquecino.) Sobre un montón de ladrillos, y en medio del*

triángulo que forman estos tres hierros, un farolillo rojo de luz parpadeante. Al lado izquierdo de la escena, sobre una plancha de acero con ruedas, un gran cono de carbón. Y al derecho, sobre una tabla, una gran pirámide de cal. Ambos montones, clavados de palas. Esparcidos por distintos lugares, cinco toneles, polvorientos, y piquetas, martillos, cubos, sacos, pedazos de raíles, etc. En penúltimo término, y haciendo bocacalle, dos vallas: una de latones mohosos y otra de maderas destrozadas. Contra el fondo negro, un poste medio tumbado, de luz eléctrica, del que pende un largo cable roto.

(I, 9.)

The diver that emerges into this bleak setting is subject to the arbitrary dictates of a Machine Age deity. The Eucharist—the sole theme of the traditional *auto*—has no reality for him. His battle will be an inner struggle, not against Temptation but against the necessity of contemplating his own victimized being. The dialogue which reflects the increasingly violent movements of his spirit is full of cognitive and sensorial verbs. It represents a desire not to see, an attempt to maintain innocence intact by eluding awareness [3].

The evolving situation of Alberti's character resembles that of Man at different stages in Western history. In the prologue he is a creature of darkness—that is, the pagan who has been promised nothing because his existence antedates the arrival of Christ. In the *acto* he is an aspirant to happiness, as is the Christian for whom penitence and salvation are vital concepts. Finally, in the epilogue he is a man who continues to desire but lacks hope—who thirsts after freedom knowing he cannot attain it and searches for explanations he realizes he will not find. At the play's conclusion, in other words, Alberti's protagonist stands at the edge of the unfathomable abyss that separates what he is from what he would like to be. Like modern man, he has glimpsed the existential absurd [4].

While Alberti's *auto* is a significant experiment, it is not always a successful one. An unclear exposition and diffuse statement of theme make the work subject to highly contradictory interpretations. In several instances the author touches upon ideas which he neither develops fully nor wholly relates to his conceptual struc-

---

[3] Here again Alberti undoubtedly echoes the German Expressionist playwrights. Like the *autos sacramentales,* their works are heavily allegorical in character. However, their dramatic conflicts are most often psychological rather than theological. See M. Gravier, «Les héros du drame expressioniste», in *Le théâtre moderne: hommes et tendances,* pp. 117-30.

[4] A. Valbuena Prat notes in passing the existential focus of Alberti's *auto (Historia del teatro español* [Barcelona: Noguer (c 1956)], p. 625).

ture [5]. Most of all, the first half of the work is markedly prosaic. Until EL HOMBRE initiates his battle against Temptation, the allegorical characters are little more than personified concepts, lacking in poetry and dramaticity [6]. In our estimation, Alberti's difficulty stems from his failure to take full advantage of the possibilities at his disposal. For example, he did not sufficiently exploit the expressive possibilities of his decor. The Expressionistic setting of the prologue is present as mere revestment. In the protagonist's first soliloquy, the scenographic images are prolonged in a series of violent metaphors and chaotic concatenations. However, there is virtually no other stylistic connection between Alberti's dialogue and his extensive theatrical trappings. When the characters allude to the world which they inhabit, they do so in the most prosaic terms which allegory will allow. A better integration of decor and dialogue would have greatly enhanced the poetic effect of the whole.

In the same vein, the author did not avail himself of a series of ironic elements which figure significantly in the early moments of the play. The first of these appears when the diver of the prologue is transformed into a young *caballero*. With the awakening of his senses, EL HOMBRE loses all awareness of his surroundings. For the audience, however, the barren setting provides a dismal counterpoint to the sleight-of-hand performance of the VIGILANTE NOCTURNO. The tripartite decor of the act makes possible a second irony. By juxtaposing a vision of paradise against an image of horror and decay, Alberti reminds us of the dual nature of the senses—that is, the reality which, unknown to EL HOMBRE, will precipitate his fall. When Temptation makes her entrance at the wall, we can construe this as a symbolic warning. The protagonist on the other hand, cannot grasp its significance : his vision only encompasses the garden.

Early in the act, there occurs a sequence which has as its focal point a pond located in the garden. When the protagonist and his wife gaze into its depths, they witness kaleidoscopic scenes of past and future bliss—a modern metropolis, a forest in the snow, and an ancient city :

> LA VISTA. — Hay ciudades que yo no he visto nunca. Esta
> es una de ellas. Sus murallas dentadas y derruidas, sus jardines

[5] This probably accounts for some of the controversy which existed among Alberti's contemporaries regarding the religious views expressed in *El hombre deshabitado*. See our note 24, p. 19. Marrast's assertion that the work is optimistic and orthodox (pp. 34 ff.) stems from his use of the author's life and *Sobre los ángeles* (a more optimistic work) in interpreting the *auto*.

[6] For a viewpoint somewhat similar to what follows, see Ruiz Ramón, *op. cit.*, pp. 229-30.

perdidos, sus habitantes andrajosos y tristes, me hacen pensar en alguna ciudad antigua hoy venida a menos. Sería dichoso yo con pasearme por sus calles ruinosas, ver de cerca la pena carcomida de sus gentes...

EL HOMBRE. — Una ciudad antigua que saldremos a buscar este verano...

LA MUJER. — ¿Y crees tú que la encontraremos?... ¿Cómo, si no sabemos su nombre?

EL HOMBRE. — Para nosotros no hay nada imposible... Es la pureza de nuestras almas la que nos hace hallar fácilmente lo desconocido.

(I, 21-22.)

Believing their innocence to be a source of strength, the couple reflects upon these visions in terms of sensual delight. At the same time the Five Senses provide a second commentary containing images suggestive of grief and pain. Here there is a third irony : the spectator is again given access to a full image of reality while the vision of the protagonist remains partial. The fourth and final irony occurs shortly thereafter in the previously cited lyric interlude. The playful behavior of the Five Senses is only witnessed by the audience. The poetic metaphors of the dialogue once more alternate beautiful images with visions of death and destruction. The game ends when EL GUSTO strangles the fish. This gesture foreshadows the end of the *acto*. After his fall, the protagonist will gaze for a last time into the pond that offered him visions of beauty ; all he will see there are a dagger and a dead fish (I, 40).

The presence of these ironies is essential to our grasp of theme. They enable us to witness the awakening of the character's consciousness by underlining the discrepancy between reality and his limited perception. The elimination of the ironic discrepancy signals his defeat, his arrival at awareness. Therefore Alberti's failure to enjoin the ironies with the painful struggle of his protagonist seems a serious oversight. The tension generated by the character's growing awareness could have been extended. If the ironies had been graduated so as to bring about a prior awakening of the spectator, considerable dramaticity might have been achieved. Yet throughout, their relationship to the dramatic process remains purely technical. In *El hombre deshabitado*, irony never transcends the level of exposition. As a result, the beginning of the work remains prosaic and excessively abstract.

Among the probable reasons for Alberti's failure to make the most of his material are some which are historical : *El hombre deshabitado* was written in several stages [7], at a time when the author's turbulent emotions could hardly have fostered critical detachment. Undoubtedly certain generic factors also contributed to the play's unevenness. It is difficult to achieve artistic unity and maintain dramatic tension in a work as ambitious as *El hombre deshabitado*; it is also easy to respond uncritically to literary vogues, merely appropriating rather than assimilating that which is borrowed. In at least one respect, however, the playwright's inexpertness seems clearly to have been at fault. In most instances, the elements overlooked were visual. They would be less apparent to a *literato* than to a genuine man of the theatre. It is unlikely that Alberti would have chosen to disregard such potentially valuable resources had he perceived them clearly; therefore we must suppose that he lacked awareness. This suggests that in 1929, he approached the problem of dramatic composition in an excessively literary fashion—with less of a sense of spectacle than would have been required to handle his allegorical language [8].

In *El hombre deshabitado*, the author attempted to breathe new life into an outmoded literary form by adapting it to the perspective and concerns of a modern audience. From the standpoint of artistic quality, the step which he took was largely a false one. Nonetheless, Alberti's *auto* is historically an important example of *tradición renovada*. Moreover, it represents a decisive step in the direction of the playwright's future experiments. Its didactic nature and ideological emphasis established a pattern for

---

[7] See our p. 13.

[8] It is worth noting in this connection that the text we have cited, first published in 1950, is a revised version of the work presented in 1931 (cf. R. Alberti, *El hombre deshabitado* [Madrid: Gama, 1930] [sic for 1931]). In addition to several minor word changes, the 1950 edition incorporates three passages which do not appear in the original:

(1) In the revised text, the spectre of EL HOMBRE's murdered wife makes a second appearance. As the protagonist begs for a sign of forgiveness that would permit him to rest from his hallucinatory state of guilt, she passes without noticing him (I, 40-45). This gives tangible form to the notion that guilt is memory and awareness, not an abstract concept.

(2) In the earlier version, the passage in which Temptation calls upon EL HOMBRE for the last time is a simple «¡Aquí! ¡Aquí! ¡Baja!» In the later text, this speech is lengthened and the appearance of Temptation and the Five Senses substituted for the sound of a disembodied voice (I, 47-48).

(3) In the original text only a series of blasphemous outcries precedes the protagonist's final collapse. In the second version, an extended sequence in which his senses are extinguished one by one again makes the characters less purely conceptual (I, 48).

Interestingly, these variants do not alter the meaning of Alberti's work, but serve instead to render the struggle of his protagonist more visual and plastic. Apparently the more knowledgeable playwright of 1950 felt a need to remedy the consequences of his earlier inexperience.

what his theatre would be during the remainder of the 1930s. His interest in allegory, especially the allegorical portrayal of a spiritual process, would encompass the works of the following decade as well. Alberti's liking for multiple sets, his taste for dramatic irony and his predilection for combining traditional and vanguard elements are already evident in this play. These tendencies and techniques would eventually become a part of his mature style.

Fermín Galán

Fermín Galán (1930) [9] has much in common with *El hombre deshabitado*. Both of these works had a discontinuous and somewhat haphazard origin, and a noisy reception. Both reflect the experimental tenor of the 1930s and echo Alberti's spiritual development as he moved increasingly toward commitment. Both bespeak the author's continuing interest in didactic composition and the innovative use of traditional elements. These latter similarities provide a basis for regarding them as the point of departure for a second ideological phase in his theatre.

In *Fermín Galán*, Alberti turned his attention once again to balladry—this time to a form which is especially theatrical and spectacular, even though it does not fall within the limits of what we normally classify as theatre. «Mis propósitos eran conseguir un romance de ciego», he writes, «un gran chafarrinón de colores subidos como los que en las ferias pueblerinas explicaban el crimen del día». True to the spirit of the original genre, *Fermín Galán* was to be «una obra sencilla, popular, en la que me atendría más que a la verdad histórica, a la que deformada por la gente ya empezaba a correr con visos de leyenda...». In keeping with the nature of his project, the didactic author's thematic material is no longer metaphysical: «Lleno de ingenuidad, y casi sin saberlo, intentaba mi primera obra política» (AP, p. 318).

The action of *Fermín Galán* focuses on the high points of the hero's life, as well as on the historical events surrounding the famous insurrection of Jaca. In Act I we meet FERMÍN as a child on the island of San Fernando. We then follow him through a training period in Morocco, where he accumulates honors and ascends in rank. Next we see him in the jail of Montjuich, where he is serving a three year sentence as a political prisoner. In Act II, Alberti recreates the different stages of the incident at Jaca—the pre-

---

[9] R. Alberti, *Fermín Galán* ([Madrid: Chulilla y Angel], 1931). Hereafter cited as FG.

parations, the uprising, the departure of the Republican troops,
and an encounter with the Monarchist forces in the sanctuary of
Cillas. In the final act, we witness the trial and sentencing of
FERMÍN and his aid GARCÍA HERNÁNDEZ before the Council of
Ministers, their execution by a firing squad, and a dance at the
palace of a nobleman. The work concludes with an epilogue in
which FERMÍN's mother eulogizes her martyred son.

Alberti's use of the conventions of the *romance de ciego* is
extensive and ingenious. In addition to having chosen as his theme
a recent and much publicized event of contemporary history, the
author echoes the traditional genre in the following important
respects:

(1)   The characteristic structure of the *romance de ciego*, with
its alternation of narrative passages and dialogue, is maintained
through the use of interior reduplication. A blind balladeer performs
in a town square before an audience of students, old folks and
diverse popular types (frame situation). As he recounts FERMÍN's
deeds and comments upon their significance, his recitation is interrupted by ten dramatic episodes (interior fiction). These are
analogous to the snatches of direct dialogue ordinarily interspersed
throughout the balladeer's narration.

(2)   Alberti has approximated the material conditions which
usually surround the balladeer. The *ciego* is accompanied by his
young helper or *lazarillo*. As in real life this character peddles
printed copies of the text to interested spectators:

> EL NIÑO.
>> ¡Compren, si quieren llorar!
>> ¡Oigan, si quieren llorar!
>> ¡Romance de Fermín Galán y
>> los sublevados de Jaca! ¡A
>> cinco céntimos!
>
>> > (FG, p. 13.)

The questions of the audience and the occasional reappearance of
passers-by are additional echoes of the traditional setting for these
rustic performances. For example, a sailor and a street vendor
cause a momentary interruption with their gross insinuations and
lascivious laughter:

> *(Enlazados por los hombros y borrachos...*
> *entran...* EL MARINERO *y* LA VENDEDORA...)
>
> EL MARINERO *(Tocándole un pecho...)*
>> ¡Ja ja! ¿Qué tienes aquí?

La vendedora.
    ¿Qué te importa a ti?
El marinero.
    ¡ Ja, ja, ja! ¡ Kikirikí!
    ¿Algo para mí?

                                        (FG, pp. 32-33.)

(3) Alberti's stage sets resemble the garish storybook illus-
trations that usually adorn the broadsides which the *lazarillo*
offers for sale. The allegorical curtain of the frame situation
simulates a title page:

> *En primer término del escenario, telón pintado: con colores*
> *populares, de aleluya callejera, el fusilamiento de Fermín Galán y*
> *García Hernández, sobre un fondo de alegoría republicana. Arriba,*
> *en la parte alta del telón, un gran letrero que dice:* «Romance de
> Fermín Galán y los sublevados de Jaca». *Abajo, en uno de los*
> *lados...* «Precio: 5 cénts.»

                                        (FG, p. 11.)

In the dramatic episodes, a comparable effect is sought through
an openly conventional use of color and lighting. The sky of
Morocco is a «cielo naranja, intenso» (FG, p. 41). The stage directions repeatedly call for a schematic arrangement of objects
and furniture. Thus the author facilitates identification but avoids
any illusion of verisimilitude:

> *Rincón solitario del muelle. Por fondo, cortinas negras o azu-*
> *les. O telón azul de cielo. A la derecha un trozo de muralla, con*
> *su escalerilla. Asoman bocas de chimeneas, respiraderos y mástiles*
> *con banderas, de los barcos fondeados. Anclas y aparejos de pesca,*
> *por el suelo.*

                                        (FG, p. 26.)

(4) The language of the narration recalls that of the ballad
in diction and tone. The *juglar* makes abundant use of the exhorta-
tive formulas of oral literature:

> El ciego.
>   Vedle por los malecones...
>   Mirad también a su madre, etc.

                                        (FG, p. 17.)

He communicates a feeling of wonder to his audience through the frequent use of exclamations :

> EL CIEGO.
> ¡ Qué niño es Fermín Galán
> niño serio, sin sonrisa,
> niño que mira a lo lejos,
> sin saber adónde mira !

(FG, p. 16.)

His ponderative attitude is reflected in details and images which surround the protagonist with marvelous attributes. For example, he endows the child FERMÍN with a prophetic intuition of his future glory and the ability to elicit an emotional response from nature :

> EL CIEGO.
> Muy lejos Fermín Galán
> tiene clavada su vista.
> ¿ En dónde? (España lo supo
> cuando en la tierra caía.)
> Las playas de arena alegre
> son de arena dolorida.

(FG, p. 17.)

(5) Traditionally, the dialogued parts of the *romance de ciego* represent the balladeer's attempt to satisfy his audience's taste for truculence and melodrama. This seems to be paralleled in the dramatic episodes of Alberti's play by a studied insistence on sentimental clichés, especially at moments of adversity. FERMÍN has witnessed the death of a fellow prisoner ; when he feels a need to rekindle his waning courage, his mother appears to him in his cell at Montjuich. About to be shot, the hero bravely refuses the offer of a blindfold ; his last wish is that one of the executioners deliver it to his mother. She, in turn, will make of her son's last gift the central symbol of her final lament :

> LA MADRE.
> ¡ Qué soledad, hijo,
> hijo, qué silencio !
> Sólo me acompaña
> tu triste pañuelo...
> Sé que por sus nilos
> andas en recuerdo...
> ¿ No es verdad que sientes
> cómo yo te beso?
> *(Besa el pañuelo.)*

(FG, p. 217.)

(6)   Like the *juglar*, the author desires to portray an exemplary hero who has become a legend in his own time, rather than a historical figure. Therefore, the language of the narration tends toward hyperbole and idealization. That of the interpolated scenes is markedly sentimental. As a result the characterization is extremely schematic. Of the ninety-seven characters mentioned in the *reparto*, only FERMÍN, his mother and GARCÍA HERNÁNDEZ figure significantly in the action. Their behavior is entirely predictable and predetermined.

Alberti's idea for *Fermín Galán* was a promising one. Lorca, with *Mariana Pineda*, and Valle Inclán, with *Los cuernos de Don Friolera*, had found in the conventions of balladry a means of liberating and revitalizing the theatre. In our opinion, *Fermín Galán* is largely unsuccessful as drama because the author lacked the insight and expertise that permitted his more skillful contemporaries to use these conventions to better advantage. Alberti is too often a prisoner of his dramatic formula—content to transfer or transpose that which should have been modified or translated into theatrical language.

By this we mean that the author's approach to his material is literal and uncritical. For example, in simulating the structure of the *romance de ciego*, Alberti reproduces a form of redundancy characteristic of balladry, whereby that which is portrayed in the dialogue is anticipated or reiterated in the narration. Thus, the pensiveness which distinguishes FERMÍN as a child is described by the balladeer before we actually meet the hero :

> EL CIEGO.
> Más le gustaba la mar
> que la escuela y que la amiga.
> Habla con los marineros,
> canta sólo por la orilla,
> piensa que la mar es libre
> y que la tierra está fija.
>
> (FG, p. 16.)

When FERMÍN appears seated on the wharf overlooking the bay, his language and his thoughtful demeanor strongly echo this narrative passage :

> FERMÍN *(Pensativo.)*
> ¿Qué le pasa al mar,
> que si triste va
> más triste se vuelve?

> Dime, mar, ¿qué tienes?
> ¿Qué te pasa, mar?
> ¿Y tu libertad?
>
> (FG, p. 28.)

A comparable phenomenon is Alberti's insistence on the precise moment for which the attack is planned. In describing the preparations for the insurrection, the blind man says:

> EL CIEGO.
> Ya Fermín pasa las noches
> velando, ya sólo cuenta
> las horas de los relojes,
> los minutos que le faltan.
>
> (FG, p. 80.)

In the episode which ensues, the stage directions call for a clock which is supposed to keep time during the final moments of waiting [10]. In addition, the hero is made to announce no less than five times with slight variants that «a las cinco en punto, nos sublevaremos». After this, the balladeer resumes the narration with «Dadas las cinco...». In these instances the author has probably taken too much from the original. In the context of the *romance de ciego* proper, the preponderance of narration over dialogue need not have unfortunate consequences. In Alberti's play it results in a marked decline in dramaticity. By relegating the dramatic episodes to a position of secondary importance, the author divests them of any element of suspense. It is impossible for the audience to experience the characters or their deeds independently of the mediating and distancing words of the narrator. Therefore they cannot affect us directly. The anti-dramatic quality of the interpolated episodes is further intensified by the scenographic conception, since its effect is to convert them into static tableaux. What drama requires to be effective is immediacy, actualization, dynamism; what we have here is precisely the opposite.

The memorialist of *La arboleda perdida* would have us believe that *Fermín Galán* was conceived primarily as an experiment with form, that its political character was a somewhat gratuitous development. Nevertheless there are numerous elements in the work which can best be understood in relation to a partisan attitude. The author has a tendency to abandon his lofty language and descend to the level of tendentious rhetoric and insults. The ideal

---

[10] The author was apparently unaware of the technical problem that this poses for a director.

proportions of the hero are thereby diminished. Political intentions would best account for the sensationalism which caused such a fuss in 1931 [11]. They could explain the existence of anti-poetic verses such as : «tumbada la tiranía / las nuevas ideas triunfan. / Nuestro ideal nos reclama, / ¡ prestémonos a la lucha ! / La revolución social / necesita vuestra ayuda» (FG, p. 114). Clearly, ideological concerns played a very significant role in the genesis of the work.

Much of Alberti's tendentious material seems to us in poor taste. Moreover it detracts from the stylistic unity of *Fermín Galán*. The appearance of the Virgin at Cillas for instance, is an echo of the supernatural interventions frequent in balladry ; as such it is intended to evoke a feeling of wonder in the audience. But the author's emphasis on factionalism and political alliances inadvertently converts the episode into a caricaturesque parody. The regrettable results of Alberti's partisan attitude are also visible in the narrative passage which follows the execution of FERMÍN and GARCÍA HERNÁNDEZ. The CIEGO's account of their burial and the events which ensue is little more than rhymed history :

EL CIEGO.
    Asesinados los héroes,
    del barro, sus tristes cuerpos
    fueron, en mantas de sangre.
    llevados al cementerio.
    El lunes 15, a la hora
    en que los sepultureros
    para siempre los aislaban
    en la tierra de los muertos,
    Queipo de Llano, con Franco,
    Rada y otros compañeros,
    sublevaban en Madrid
    la base de Cuatro Vientos...
    Pero por indecisiones
    fracasaba el movimiento.
    Los jefes republicanos...
    fueron conducidos presos.
    ¡ Cuántos futuros ministros
    guarda la Cárcel Modelo !
    Niceto Alcalá Zamora,
    Presidente del Gobierno,
    con Fernando de los Ríos,
    Maura y Largo Caballero.
    Don Marcelino Domingo,

[11] See our pp. 19-20.

Lerroux e Indalecio Prieto,
huidos y a duras penas
pasaron los Pirineos.
La Ley Marcial se proclama,
sobrecogiendo los pechos.
Se establece la censura,
se clausura el Ateneo.

                                    (FG, pp. 183-84.)

The prosaic nature of this passage is all the more striking when
contrasted with what we might normally expect to find at this
point in the recitation. The author chooses to abandon his characters and talk about the political situation at precisely the moment
when most balladeers would apotheosize their heroes.

As in *El hombre deshabitado*, it is difficult to believe that
Alberti would wittingly have fallen into this trap. Therefore we
can assume that the presence of excessively prosaic and discursive
political commentary is the result of an unconscious process. It is
possible that at the time he wrote *Fermín Galán*, Alberti's energy
was being pulled simultaneously in two directions. He was unable
to choose between his growing vital commitment and his role
as a champion of formal renovation. This is consistent with what
we know of his life between 1928 and 1931. A duality of purpose
—that is, a need to expound, running counter to a desire to experiment—might also explain the overemphasis on ideology in his
auto.

In two instances—two comic vignettes in which he exhibits a
marked talent for caricature—the author's propagandistic zeal had
a more fortunate effect on his artistic judgment. The first is a
satire of the military establishment. Its representatives—Fermín's
superior officers in Morocco—are portrayed as lewd and boastful
drunkards. As they parade about to the tune of the «Marcha Real»
in the presence of an irreverent French whore, they mix pious
affectations with mock ferocity and lascivious innuendos:

> *(Cogidos por la cintura* [con] El alto comisa-
> rio... *delante... giran, rítmicos y marciales, alre-*
> *dedor de la mesa.)*
>   Todos *(Cantando...)*
>   ¡ La Virgen María
>   es nuestra protectora,
>   nuestra bienhechora !
>   ¡ No hay nada que temer !
>   ¡ Guerra al mundo,
>   demonio y carne,

guerra, guerra, guerra
contra Lucifer!

EL ALTO COM. *(Parando y simulando un combate.)*
¡Tararí! ¡Pin! ¡Pan! ¡Los moros!
¡Cuerpo a tierra!
(Todos menos él se tiran al suelo, de frente al público.)
¡Tararí!
(Hinca una sola rodilla detrás de LA COCOTTE.*)*
¡Apunten!
(Todos, menos él, fingen el fusil con los brazos.)
¡Fuego!

TODOS.
¡Pin, pan!

EL ALTO COM. *(Pellizcando a* LA COCOTTE.*)*
¡Pin, pan!

LA COCOTTE.
¡Ay!

EL CORONEL Y EL GENERAL.
¡Pin, pan!

EL ALTO COM. *(Volviéndola a pellizcar.)*
¡Pin, pin!
¡Arriba, bravos, arriba!
(Se levantan.)

(FG, pp. 49-50.)

The clergy and the aristocracy fare no better than the military during the final scene in the Duke's palace [12]. Here too the dominant notes are lewdness and alcohol. The frivolous conversation of the noblemen mingles with the fractured Latin phrases and blasphemous couplets of a drunken Cardinal Segura:

EL CARDENAL *(Levantando una copa).*
Nos, repudiam anarquistas,
repudiam sindicalistas,
despreciavit comunistas,
et amavit catequistas.
(Se la bebe. Dentro, se oyen aplausos y voces que dicen: ¡Viva! Sigue el vals.)
EL DUQUE *(Apasionado).*
¡Quién naufragara, Condesa,

12 See our p. 19.

por el canal de tu pecho!
¡Quién, Condesa, se perdiera!
LA CONDESA.
¡Oh, si el Conde se durmiera!

FG, p. 193.)

This scene concludes with the arrival of a certain SEÑORITA GUIRI-
GAY, who turns the merriment into a fracas with her partisan
behavior:

(*Por la izquierda, entra, mareada, lle-
vando clavada en la cabeza una banderita
republicana,* LA SEÑORITA GUIRIGAY.)
SRTA. GUIRIGAY.
¡Viva la República!
¡Vivan los republicanos!
¡Viva Galán!
(*Las parejas dejan el baile. La música
aumenta.*)
LA DUQUESA.
¡Fuera! ¡Toma!
¡Galán está condenado!
(*Le da una bofetada, quitándole la ban-
derita y rompiéndola.*)
EL CARDENAL (*Aburrido*).
Toma la llave de Roma,
porque...
SRTA. GUIRIGAY (*Dándole otra bofetada
a* LA DUQUESA).
¡Abajo los monárquicos!...
LA DUQUESA.
¡Que la echen mis lacayos!...
EL CARDENAL.
... En la calle hay un palacio,
en el palacio una alcoba...

(FG, pp. 197-98.)

These skillfully crafted scenes prefigure Alberti's future development in two ways. His comic vision is still heavily rooted in the
guiñol. Nevertheless it begins to evolve toward something we can
call esperpentic. The author's use of caricaturesque elements as
an instrument of social satire is equally important. Along with
the play-within-a-play structure and the tendentious thematic
material, this was an innovation that would have major repercus-
sions for a whole sector of his theatre.

Alberti's enterprising nature and seriousness of purpose notwithstanding, *Fermín Galán* is a work of limited artistic value. Its glaring technical defects indicate that in 1931, the playwright's ambition was not matched by his skill. Nevertheless, *Fermín Galán* is the first of Alberti's 'social plays'. As such, it possesses a unique significance in relation to the rest of his dramatic opus.

Dos farsas revolucionarias

In the *Dos farsas revolucionarias* (1934) [13] Alberti attempts to address himself to the popular audience about which he had spoken for the first time a year earlier. The simplicity of conception and improvisational quality of these two works represent a departure from the tendencies explored in *Fermín Galán*. At the same time, the author's search for a theatre of the masses takes place within the framework of his already evolving style. What he has done, in effect, is dislodge from their cumbersome framework the self-contained comic scenes of his earlier play.

1. *Bazar de la Providencia.*—The first and simpler of the two farces is a short puppet play, in which Alberti pokes fun at those high church officials who enrich themselves at the expense of their credulous parishioners. A Bishop peddles relics in a town square. He attempts to dupe his popular audience into buying his products by extolling their extraordinary properties and working some sleight-of-hand miracles with the aid of an assistant. The prospective customers are not so easily deceived, however. Upon discovering the ruse they take revenge on both the tricksters, putting them to death in return for their fraudulent behavior.

The source for *Bazar de la Providencia* is the last poem of a work entitled *A velhice do padre eterno* by the nineteenth-century Portuguese poet Guerra Junqueiro. Alberti has modeled his work closely on the original; Guerra Junqueiro must be credited with the general situation of the play, much of the blasphemous, scatological and macabre imagery, the anti-clerical and anti-establishment emphasis and most of the Bishop's declarations. Thus, the Portuguese poet is directly responsible for a good part

---

[13] R. Alberti, *Bazar de la Providencia (negocio): dos farsas revolucionarias* (Madrid: Ed. Octubre, 1934). Also contains the *Farsa de los Reyes Magos.* Hereafter cited as DFR. Except for a couple of isolated scenes from the latter work, Marrast was not familiar with these texts at the time he wrote his thesis. Thus, he underestimates their complexity and fails to note their importance to an understanding of Alberti's theatre as a whole.

of the comic effect. Much of the humor of this brief sketch is contained in the inventory of objects for sale:

OBISPO.

¡Agua fresca de Lourdes! ¡En pipas, en botijo!
Siempre exigir la marca—no lo olvidéis—DIOS-HIJO,
y en la etiqueta, a fuego, grabado, PROVIDENCIA,
la verdadera sólo se vende en esta agencia.
Cuarenta años de éxitos y millones de curas.
Buena contra la caspa, contra las mordeduras
de víbora y de perro por las pulgas comido.
Ladillas y piojos los deja sin sentido.
Hace nacer a un tiempo el apetito, el pelo.
Cura las almorranas más rebeldes al vuelo.
Reumatismos, tercianas y otras molestias varias
los quita, consiguiendo que hasta las solitarias
se expulsen. ¡Es la reina de todos los purgantes!

(DFR, pp. 9-10) [14].

The Bishop's wares, ridiculous in themselves, are intended for very extravagant uses. An added source of humor is the sing-song effect and abominable rhyme scheme of Alberti's *versos pareados.* Here too our author is indebted to his source.

At the same time, the conversion of poetic text into a play involved considerable invention. In Alberti's version, the Bishop's performance provides the context within which the real action unfolds. Periodically the character is interrupted by the questions, reactions and requests of his clientele and there ensue dialogued exchanges. The diverse 'gags' by means of which the Bishop attempts to sell his wares contain the substance of the work. In all cases, the idea for these episodes is Guerra Junqueiro's, but the theatrical version is Alberti's. For instance, the episode which results in the unmasking of the tricksters is an expansion of two verses from the poetic text:

14 Cf. the original on which this passage is based:
Água de Lourdes, fresca. Em pipas, ao quartilho
E em garrafa. Exigir a marca—Deus & Filho—
Na etiqueta, e na rôlha, a togo—Providência—
Genuina só a há à venda nesta agência.
Dez anos de sucesso e mil milhões de curas!
Eficaz contra a caspa e contra as mordeduras
De cobra cascavel ou cão danado ou pulga
Ou percevejo. Faz, Tartufo assim o julga,
Nascer ao mesmo tampo [sic] o apetite e o cabelo.
Bôa no hemorroidal e útil no sarampelo.
(Guerra Junqueiro, *A velhice do padre eterno*
[Porto: Livraria Chardron (n.d.)], p. 255).

Uma perna amputada unta-se, e em dois instantes
Torna a crescer e fica maior que dantes [15].

Elaborating upon these lines with imagination and a fine sense
of the absurd, Alberti invents a lame Beggar, who pretends to
respond to the offer of a miraculous cure. Really the Beggar is
the Bishop's assistant:

> (*Asoma un* cojo, *mendigo, enmarañado: largas barbas. Le fal-*
> *ta toda una pierna.)*
>   (DFR, p. 10.)

Joining in the masquerade, the cleric mumbles the appropriate
abracadabras in garbled Latin phrases, applies holy water to the
Beggar's stump, and proceeds to perform his sleight-of-hand:

> Obispo *(Mientras dice los siguientes latines, va frotando*
> *con agua el muñón).*
> Acqua, piernis hominibus triste prolongaveribum.
> Primus, secundum, tercius y... ¡zas!... piernis
>   creceribum.
> *(Le tira, rápido, del muñón, sacándole una pierna larguí-*
> *sima, mucho mayor que la sana.)*
> Cojo.
> ¡Aaah! ¡Milagro, Ilustrísima! ¡Oh!
> Obispo.
>   Levántate y anda.
> La niña Bernardita de Lourdes te lo manda.
> Cojo *(Intentando levantarse).*
> ¡Oooh! ¡Milagro, milagro!
> *(Va a ponerse en pie, pero cae.)*
>   (DFR, p. 10.)

For obvious reasons the Beggar is as lame as ever. Thus, the
Bishop seeks another remedy for his client's affliction:

> Obispo *(Dibujándole con el dedo una cruz en la pierna).*
> Prolóngate, y álzate, alma devota.
> *(Le tira, rápido, de la pierna, alcanzando la largura de la*
> *otra. El* cojo *se levanta, hecho un gigante.)*
> Cojo *(Tirando las muletas y alzando los brazos al cielo).*
> ¡Milagro nunca visto desde que Dios fue eunuco!
>   (DFR, p. 12.)

This new solution, even more grotesque than the previous one,
occasions a histrionic display of false piety:

---

15 *Ibid.,* p. 256.

Obispo *(Sonando la campanilla, jubiloso).*
¡Milagro verdadero, sin ventajas, sin truco!
¡De rodillas, hermanos! Y comprad desde ahora
el agua curandera, divina, bienhechora.
Y tú, pobre tullido, pobre alma mendicante que
a ras del suelo fueras, convertida en gigante
puedes por las barracas vivir de exhibiciones o
hurtando de los árboles los nidos de gorriones.

(DFR, p. 12.)

At this point, several of the spectators whom the Bishop has not
succeeded in deceiving denounce the charlatans and put an end
to their tricks. Several other episodes come about in an identical
fashion.

In keeping with the *agitprop* character of his play, Alberti
has tacked on an original ending. Following the exposure of the
Bishop's trickery, his cries for help are answered by a contingent
of archangels dressed as Civil Guard. Immediately the culprits are
shot and carried off amidst rabidly anti-clerical pronouncements
and Marxist references to class struggle:

[Se] *levantan en alto los cuerpos difuntos. Un campesino va
delante, puesta la mitra del* OBISPO. *Dos detrás, con los tricornios,
y en los labios, los bigotazos arrancados a los guardias civiles.
Otros llevan alzadas las muletas del* COJO. *Los demás, a continua-
ción, con las estacas, los rastrillos y las hoces en alto. Van desfi-
lando, en forma de procesión, por el primer término de la esce-
nilla.*

EL CAMPESINO DE LA MITRA *(Cantando larga-
mente; fingiendo la voz del cura en la misa).*
¡Señoras burguesas!
¡Señores burgueses!
¡Grandes señoras y señores!
¡Enterremos por siempre a los obispos
y a todos sus cochinos servidores!
TODOS.
¡Aaaaméééééén!

(DFR, p. 15.)

We cite this finale because the guiñolesque procession will become
a familiar element in Alberti's theatre. Here it is probably the
least effective part of the play. Its tendentious content is unnecessary, as Alberti's message is already perfectly explicit. Structurally,
it appears to have been an afterthought.

In *Bazar de la Providencia,* the most perceptible sign of
Alberti's growing skill is the self-contained expressiveness of his
theatrical language. Throughout most of the play, the spectacle

is the sole means of satirizing the characters. Alberti has seeded the Bishop's speeches with the pat phrases of radio commercials. He has his character entone the rhetorical formulas of pulpit oratory with the air of a circus barker. By alluding ironically to these forms of cheap entertainment and contemporary advertising, he converts the cleric into a salesman and a clown. Thus Alberti calls attention to the exploitative nature of the Bishop's venture. The author conveys his message effectively without the aid of a commentator.

In this work, Alberti again makes use of interior reduplication. The dialogued exchanges between the Bishop and his audience arise as do the snatches of conversation in *Fermín Galán*. Here however, they have gained in complexity. They possess a plot line and permit the author to develop his characters. In this sense, they assume the status of interior fictions. This contributes to the existence of a highly theatrical form of irony which Alberti would use on several occasions. The two tricksters are portrayed in an openly conventional and unconvincing style. Their behavior is clearly histrionic. As the tricks succeed one another in quick succession, each constituting a complete action, we become increasingly aware that they are performers. Thus, the author has used structure in a more purposeful manner than previously. In *Fermín Galán*, the episodic structure and the play-within-a-play were merely imitative; by *Bazar de la Providencia* they have become functional.

Bazar de la Providencia is another example of *tradición renovada*. In this brief *agitprop* play, Alberti rejoins the *entremés* tradition of Spanish literature. The pitting of deceitful master against supposedly gullible commonfolk echoes a favorite theme of the classic authors—that of human credulity versus self-interest. Moreover, the author's use of formal irony as a means of exposure calls to mind Cervantes' treatment of the illusion and reality theme. In *Bazar de la Providencia*, for the first time, Alberti used the play to make a statement about playing. In *El adefesio*, he would do the same.

2. *Farsa de los Reyes Magos.*—In the second of the *Dos farsas revolucionarias*, Alberti satirizes opportunistic clergy who seek to further their anti-republican and anti-communist ends by exploiting the credulity of the peasants. The action is set in rural surroundings on the eve of Epiphany. A wealthy landowner, a town priest and his sacristan wish to safeguard the faith of the commonfolk against the atheistic ideas of the radical left. They plan to masquerade as the Magi and call upon several families of the village. A student,

a worker, and a peasant learn of the plot and decide to terrorize their enemies with a scarecrow-like figure representing a Bolshevik. Soon there ensues a battle of wits, in which the proletarian elements of society win out over the representatives of the bourgeoisie. In the end, the student and his two friends expose the false kings. They disarm their entourage of Civil Guard and thrash the imposters, while inciting the peasants to rise up against the forces of reaction.

The *Farsa de los Reyes Magos* resembles *Bazar de la Providencia* in theme and form. A major part of the action is taken up by two extensive and self-contained episodes—the encounter with the Bolshevik and the arrival of the Magi. In presenting these two ruses by means of which the opposing factions seek to outwit one another, Alberti has placed a good deal of emphasis on surprise revelations, masquerading and unmasking. Again we can consider each scene as an interior fiction within a larger frame situation, and the entire work as a play-within-a-play.

The first of these two principal episodes hinges on a comic reversal. At the very moment when the CURA and the AMO are planning to disguise themselves as the Magi, they are beaten at their game of deception by the Student and his allies. A grotesque figure surges forth out of the darkness of the countryside ; his all-but-convincing appearance is the facade behind which the revolutionaries carry on a masquerade of their own—replete with appropriate histrionic and ventriloquistic effects :

> (EL OBRERO *hace el canto del gallo.* EL ACEITUNERO, *desde su escondite, tira de la cuerda y queda pendiente interceptando el camino, un gran* ESPANTAPÁJAROS. *Por una cara representa la figura de un bolchevique; gorro de astracán, un largo capisayo, botazas, bigotazos rojos de estopa, una estrella en el pecho y en la mano, una hoz y un martillo.* EL ESTUDIANTE, *con una voz cavernosa y terrible, hablará por* EL ESPANTAPÁJAROS. EL ACEITUNERO *le dará expresión y movimiento.)*
>
> EL CURA Y EL AMO.
>   ¡ Oooooh !
> EL ESPANTAPÁJAROS.
>   ¡ Aquí, señores, estoy yo !

(DFR, pp. 28-29.)

For the duration of the scene, the action and the stage business return repeatedly to the related notions of costume, mask, and role. First the CURA and the AMO attempt to outwit the Bolshevik by surrendering their clothes—supposedly all their worldly goods—in exchange for clemency :

EL CURA.
                    Don bolchevique,
no se avinagre, no se pique.
Todos mis bienes son latines.
un par de sucios calcetines,
cuatro novenas, diez sermones,
trescientas diez genuflexiones,
ayunos, toques de campana
y esta pobrísima sotana.
¡ Por don Lenín y su señora,
tómela, es suya desde ahora!
(Se quita la sotana y la tira, temeroso, a los pies de EL ESPAN-
TAPÁJAROS, *quedando con unas impropias y ridículas enaguas*
blancas.)
         EL ESPANTAPÁJAROS (A EL AMO).
            ¡ Oooooh!
            ¡ Sus pantalones quiero yo!
                                            (DRF, pp. 30-31.)

After appearing to yield, the assailant suddenly does a literal
about-face, displaying another costume and claiming to be the
Governor :

         (Da la vuelta EL ESPANTAPÁJAROS *y aparece por la otra cara*
         la figura de un grande y gordo señor, vestido de frac y con som-
         brero de copa. EL ESTUDIANTE *finge una voz afeminada...)*
         EL ESPANTAPÁJAROS.
            Soy el señor gobernador.
                                            (DFR, pp. 31-32.)

At this point, the CURA and the AMO abruptly change their tactics,
complaining indignantly that the Bolshevik has stolen their
clothes :

         EL AMO.
            Muy buenas noches, excelencia.
            Es un abuso...
         EL CURA.
                              Una indecencia...
         EL AMO.
            Un atropello...
         EL CURA.
                              ¡ Exactamente!...
            que en calzoncillos y al relente...
            sin que un porqué lo justifique,
            un comunista, un bolchevique...
         EL CURA.
            con una hoz, con un martillo...

EL AMO.
¡me haya dejado en calzoncillo!...
EL ESPANTAPÁJAROS.
¿Y cuánto, amigos, cuánto, cuánto?
EL AMO.
¿Cómo que cuánto?
EL ESPANTAPÁJAROS.
Quiero un tanto.

(DFR, pp. 32-33.)

The equally opportunistic Governor demands a bribe. Having obtained it, he reverts back to his earlier role as Bolshevik. As he is about to beat his adversaries with a hammer and sickle, he falls to the ground, apparently put off by the sign of the cross. This final fiction enables the two victims to scurry off with their clothes.

The scene in which the three bourgeois attempt to carry out their ingenious plan is constructed along similar lines. A comic reversal is again the principal means of advancing the action. As the awe of the gullible onlookers increases in response to the histrionics of the false kings, the Nativity scene before which they pause—and pose—comes to life:

> *(Se abre, como una tapadera redonda, la cara del Niño-Dios y asoma un brazo de soldado que arranca la careta al* REY MELCHOR, *al mismo tiempo que avanzan de la pared las cabezas de* LA MULA *y* EL BUEY.)
> EL BUEY. — ¡Múúúú!
> LA MULA. — ¡Ru-rú, ru-rú, ru-rú!
> EL SOLDADO *(Asomando la cara por la del Niño-Dios)*. — Sinvergüenzas, farsantes, embusteros, explotadores!...
> EL BUEY. — ¡Muuuuu! *(Se quita la cabeza y aparece la cara de* EL OBRERO.)

(DFR, p. 44.)

With the aid of a soldier, the proletarian characters have once more succeeded in denouncing their opponents by causing their plot to backfire. This time the reversal is even more pronounced. Again the desire to expose one masquerade occasions another. Furthermore, the means employed to strip the 'actors' of their disguises are the very trappings with which they had hoped to accomplish their ends. The Nativity scene—that is, the stage set which they have chosen for their performance—turns out to be a hiding place where the enemy lies in ambush.

This second of the *Dos farsas* is a longer and more ambitious play than *Bazar de la Providencia*. In it, the principal features of the simpler work grow more pronounced. The relationship with the *entremés* tradition is also more apparent. The country bumpkins of this work are clearly descended from the gullible rural types of the *prelopistas*. Alberti's combination of nominally religious subject matter with largely secular action can be viewed as a *versión a lo divino* in reverse. Moreover, the Cervantine play on illusion and reality is more complex than in *Bazar de la Providencia*, involving a number of ironic devices in addition to those we have mentioned. The credulity of the peasants functions in counterpoint to the patent falseness of the tricksters' performance. The theatre audience witnesses the planning of both pranks ; thus there is no doubt as to what is occurring. Finally, there is a marked increase in the conventionality of the spectacle during the enactment of the hoaxes ; since the use of verse is limited almost entirely to these two episodes, there is an abrupt and audible transition between the frame situation and the interior fiction.

In the *Farsa de los Reyes Magos*, the episodic structure of *Fermín Galán* has given way to a more unified whole. The author has successfully integrated two distinct planes of action : the interior fiction with its broad thematic emphasis on human credulity and self-interest, and the frame situation, where the religious celebration becomes the occasion for a more topical statement. In each masquerade, the deceptions are motivated and their form suggested by the political alignments and attitudes of the intended victims. Thus the idea for the ESPANTAPÁJAROS obviously derives from the AMO's obsessive fear of Bolsheviks :

> EL CURA. — Bolcheviques... Yo no los he visto ; pero creo que son colorados... y con unos grandes bigotazos caídos... y llevan puesta no sé dónde una estrella roja...
> EL AMO *(Temblando).* — ¡Horrible, horrible, señor cura ! ¡Y en una noche como ésta ! Habrá que avisar a la Guardia Civil... *(Temblando con violencia, cómicamente.)* Bolcheviques, bolcheviques, bolcheviques...
>
> (DFR, p. 25.)

Similarly the hammer and sickle with which the ESPANTAPÁJAROS purports to beat his adversaries is an allegorical reminder of the source of the hostility which it expresses.

The culprits' plan to impersonate the three kings also has a political origin. It is a response to the naive questioning of the peasants *and* to the defiant mockery of one of their number :

7

LA MUCHACHA. — ¡Queremos ver la estrella de los Magos, señor cura!... Nos han dicho que es verde y que se la ve caminar por el cielo...

EL CURA (En voz baja). — ¡Vaya conflicto!... Preguntan ahora por la estrella verde de los Magos, y el sacristán, lo está usted viendo, se ha olvidado ponerla sobre el monte, como le dijimos. (Silba. Luego se dirige a los Pastores.) Sí, es una gran estrella... muy hermosa... (Vuelve a silbar.) ¡Cabrón de sacristán!... Verde... una grandísima estrella verde...

(Sobre la punta de un palo, sube, tras el monte, una gran estrella roja de cinco puntas.)

EL CURA. — ¿Qué? ¿Cómo?...

LA MUCHACHA. — Esa estrella no es verde, señor cura...

EL CURA (Desfigurado por el miedo). — No... no... no... es roja... Lo veo... roja... Ya lo véis ...Se trata de un milagro... sin duda... de un gran milagro...

(Silencio, lleno de espanto las caras.)

EL ABUELO. — ¿Por qué calla la gente? ¿Qué ha sucedido? ¿Es que ese renegado de yerno ha cometido alguna mala cosa?...

EL CURA. — ¡Los Santos Reyes, que son muy milagrosos!... Hoy... llegan... de Oriente los benditos monarcas...

PASTOR 1.º. — ¿Vd. los ha visto, señor cura?

EL CURA (Desconcertado). — Sí... sí ...qué duda cabe... A la madrugada puede vérseles...

(DFR, pp. 25-26.)

The same peasant who tampers with the star of Bethlehem will subsequently eavesdrop on the conversation of his enemies and discover their plan for the masquerade. Thus the final denunciation of the imposters is presented as a counter-retaliatory measure. Through this integration of diverse thematic elements and structural levels, Alberti has enhanced considerably the effectiveness of his satire. Our awareness of the real identity of the 'actors' enables us to view their performance as tacit commentaries on the merits of the two opposing ideologies. In the encounter with the Bolshevik the intentionally trite rhymes and rhythms of the verses, the absurd content of the dialogue, and the ridiculous fawning of the victims all create a lack of sympathy for the 'masters'. In the scene of the Magi, the caricaturesque elements become an indirect attack on the political attitudes of the Monarchists. Needless to say, there is a judgement implied in the repeated failures of one party and the repeated successes of the other. The painstaking elaboration which this required suggests a singularity of purpose unprecedented in Alberti's earlier work. In the Dos farsas the author's use of traditional elements is less academic than formerly ; these elements have become a means of furthering his didactic ends.

In the *Farsa de los Reyes Magos,* Alberti's favorite conventions enable him to meet the specific technical requirements of a successful *agitprop* play. This too implies greater awareness. The iconographic, non-representational quality of his set serves the interest of simplicity. He uses a multiple stage to facilitate a desirable rapidity of action. A mere shift in lighting suffices to transport the spectator from countryside to household :

> *A un lado se ve el campo. Un olivo. Una línea ondulada que indica las montañas del fondo. Al otro lado se adivina el quicio de una casa, del que sobresale el brazo de un farol, de luz amarillenta, y el marco iniciado de una puerta. Del interior no se dibuja nada.*

> (DFR, p. 19.)

The playwright has also made use of improvisation to supply that which the setting lacks in detail. This is extremely appropriate to guerrilla theatre, with its lack of available tecnical resources :

> *Se hace el oscuro y el silencio en la casa, y salen, borrachos,* EL CURA *y* EL AMO. *Mientras dialogan,* van andando, a tumbos, alrededor de la escena, fingiendo el camino [our emphasis].)

> (DFR, p. 28.)

Above all, the direct expressiveness of Alberti's guiñolesque characters is admirably suited to the difficult material conditions in which the *agitprop* play is often performed. Their elemental psychology, broad gestures and slapstick behavior guarantee effectiveness in the briefest of encounters, in the noisiest of surroundings and before the least cultured of popular audiences.

Nevertheless, this play is not free of the technical defects which we have noted in Alberti's previous works. In fact given its complexity, its weaknesses seem all the more telling. Evidently, in 1934 the author's artistic integrity and his commitment were still in conflict. He appears to have been reluctant to rely exclusively on his ironic language as an instrument of propaganda. He has overemphasized scatological detail and blasphemous elements. Frequently he uses his characters as mouthpieces. This results in a totally anti-climactic finale. The playwright should have limited his tendentious commentary to the literal unmasking of the false kings and the figurative unmasking of their entourage of Civil Guard :

GUARDIA CIVIL 2.º. — ¡ Perros !
(EL MARIDO *le arranca de un tirón los bigotes y se los pega él
sobre su boca.*)

(DFR, p. 47.)

Not content with these appropriately absurd and theatrically
effective signs of domination, Alberti concludes instead with the
sparsely motivated conversion of the peasants to the atheistic
Marxist position, a flood of doctrinaire rhetoric, and an allegorical
battle between the red star of the Bolsheviks and the green star
of Bethlehem. The latter is carried out amid tendentious symbols,
trite light effects and martial music :

> (*La estrella roja, que ha luchado continuamente con la verde,
> queda vencedora, única, en el cielo. Bajo ella, grandes, se iluminan,
> también de color rojo, la hoz y el martillo. La escena se va alum-
> brando de amanecer.*)
>
> EL OBRERO. — ¡ Camaradas !: La farsa ha concluido, como
> véis, con la victoria de los trabajadores. La dictadura del proleta-
> riado empieza ahora, con el amanecer del nuevo día. Campesinos y
> obreros de este pueblo, familias pobres y explotadas, ya no hay
> estrella verde que os engañe, ni monarcas celestes ni terrestres, ni
> burguesía... que os aniquilen. Sobre el cielo que nace... sólo alum-
> bra una estrella... del firmamento helado de la Unión Soviética...
> Se oye un rumor de espigas que crecen y un estruendo de fábricas
> que se levantan. Las hoces y los martillos no dejarán ya nunca de
> cantar alegremente en vuestras manos... ¡ La internacional para
> celebrar el triunfo !
>
> (*Levanta el brazo a modo de batuta, para dirigir el himno re-
> volucionario.*)

(DFR, p. 49.)

Finally, in the *Farsa de los Reyes Magos*, Alberti has also
introduced extraneous poetic material. In this play there is a
re-creation of popular Chrismas art which has far more to do with
the *Belenes* of his childhood and the pastoral world of the *prelopistas* than with political satire. Thus despite the extent of his
commitment in 1934, Alberti failed to be rigorously selective in
his use of source material. He persisted in treating the stage as
a poetic vehicle. Apparently he was still struggling against his
basically lyric temperament.

Teatro de Urgencia

Alberti's formula for guerrilla theatre, as stated in the *Boletín de Orientación Teatral* in 1938 [16], could easily serve as a description of the *Dos farsas revolucionarias*. It aptly characterizes the comic scenes included in *Fermín Galán* as early as 1931. Thus, the two plays in which the playwright applied his formula are continuous with the rest of his works.

1. *Los salvadores de España.*—All we know of *Los salvadores de España* derives from two brief items which Marrast has located in the pages of *El Mono Azul*. In a note written in 1936 immediately following one of its many performances, we are told that this play was an «'ensaladilla' en un cuadro con música de Acario Cotapos» [17]. From a review which appeared the next day, we can deduce that it greatly resembled the three short plays for which the texts are extant.

The critic who wrote at length about Alberti's play describes the experience of seeing it performed in the following manner:

> Todos reaccionamos con entusiasmo sólo al levantarse el telón y ver el abigarrado conjunto de generales andalucistas de feria, moros, y comparsas, presididos por un obispo al que rodean sacristanes y cánones. Los latines del obispo bendiciendo a italianos, portugueses y alemanes, los tipos ridículos de éstos y sus discursos dieron motivo a Alberti para que luciera su ingenio y su asombrosa habilidad y gracia en el manejo del trabalenguas. Al final un desfile brillante de la soldadesca, heroica y bendita bajo una lluvia de rojos claveles, que lanza al lado de unos señoritos borrachos la mujer de cartel, de españolada, de generales chulos [18].

The characters of *Los salvadores de España* are clearly related to those of the other short plays. The *generales chulos* can be traced to *Fermín Galán* and the bishop with his garbled Latin phrases to that work and *Bazar de la Providencia*. The *mujer de cartel* and the drunk dandies would reappear in *Radio Sevilla*. Other familiar elements in the critic's description are the tongue-twisters and the ceremonious parade. These are standard guiñolesque gags for which the author would continue to demonstrate a marked fondness. Some additional remarks by this same critic

---

[16]   See our p. 27.
[17]   S., «Teatro Español: Presentación de Nueva Escena», *El Sol*, 21 Oct. 1936.
[18]   A[ntonio] S[ánchez] B[arbudo], «[Review of] *Los salvadores de España* de Rafael Alberti», *El Mono Azul*, 22 Oct. 1936.

86 LOUISE B. POPKIN

call attention to the grotesqueness and sheer theatricality of the spectacle :

La «ensaladilla» de Alberti, puro espectáculo, no es para contada, pero fue un acierto indudable que regocijó enormemente al público y no defraudó en nada a los admiradores del gran poeta del pueblo, animador de nuestro teatro grotesco y poeta satírico que enlaza con la mejor tradición popular española de este género.

These words are equally applicable to the other short plays. Evidently, *Los salvadores de España* was another brief satirical piece written in the comic vein characteristic of this period. As Marrast suggests, Alberti probably wrote it to poke fun at those sectors of the establishment that laid claims to being the «saviors of the nation» [19].

2. *Radio Sevilla.* — *Radio Sevilla* (1937) [20] is another brief satire directed against the so-called *salvadores de España*. In this instance, Alberti focuses his attention on the radio broadcasts of the Falangist general Queipo de Llano. Queipo's drunken voice could be heard nightly during the Civil War ; his lewd performances over the Andalusian station won him universal notoriety.

The work opens with a conversation between a young woman and a Nationalist soldier. The Woman's father and brother have been killed by the Franquist forces. The Soldier has been drafted by force and plans to desert to the enemy camp. Just as these two are deciding to flee together, the voice of a radio announcer is heard over a loudspeaker. The Soldier invites his companion to witness the spectacle which is about to begin. Immediately the curtain that has served as a backdrop for the prologue is pulled aside, disclosing a matchbox decorated in gaudy turn-of-the-century style. Inside the matchbox is the studio in which most of the action takes place :

(Al descorrerse las cortinas, surge, abriéndose lentamente, dentro de una gran caja de cerillas de la época monárquica, la sala de la emisora sevillana. Un micrófono. Adornando las paredes: carteles taurinos, una cabeza de toro de cartón, banderillas, dos capotes extendidos y un gran rejón de lujo. Sentado, un tocador de guitarra. Rodeándolo en diversas posturas de cuadro flamenco las SEÑORITAS *1, 2 y 3, con los* SEÑORITOS *1, 2 y 3, falangistas en*

19 Marrast thesis, p. 58.
20 We cite page number and column from No. 45 of *El Mono Azul*, May 1938, pp. 6-8.

traje corto. Sobre las rodillas de QUEIPO, *en uniforme,* CLAVELONA, *con bata de cola, y flores en la cabeza.)*

(p. 6, col. 3.)

In the early part of the studio sequence, the emphasis is on QUEIPO's swaggering and boastful pretentiousness, his crass ignorance and extreme vulgarity:

> CLAVELONA.
> Queipo, Requeipo
> Queipo, Queipillo,
> me tiene muerta tu bigotillo.
> QUEIPO *(Brusco).* — Bigotazos, querrás decir, Clavelona. ¡Bigotazos!... Si pudiera contemplarme Franco, se moriría de envidia. Soy el rey de la Bética. Un verdadero Moro...
> SEÑORITA 1. — ¡Viva Boabdil el Chico!
> QUEIPO. — ¿El chico? ¿Por qué el chico?
> SEÑORITA 2. — Así lo llama la historia.
> QUEIPO. — ¡Ah! Creí que era un insulto.
> TODOS. — ¡Viva!
> EL SPEAKER. — ¡Majestad! Al micrófono... Los rojos no pueden pasar una sola noche sin escucharle... Es Vd. el asombro de Europa...
> SEÑORITA 1. — Empiece, general, que tu voz me deleita...
> SEÑORITA 3. — ¡Qué bella transparencia de arroyuelo!...
> QUEIPO. — Basta, basta. Silencio. No me ruboricéis. ¡Ejem! Voy a empezar. *(al* SPEAKER*)* A ver, tú, descorcha ese micrófono y anúnciame. Vamos. ¡Pronto! Que esta noche me siento inspirado.

(p. 6, cols. 3-5.)

The general is totally susceptible to the transparent adulation of his crowd of hangers-on. Thus, following his initial display of vain posturing, he begins the broadcast by imitating a horse:

> QUEIPO *(Imitando los gestos de un caballo).*
> Ya se me atiranta el lomo,
> ya se me empinan las ancas,
> ya las orejas me crecen,
> ya los dientes se me alargan,
> la cincha me viene corta,
> las riendas se me desmandan.

(p. 7, col. 1) [21].

At the general's instigation, he is joined by the other characters. A protracted series of animal impersonations culminates in a

---

21 This is part of the ballad from which the dramatic text was derived.

simulated *corrida*. QUEIPO's girl CLAVELONA plays the bull. His aide and sidekick CATITE is the *rejoneador*:

> EL SPEAKER. — ¡Atención, señores radioyentes! El famoso rejoneador, Catite, en ancas del excelentísimo señor don Gonzalo Queipo de Llano, sultán de Sevilla, va a ejecutar... la difícil y airosa suerte del rejón. El toro, más propiamente dicho, la vaca que le acomete correrá a cargo de la distinguida señorita Clavelona...
>
> CLAVELONA *(Histérica, cogiendo de la pared la cabeza de toro y poniéndosela a modo de máscara)*. — ¡Mu, muu! ¡Que embisto! ¡Que embisto!...
>
> CATITE.
>
> > Vengan pronto los peones.
> > Corre a la vaca...
> > ¡Al toro, al toro, alazán!
>
> CLAVELONA *(Acercándose)*. — ¡Muuuuu!
>
> (p. 7, cols. 2-3.)

In the action which follows this questionable demonstration of courage and skill, Alberti pokes fun at Queipo's allies as well as his followers. The *corrida* is interrupted by the appearance of a German and an Italian official. The former arrives issuing peremptory orders to which QUEIPO responds first with noisy protests and then with a display of fawning subservience. Presently, there ensues a raucous confrontation. The false bravado of all the interested parties is exposed by means of some highly amusing reversals. At the repeated instigations of CLAVELONA, the Spaniards provoke a none-too-convincing showdown. The foreign officers are all too willing to beat a hasty retreat:

> CLAVELONA *(En jarras)*. — Pero, ¿qué significa esto? (A TODOS) ¿A qué esperáis? ¿Qué hacéis? ¿Dónde está vuestra raza, su poder, su empuje? ¡Venga! ¡Todos a una!
>
> TODOS *(Menos QUEIPO, inclinando la frente en actitud de embestida, y arrancándose contra los oficiales extranjeros)*. — ¡Muuuuuuuuu!
>
> OFICIAL ALEMÁN *(Retrocediendo con el ITALIANO)*. — ¡Quietos, quietos, berrendos españoles! Guárdense bien guardados sus cuernos, que nosotros nos vamos.
>
> (p. 8, col. 3.)

At this point it is the Falangists who back down. They are horrified at the thought of having to fight their own battles:

> TODOS *(Espantados, como de piedra)*. — ¿Eh?
> OFICIAL ALEMÁN. — A Berlín.

OFICIAL ITALIANO. — A Roma.
QUEIPO *(Desfalleciendo)*. — A Berlín... A Roma... Pero...
OFICIAL ALEMÁN. — ... para no volver. ¡ País poco científico !
TODOS *(De rodillas, suplicantes)*. — ¡ No, no, no !
QUEIPO. — Imposible, imposible... Señoritas y caballeros, mostrad en todo instante a estos buenísimos señores el hondo agradecimiento que tenéis, el respeto profundo que les guarda mi España, mientras que yo, con mucho gusto... *(Se arrodilla, y sacando otra vez el pañuelo les da varias pasadas por las botas.)*

(p. 8, cols. 3-4.)

Following this timely capitulation, the wooden creatures on stage are joined by a puppet-like *cortège* of foreigners in a noisy parade. The event signals a final reconciliation :

(Entran tres SOLDADOS ITALIANOS, *de negro, facinerosos, bigotudos, llenos de plumas los sombreros, pistolones al cinto y un inmenso sable desenvainado. Van seguidos por tres* SOLDADOS NAZIS, *finos, rubios, afeminados, depiladas las cejas, pintados los labios, etc. La guitarra, mientras evolucionan por la escena, empieza a rasguear sordamente.)*

OFICIAL ITALIANO.
      A Benito le piden
      las sevillanas
      a cambio de Sevilla
      gente de Italia.
      Hombre, que llega
      señorita bailando
      que se le entrega.
Señoritas, haced honor a la raza del Duce...
      (Cada una se coge del brazo de un facineroso italiano, mientras continúan las evoluciones de los tres SOLDADOS NAZIS.)

OFICIAL ALEMÁN.
      Cuando a Sevilla llegan
      los alemanes
      pierden sus pantalones
      los «nacionales».
      Nazi que llega,
      falangista bailando
      que se le entrega.

(p. 8, col. 4.)

In the midst of this ceremonious display, the sequence is brought rapidly to a close. An abrupt transition places us before the static *tableau* which introduced us into the studio :

*(La guitarra rasguea fuertemente, quedando todos los personajes,
a un golpe seco y fuerte de la misma, en una retorcida y trágica
postura de baile flamenco.)*

(p. 8, col. 5.)

The conclusion of *Radio Sevilla*—aptly characterized by Marrast
as a «finale pour marionettes» [22]—is as original as it is hilarious.
The box closes catching QUEIPO by the neck so that his head
remains hanging out ; as the Soldier of the prologue addresses the
theatre audience and incites them to rebellion, the culprit is
appropriately chastised at the hands of the *pueblo* :

> EL SOLDADO.
> > ¡Venid, vecinos, vecinas,
> > madres fuertes de Triana,
> > cigarreras, hombres, todos,
> > venid, que Sevilla os llama!
> > Solamente esa cabeza
> > el pueblo puede juzgarla.
>
> *(Entran gentes armadas de palos, escobas, escopetas, etc., y
> golpeando en ronda la cabeza de* QUEIPO, *cantan el «Trágala»,
> mientras cae el telón.)*

(p. 8, col. 5.)

In *Radio Sevilla*, Alberti satirizes his characters by surrounding
them with the tasteless accoutrements of the *España de pandereta* tradition. As the Soldier remarks in the prologue, the spectacle we witness is «un triste cuadro flamenco... toda la gran pandereta de esta estropajosa España cuya vil representante... se
nombra Queipo de Llano» (p. 6, cols. 2-3). This hackneyed version
of typical Spain in contained in the garish matchbox cover and
the trite objects which adorn the walls of the studio. It is present
in the antics and *olés* of QUEIPO's gang of followers, as they
applaud him with false vehemence and strut about to twangy
pasodoble music :

> SEÑORITO 1. — ¡Olé con olé!
> SEÑORITO 2. — ¡Viva el sultán de Persia!
> SEÑORITO 3. — ¡Vivan los hombres!
> TODOS. — ¡Vivaaa!
> QUEIPO. — ¡Música, música, y vuelta al ruedo! (QUEIPO *coge
> del brazo a* CLAVELONA, *las* SEÑORITAS *a los* SEÑORITOS, *y forma-
> dos en cuadrilla torera, giran alrededor de la sala, mientras el gui-
> tarrista rasguea el pasodoble «Joselito».)*

[22] Marrast thesis, p. 67.

CLAVELONA *(Con la melodía del pasodoble).*
Muy pronto en la Puerta del Sol...
TODOS *(menos* QUEIPO*).*
entrará Queipo
sobre una escoba.
(El pasodoble continúa.)

(p. 6, col. 3.)

The general's crude displays of *machismo* and obsessive insistence on his Moorish ancestry also echo the worn clichés of the European Romantics. So does the burlesque reenactment of the *fiesta brava*, from which Alberti derives many highly theatrical comic effects.

From a thematic standpoint, this use of the *españolada* is an indirect form of name-calling. In the simulated *corrida*, where that function is most apparent, the ludicrousness of the participants is directly linked to their «animal-like behavior». In addition, there are several visual and verbal puns transparently allusive to cuckoldry :

SEÑORITA 3. — ¡ Ay, don Gonzalo, que le cornean !
SEÑORITO 3. — ¡ Que le empitonan, mi general !

(p. 7, col. 3.)

Included in the author's list of epithets are several intended for the foreign officers. Arriving in time to witness the climax of the performance, they react as though they were experiencing the essence of Iberia. This is the first of a series of uncritical reactions that gives rise to an ebullient satire of national stereotypes :

OFICIAL ALEMÁN *(Rígido, inconmovible, saludando a lo fascista).* — ¡ Oh, la España romántica !... ¡ Los toros, las mujeres hermosas, el sol, el vino... ! Pero haga el favor de arrodillarse, general. Poco científica, esa postura.

(p. 7, col. 3.)

By portraying this gang of officers, dandies and painted women as vulgar types whose forbears might have frequented the environs of Carmen's cigarette factory, Alberti has once more made an ironic statement about falseness, hypocrisy, insincerity. A notable feature of the studio sequence is its parodic quality, achieved through an emphasis on rhetoric and overstatement. Exchanges such as the following would seem unconvincing and literary even if one attempted to 'play them straight' :

CLAVELONA. — ¿Que no es un general mi general? *(Abrazán-dolo, y besándolo, de rodillas)* ¡Mío, mío, remío, requetemío!
(Declamatoria e idílica)
  ¡Mi sultán del Alcázar,
  mi rey de Andalucía,
  mi moro de Granada!...
  ¡mi bravo bigotazo,
  bigotillo del alma!
QUEIPO. — ¡Clavelona de ensueño!
CLAVELONA. — ¡Mi salvador de España!

(p. 7, col. 4.)

Owing largely to the utterly trivial and superficial imagery of the *España de pandereta* tradition, the characters seem to exhibit an awareness of their own histrionic nature. As in Valle Inclán's *esperpentos*, this serves as a sign of their inauthenticity—a warning that the spectator is not to take them seriously.

In *Radio Sevilla* Alberti has again written a play-within-a-play, this time with several interior fictions arranged in a manner resembling a Chinese box. As the prologue (original frame situation) concludes and we enter the broadcasting studio via the matchbox cover (original interior fiction), the concentric arrangement of the theatrical space is carried out by means of a number of histrionic and scenographic details: the prominently placed microphone, the cheers and applause of the onlookers, the SPEAKER's admonitions regarding the late hour, his protests about the vast amount of ad-libbing which can be heard on the air, noisy discussions between the actors over who will play what part. All of these elements enable us to distinguish the broadcast proper (new interior action) from that which is to be construed as taking place behind the scenes (new frame situation). This careful differentiation of 'onstage' and 'offstage' action coincides with an insistent use of parallelism. The characters' overt involvement in several roles during the broadcast is matched behind the scenes by frequent and abrupt shifts in their attitudes and the focal points of the action. Through this proliferation of poses and structural planes, their allegedly real behavior is likened to their playing; it is infused with a quality of sham and pretense. Increasingly we perceive the characters as vain and hypocritical creatures—as lacking in spontaneity and devoid of substance as the exaggeratedly posed figures that adorn the cheap commercial covers of matchboxes.

From the standpoint of theatrical technique, *Radio Sevilla* is the most complex and carefully executed of the surviving *agit-prop* plays. Only in the prologue and the epilogue are invectives and tendentious commentary a source of esthetic diffuseness, as they are in *Fermín Galán* and the *Dos farsas*. In the tightly conceived and stylistically consistent studio sequence, they have become a form of characterization. Like all the other technical resources of this brief playlet, they convey a more vivid impression of QUEIPO's empty posturing and the brazen insincerity of his followers. *Radio Sevilla* is also another 'play about playing'. A statement about posturing, illusion and reality underlies and transcends the topical thematic material. Alberti's technical handling of these themes bespeaks his sophistication and his growing command of theatrical language. This brief playlet takes us beyond the comic scenes of *Fermín Galán* with their incipient esperpentism, and the *Dos farsas* with their relatively simple use of interior reduplication and masquerade.

Probably in all the *agitprop* plays, a limited format supplied the discipline which Alberti still lacked for more ambitious undertakings. As his subsequent relapse into former excesses would indicate, *Radio Sevilla* does not represent a definitive breakthrough in his career as a dramatist. Nevertheless, it brings us one step closer to the mature comic style of *El adefesio*.

De un momento a otro

De un momento a otro (1938), subtitled «drama de una familia española, en un prólogo y tres actos», is the only play in which Alberti employed a basically fourth-wall esthetic. In this work he attempts to portray the situation of Spain on the eve of the Civil War by exploring the effects of ideological differences on human relationships in an Andalusian town.

GABRIEL, an idealistic youth, returns from Madrid imbued with Marxist philosophy. He becomes involved in a series of confrontations with his bourgeois relatives, his former school companions, his Jesuit teachers and the very workers with whom he has allied himself. His attempts to gain sympathy for his political views are repeatedly met by opposition, mistrust and incomprehension, until at the end he dies in a street skirmish at the hands of his brother IGNACIO. In death, GABRIEL succeeds in winning the confidence of the workers and regaining the well-intentioned but ineffectual love of his mother and his sister ARACELI. By then, however, his ideological and sentimental victories are of questionable value. A parochial mentality has effectively done away with him, and his idealism holds little promise for society.

In this highly pessimistic play, Alberti's vision of provincial

life is almost totally negative. The leading citizens of the town
espouse ideals which are worn and outmoded. They are staunch
defenders of 'decency' and intransigent in their support of the
status quo. They resist innovation with a blindness that is only
matched by their complacency. Any idea that comes from outside
is held by them to be immediately suspect. As a means of ensuring
total conformity—lest they be contaminated by 'worldly interests'—they resort instinctively to inquisitorial tactics: they
eavesdrop behind closed doors and rummage through pockets.

In the conduct of town affairs and their own lives, these
narrow-minded beings exhibit a short-sightedness and indifference
which renders even their good intentions impotent. They are
content to practice a form of charity which spends itself in pious
gestures; and quick to label GABRIEL a monster when he attempts
to delve into causes. Thus, they strike at the symptoms but never
the roots of a problem. A breakfast for beggars is deemed an
effective means of combatting poverty, even though at its conclusion the guests abscond with the silverware amidst obscene
shouts and lewd laughter. A tenderness born of parental and filial
ties gives rise to a desire for comprehension, but only after it is
too late for bloodshed to be avoided; in order for GABRIEL's mother
and sister to attempt to decipher his message, they have first to
confront his corpse. The negative vision of provincial life encompasses the lower classes as well. The workers especially are portrayed as ignorant, violent and resentful creatures. Automatically
mistrustful of GABRIEL and his kind, they undertake the class
struggle more out of rancor than idealism. In short, GABRIEL, who
dreams of the triumph of the proletariat amidst shouts of joy,
encounters nothing but hostility. This seems to suggest that his revolution is doomed to failure. In a brief prologue, two chorus-like
characters speak of «la [gran] aurora que aguarda a todos los
que... merezcan la vida» (II, 86). Nevertheless one is left with the
impression that the dawn will be long in coming; the struggle
will be less productive of grandeur than of grief.

In *De un momento a otro* Alberti has equated the class struggle
taking place in the nation at large with the process of disintegration
that occurs in one family. He has made of GABRIEL's house a mi-
crocosm, in which the rapid dissolution of personal ties echoes the
erosion of political and social institutions. To this end, he avails
himself of a number of symbolic details:

(1)   The worn furniture of GABRIEL's family's living room with
its «gusto retrasado de la provincia» mirrors the outmoded ideas
of the bourgeoisie.

(2)   A similar function is fulfilled by the abject physical ap-

pearance of the protagonist's uncle VICENTE—a senile and absent-minded character who plays incessantly with a pet parrot and displays an obsessive hate of Voltaire and the Masons.

(3) The names of the two brothers echo their opposing ideologies. GABRIEL—the angel of the Annunciation—is the bearer of a new message to humanity. IGNACIO—Ignatius of Loyola—is the militant Jesuitic type who represents the forces of reaction.

(4) During the course of the action, a portentous storm causes the walls of the family dwelling to literally crumble and fall apart. This event becomes a central element in the dialogue. «Hay quienes ven ahora que la casa va a derrumbarse», says a worker, «y quieren ponerse a salvo pegándose a nosotros» (II, 107). Thus GABRIEL's house takes on a vertical and a horizontal projection reminiscent of similar usages in the works of Ibsen, Lorca and Poe.

(5) In order to further underline the identity between national crisis and domestic strife, Alberti uses his characteristic juxtaposition of two planes of action. This is especially noticeable following the outbreak of hostilities. Throughout the last act, the entrances and exits of the principals, and the constant movement between street and interior become indispensable adjuncts to the dialogue. An awareness of the whereabouts of the brothers is essential to our knowledge that IGNACIO is GABRIEL's slayer, hence to our perception of the larger conflict as a fratricidal struggle.

Although the use of symbols in *De un momento a otro* is somewhat obvious and heavy-handed, the playwright's intention is commendable and his results partially successful. Alberti understood that the interests of drama could best be served by portraying his ideological and social conflict within a specific human setting. Thus, he shifted the emphasis from a national context to an individual household, interweaving ideological and highly emotional factors. By stressing the peculiarly tragic nature of a war that pits brother against brother, he achieves a considerable degree of dramatic concentration.

In the first act, the author evidences a growing ability to create complex characters. By means of a series of particularly effective encounters between GABRIEL, his brother, his mother and his uncle, Alberti portrays diverse and complex aspects of the protagonist's feelings. He conveys a sense of painful incomprehension among loved ones. The dialogue between GABRIEL and IGNACIO has an inquisitorial tone ; IGNACIO is the accuser and GABRIEL the accused. This provides a fine contrast to more poignant exchanges between mother and son. After one of these, there follows the most psychologically convincing scene in the play. The protagonist has just seen his mother destroy one of his political pamphlets. Now

he attempts to dissipate the tension which has arisen between him
and his uncle:

> GABRIEL. — Tío ¿cuántos años va a cumplir el lorito? ¿Es ma
> yor que tú, no?
> Tío VICENTE *(siempre entretenido con el loro, sin mirar a
> Gabriel).* — Haces mal, niño. Tu abuelo te quería mucho. Llevaba
> siempre en la cartera un retrato de cuando eras pequeño, montado
> en un mastín. «Este es mi único nieto», decía riéndose. «Le deja-
> ré en herencia un barril de solera del siglo XVIII.»
> GABRIEL. — Va a cumplir en octubre los setenta y cinco. ¿No,
> tío? Tiene dos años más que tú. Ya es viejo el loro.
> Tío VICENTE. — Hacía largos viajes, y siempre hablaba de lle-
> varte a ver Londres, Noruega y Dinamarca. A esos países expor-
> taba sus mejores vinos. Hoy, estoy seguro, no te hubiera llevado.
> El era religioso y gran amigo de los jesuitas. Tú haces mal, niño,
> en no imitarle.
> GABRIEL. — Tío, nunca me contaste si algún loro vivió más
> de quinientos años.
> Tío VICENTE. — Tu abuelo odiaba todo lo que fuera propagan-
> da masónica. Y yo también, ¿comprendes? Yo, también. Soy su
> hermano. Y tú no eres su nieto.
> GABRIEL. — ¡Pero si tú no sabías, tío, lo que había escrito
> en ese folleto que han roto!
> Tío VICENTE. — Ni me hace falta. ¡Déjame! Alguna bárbara
> calumnia contra la religión. Hoy no me hables. ¡Déjame!
>   (II, 91.)

As a consequence of these painful confrontations, GABRIEL experiences a strange schizoid split. He is tormented by feelings of
failure as a man, by the guilt that stems from his repudiation of
religious teachings and family ties, by the knowledge that the
workers despise him. Driven to the point of suicide, he carries on
a dialogue with two mysterious voices—really the disembodied
projections of his turbulent emotions:

> Voz 1.ª — Avergüénzate, Gabriel. Arráncate la cara y tírala
> en un charco, donde las herraduras de los mulos la transfiguren,
> hundiéndola.
> Voz 2.ª — Olvídate de tu nombre, de tu apellido. Vete de
> aquí. Huye. Eres un canalla.
> GABRIEL. — Es verdad. Hundidme. Quitadme el poco aire que
> aún me queda. Os lo pido.
>   (II, 99.)

The language in this sequence is somewhat turgid and as a dramatic device, the *auto-diálogo* is a bit contrived. Nevertheless,

it is a reasonably effective way to express the protagonist's confusion. Here GABRIEL comes close to conveying an impression of the crippling effect of inert and stifling surroundings on youth, purity, innocence and idealism.

Aside from these details, we consider *De un momento a otro* to be one of our author's least successful plays. This is due largely to the reappearance of Alberti's most characteristic excesses. A familiar mixture of high-flown rhetoric and pedestrian prosaicness delays the action and destroys the characters, in spite of their potential. The following exchange between GABRIEL and ARACELI exemplifies the author's clumsy handling of the dialogue:

> (*Silencio. Suena, lejana, la sirena de un barco.*)
> ARACELI. — Gabriel: hoy estamos a ocho. ¿Qué te recuerda esa sirena?
> GABRIEL (*abstraído*). — Hay hombres en el mar, hombres desnudos, tiznados, miserables, perdidos en el fondo de los buques...
> ARACELI. — Íbamos a la playa, hasta Punta Bravía. Cuando sonaba esa sirena, los dos salíamos de casa. Siempre nos daba tiempo de llegar hasta el cabo...
> GABRIEL. — ... hombres rotos, cansados, tirados, fuera de la vida, rodando por los muelles y las estaciones...
> ARACELI. — Gabriel, no me escuchas.
> GABRIEL. — Te escucho. Estoy hablando de ellos, de mi nueva familia...
> ARACELI. — Dime, Gabriel. Una cosa: ¿en esa nueva familia tienes hermanas tú?... ¿Como yo, Gabriel?
>
> (II, 97.)

Except in isolated instances, GABRIEL and ARACELI fail to convince us of the depth of their feeling or the extent of their loyalties. Neither the resounding Marxist phrases of the one nor the naive clichés of the other ring true. Marrast seems to have noted a similar problem with respect to GABRIEL's brother when he observed that IGNACIO gives the impression of being a prosaic police-inspector type [23]; had Alberti endowed his character with a certain grandiosity, his evil could have been truly inquisitorial.

Another major defect of *De un momento a otro* is the familiar presence of stylistically intrusive satirical elements. In this basically realistic play, there are two groups of characters whom the author presents by means of a technique of grotesque stylization. One of these is the collection of Beggars who figure principally in the aforementioned scene of the charity breakfast. Typical of

---

[23] Marrast, p. 85.

their grotesqueness are the lewd rhymes and dancelike movements
with which they conclude the episode :

> *(Irrumpen en fila, en el salón, todos* LOS MENDIGOS. *Van giran-
> do como borrachos, alrededor de la mesa, persiguiendo a* EL BEATO
> *que va delante.)*
> MENDIGA 1.ª. — ¡Son de plata, de plata!
> MENDIGO 2.º. — ¡Las lleva dentro de las botas!
> MENDIGO 1.º. — ¡Por eso anda como los patos!
> MENDIGA 2.ª. — ¡Se le van clavando en las pezuñas!
> EL BEATO. — Igual que el pato o que la pata, lo cierto es que
> son de plata.
> *(Giran en dirección contraria.)*
> MENDIGA 2.ª. — ¡Manos largas!
> MENDIGO 1.º. — ¡El coñac se las hizo crecer !
> MENDIGO 2.º. — ¡Se tragó las cucharas con el chocolate!
> MENDIGA 1.ª. — Y luego se le bajaron por los calzones.
> EL BEATO. — Pero al bajar por los calzones, me platearon los...
> MENDIGA 1.ª. — Te arrastraré como no me des una.
> MENDIGA 2.ª. — Como no repartas el dinero...
> MENDIGO 2.º. — Te destriparemos como a un sapo.
> EL BEATO. — ¡Ojo, ojo, que también llevo aquí el cuchillo de
> la cocina! *(Sacudiéndose a sus compañeros, saca de la cintura un
> enorme cuchillo.)* ¡Ahora veréis con lo robado, llegar la sangre
> hasta el tejado!
> LOS CUATRO MENDIGOS *(con terror)*. — ¡Uuuuuuuuuh! *(Des-
> aparecen, huyendo, perseguidos por el cuchillo. Silencio.)*

(II, 105-6.)

The second group of grotesque personages are GABRIEL's aunts,
three eccentric spinsters who fancy themselves protectors of the
poor ; and exhibit as their most conspicuous characteristic a bizarre
mixture of religiosity and eroticism. Their aberrational psychology
manifests itself chiefly on the night of the storm. As they franti-
cally entone the *trisagio*, they punctuate their pious phrases with
increasingly libidinous snatches of conversation. Revelling maso-
chistically in the details of her narration, TÍA GERTRUDIS recalls
a similar occasion. «Tuve tal miedo sola en mi cuarto», she says,
«que al cerrar el cajón de la cómoda donde guardaba la vela mila-
grosa, me cogí de golpe el pecho izquierdo, lastimándomelo horri-
blemente» (II, 127). Then, as her superstitious mumbling gives
way to a hysterical outburst, TÍA JOSEFA speaks of Jesus Christ as
her carnal husband :

> TÍA JOSEFA. — ¡Oh, qué lecho amoroso, presidido por su ado-
> rable hermosura! En la noche, sus rayos celestiales bajarían sobre

mi esposo y sobre mí, abrasándonos... ¡Los veo! ¡Los siento! Ya
es la hora. ¡Venid!... Se me agrieta la carne. Me arden los cabellos. Por todas partes, quemaduras, arañazos de llamas: por los
hombros, las piernas, los costados...

(II, 128.)

Her imagination stimulated by her own fantasies, JOSEFA grows
even more daring. She bangs on the doors of the male members
of the household. She responds to the overtures of EL BEATO, who
recites obscene verses under her window until somebody empties
a chamberpot on his head. Soon however, the spirit triumphs
over the flesh. Hurriedly the sinner buries her frustrations beneath shallow cries of repentance:

> TÍA JOSEFA. — Oh, ¡qué gran pecado, Dios mío! ¡Qué remor-
> dimientos! Estoy endemoniada. ¡Un pecado mortal! ¡Corazón de
> Jesús, señor de las Olivas, libradme de estos malos deseos, de esta
> víbora que me quema la sangre y me atormenta por las noches!
> Ya no querrás entrar nunca en mi pecho, Jesús mío, ni habitar
> en mi alma, más tenebrosa y negra que los carbones del infierno...
> ¡Perdón, perdón, perdón!

(II, 131.)

Alberti has made explicit and extensive use of autobiographical
material in *De un momento a otro*. Marrast has noted that many
details of *La arboleda perdida* have exact counterparts in the dramatic text [24]. The war games which Alberti recalls having played
with his sister (AP, pp. 73, 90-100), his dog Centella (AP, p. 93),
the charity breakfast that was a custom in the Alberti household [25], the family wine cellars, the Jesuits of the Colegio de
San Luis Gonzaga all reappear in this work. So does the house
of the author's favorite uncle, Vicente:

> Aquella vivienda, como la familia que la habitaba, se iba vi-
> niendo abajo todos los días un poco, hasta llegar a la mayor ruina.

(AP, p. 28.)

Just as striking is the resemblance between several of the more
extravagant characters in the play and people whom the author
knew as a child in El Puerto. Among his acquaintances there was

---

[24] *Ibid.*, pp. 75-79. Arrived at independently, our conclusions on this matter
accord with Marrast's.
[25] Marrast mentions this as an autobiographical detail *(ibid.*, p. 110). We
were unable to locate his source.

a real beggar named Andrés el Beato, on whom the fictional character is based :

> Andrés el Beato, uno de los pobres protegidos de mi familia...
> afirmaba ser una pulga y haber luchado, en la plaza de toros, con-
> tra Palomo el farmacéutico, perdiendo éste la pelea, a pesar de
> arremeterle convertido en elefante blanco.
>
> (AP, p. 66.)

GABRIEL's aunts appear to have been inspired by the collection of
eccentric and fanatical *beatas* who devoted their energies to pro-
tecting the poor, praying for the lost souls of free thinkers and
spying upon their nephew [26]. There is a particularly obvious parallel between the JOSEFA of the play and the real Vicente's daughter ;
the real Josefa is described by Alberti as a frustrated spinster,
«cuya avanzada soltería fue derivando poco a poco en un extraño
amor hacia los santos y los gitanos pobres del barrio de la Rosa»
(AP, p. 26). The Tío VICENTE of the play is modelled on Alberti's
uncle :

> ¡ El tío Vicente ! Nunca me cansaré de recordarle y extraer, de
> él, sustancia y materia continuas para mi poesía teatral, ya lírica
> o dramática.
>
> (AP, p. 26.)

The memorialist remembers Vicente as «una maravilla de locura,
de raro saber, invención y gracia» (AP, p. 26). His combined extravagances and exotic talents were an endless source of fasci-
nation and amusement for the author as a child. This bizarre
creature shared the fictional character's fondness for parrots and
his obsessive fear of Voltaire :

> Retazos de recuerdos o historias de su vida, que él mismo nos
> contara al atardecer jugando con un eterno loro, me resonaron en
> los oídos... Tío Vicente sabía muchos idiomas, incluso el árabe y
> el hebreo... Era enemigo acérrimo de Voltaire, a quien calificaba
> furiosamente de 'impío'.
>
> (AP, pp. 28-30.)

Conversely, GABRIEL's uncle is depicted by EL BEATO as a rare
collection of abilities and skills :

> EL BEATO. — Hace versos, domina muchas lenguas, conoce
> muchos pájaros, muchas plantas, caza murciélagos por las tardes,
> colecciona los sellos del estanco, reza, canta, ha dado la vuelta al
> mundo...
>
> (II, 93.)

[26] See our p. 3.

While in remaining instances the transposition from life to art is less direct, a perusal of available source material reveals the autobiographical origin of numerous other details of characterization. To complete his portrait of Tío VICENTE, Alberti evidently availed himself of the peculiarities of two relatives who figure in an autobiographical poem called «Indice de una familia burguesa española» :

> Rafael, trapajo sucio en la punta de un palo, derribando murciélagos al toque de Animas, emigrado y perdido en el trayecto ciego de su sangre.
>
> ... ...
>
> José María, llamado el triste, beocio, filatélico y habitante en una pajarera [27].

In a more general way, we can trace the reactionary attitudes, the ignorance, and the sterile, repressive religiosity of the bourgeois characters of the play to several of Alberti's other uncles : Javier, who in his eagerness to comply with Christian obligations unfailingly held his missal upside down (AP, p. 31) ; Guillermo, the somewhat renegade priest, whose hypocritical and non-committal *cara de santo* made him the favorite confessor of *beatas* and gay blades alike (AP, p. 60) ; and Jesús—«la imagen del terror, del respeto obligado y el forzoso agradecimiento»—who alleviated the family's financial difficulties «no sólo con dinero, sino con ropa, trajes para arreglar, ya gastados por él o por sus hijos» (AP, p. 64). The seminal element for the dramatic confrontation between a liberal spirit and a narrow provincial mentality may well have been supplied by Alberti's adventurous and daring tío Tomás and his son. Tomás had been a hero in Garibaldi's army. His offspring, an atheist and free thinker nicknamed *El Republicanote*, was regarded in the Alberti household as a blight upon the family name (AP, pp. 78-80) [28].

These striking parallels between the author's personal recollections and the thematic material of his play suggest that the town in which the action is set was originally El Puerto and the family Alberti's own. Marrast has noted that GABRIEL, a young intellectual in the midst of a crisis, is twenty-six years old—that is, precisely the age of the author in 1928. There is a marked stylistic similarity between the language and the content of *De*

[27] From *Un fantasma recorre Europa* (Madrid, 1935), pp. 14-15, cited in Marrast, p. 77.

[28] Marrast also feels that Alberti's sisters provided the models upon which the character of ARACELI is based. He disclaims any knowledge of IGNACIO's origin on the grounds that little is said about Alberti's brothers in AP.

un momento a otro and that of Alberti's early social poetry [29]. This further relates his play to the crisis which he is known to have suffered largely as a result of painful childhood experiences. In this sense, *De un momento a otro* corresponds to at least two moments in the playwright's career—its date of composition, and the years between 1928 and 1931.

This provides a possible explanation for the defective quality of the dramatic text [30]. Alberti may have returned to a play on which he had already begun work ; or he may have been hampered simply by the anguish of reliving past ordeals. Given the anger and frustration occasioned by his exile, the difficulty of maintaining critical distance was certainly considerable. Undoubtedly, this difficulty was compounded by the extent of his involvement with his subject matter. Earlier we suggested that at the time Alberti composed *El hombre deshabitado* and *Fermín Galán*, he was probably uncertain as to whether he intended to write a play or an ideological treatise. He insisted on making a public spectacle of his inner turmoil. In 1938, a similar duality of purpose seems once again to have led him to overlook important esthetic considerations. This conclusion seems inevitable when we note how many of the play's weaknesses appear at precisely those moments when he draws upon his most unpleasant memories. Evidently Alberti most lacked detachment when it would have been hardest to achieve—that is, when the man was least capable of being objective and most likely to frustrate the efforts of the artist.

In *De un momento a otro*, the activist playwright returned to the broad dimensions of *El hombre deshabitado* and *Fermín Galán*. After his more successful experiments with guerrilla theatre, he demonstrated his continuing inability to cope with the technical problems of a major work. Nevertheless one should not take lightly the seriousness and breadth of Alberti's undertaking. Although *De un momento a otro* is the most strictly personal and heavily tendentious of his works, it is also the least topical of the social plays of the 1930s. It is the only one which can be designated as *littérature engagée* in the ideal Sartrian sense [31].

---

[29] Especially the «Elegía cívica» and the poems of the volume similarly entitled *De un momento a otro*. Note the resemblance between the title of the former («Con los zapatos puestos tengo que morir») and a speech of GABRIEL's :

> Yo moriré de pie, con los zapatos puestos,
> en la calle, como los héroes... Todo
> se me ilumina de pronto.

(II, 102.)

[30] Ruiz Ramón touches upon the excessively autobiographical character of this work, but only notes the problem in passing *(op. cit.,* p. 233).

[31] Because this term has been bantered about uncritically, some clarification

For nearly a decade, the playwright had devoted his energies to extremely dated works. This play marks a return to the greater universality of *El hombre deshabitado* and points ahead to the works of the 1940s.

In *De un momento a otro* we can also identify several prominent thematic and technical elements which recur in Alberti's mature works. The fratricidal struggle between GABRIEL and IGNACIO prefigures the more poetic fraternal rivalry of *El trébol florido*. The surrealistic projection of psychological conflict, as exemplified in GABRIEL's *autodiálogo*, anticipates the complex techniques of *La Gallarda*. Above all, the Beggars and the spinster Aunts of *De un momento a otro* reappear in *El adefesio*. There, they are no longer transparently personal or productive of esthetic hybridism. In our estimation, the transformation of these grotesque characters is central to an understanding of the playwright's development. The reappearance of technical and thematic elements bespeaks his increased capacity to transmute life into art.

* * *

The seven plays which Alberti wrote between 1929 and 1938 have a great deal in common with the rest of his dramatic works. The author's experimental attitude is apparent in all the plays of this period. The wedding of traditional and contemporary art forms explains their originality. With the exception of *De un momento a otro*, they are all openly conventional works. Finally, except in the *auto*, grotesque caricature plays a significant role in all of them. From the outset, Alberti shows a marked gift for comic stylization. Particularly in the *agitprop* plays, he already attains considerable complexity.

The works of this period constitute a group by themselves. A preponderance of tendentious or didactic elements distinguishes them thematically from the works that immediately precede and follow. They also have in common a set of shared formal defects: a discursive and anti-dramatic dialogue, structural diffuseness, stylistic inconsistencies. In the *agitprop* plays, these defects are of slight importance; the author's dramatic formula appears to

may be in order. Sartre argued that, given the relationship which exists by definition between the writer and his circumstances, any failure to take a stand on specific issues is an evasion of responsibility. Conversely, even a partisan work such as *De un momento a otro* can, through its very topicality, express commitment to Man and the Human Condition. The ideal in Sartre's own words, is «une littérature qui rejoigne et réconcilie l'absolu métaphysique et de la relativité du fait historique... littérature des grandes circonstances» (J. P. Sartre, *Situations*, 11 [Paris: Gallimard (c 1918), 251]).

have worked in his favor. In the three longer works however, they are especially evident. *El hombre deshabitado*, *Fermín Galán* and *De un momento a otro* have an intriguing conception, but a weak execution.

The thematic content of these plays echoes Alberti's passage from crisis to commitment. His spiritual development can be documented in his dramatic works as well as in his poetry. *El hombre deshabitado* reflects the religious phase of the crisis of 1928-29. *De un momento a otro* echoes the author's discontent with political and social conditions. In the text of *Fermín Galán*, we noted Alberti's ambivalence with respect to the nature of his task: while this play is not about his confusion, it shows him to have been confused about his role when he wrote it. Finally, the *agitprop* plays correspond to a moment of new spiritual clarity. They are the work of an author for whom writing is a wholly committed act, a gesture of solidarity, a means of changing the world around him.

During this period, Alberti's difficulty appears to manifest itself as a continuing failure to recognize the nature of the task at hand. In the 1920s, he used the stage as a poetic vehicle. In the 1930s, he uses it as a tribunal. In both cases he was evidently unable to avoid being distracted by non-dramatic considerations. As we demonstrated with respect to *El hombre deshabitado*, this may have been partly the result of his inexpertness. In the main, however, his clumsiness should probably be attributed to other sources. It seems that for the playwright at this time, art and ideology were incompatible; thus the defective quality of these plays is directly related to their heavily ideological emphasis. Esthetic detachment must have been impossible given Alberti's state of mind. First his self-involvement, then his revolutionary zeal apparently had an adverse effect on his artistic judgement. Thrusting themselves upon his consciousness, they obstructed his vision.

At the time Alberti wrote the works of the 1930s, he had yet to attain the status of a mature playwright. Not until the following decade would the artist prevail over the activist, and the dramatist over the lyric poet.

CHAPTER IV

MASTERPIECES, AND THE EMERGENCE OF A STYLE: THE 1940s

El trébol florido

In *El trébol florido* (1940) Alberti abandons the realistic techniques and contemporary setting of *De un momento a otro*, leaves behind the ideological preoccupations of the 1930s and returns to the allegorical emphasis of *El hombre deshabitado*. Transporting us to a sunny island whose inhabitants lead simple, tradition-bound lives in close proximity to nature, he weaves a tale of amorous rivalry into a myth about the fatal attraction and opposition of land and sea.

The action of this work was probably suggested by a *romance piscatorio* of Góngora's, in which the fisherman Alción is spurned by a beautiful woman of the sea named Glauca:

> Las redes sobre la arena,
> y la barquilla ligada
> a una roca a quien las olas
> convierten de piedra en agua,
> el pobre Alción se queja
> por ver a la hermosa Glauca,
> fuego de los pescadores,
> y gloria de aquella playa.
> Buscándola con los ojos
> en altas voces la llama:
> —Glauca, dice, ¿adónde estás?—
> ¿Por cuál nueva ocasión tardas?, etc. [1].

AITANA, daughter of the blind miller SILENO, is courted by MARTÍN and ALCIÓN, sons of the fisherwoman UMBROSA. Secretly preferring

---

[1] Agustín Durán, *Romancero general*, BAE, No. 16 (Madrid: Impr. de los Sucesores de Hernando, 1924), pp. 494-95, partially cited in Marrast, p. 91. The French critic *(ibid.)* also calls attention to another probable source, the well-known «Romance del marinero» which begins «Mañanita de San Juan   cayó un marinero al agua.» (Durán, *op. cit.*, BAE, No. 10, p. lxvi). This ballad is recited by ALCION in Act One (I, 66-67).

ALCIÓN to her official fiancé MARTÍN, AITANA hesitates, stalls and toys with the feelings of both suitors. The situation of the lovers is complicated by the hidden subterfuges of their parents. SILENO is the victim of an incestuous passion ; UMBROSA is reluctant for her seafaring sons to marry a miller's daughter. Both are intent upon preventing any union between the two families (Act. I).

ALCIÓN decides to leave rather than to nourish the growing hatred which he and his brother have come to feel for one another. MARTÍN is to marry AITANA. Knowing that their open opposition will be met by resistance, the two old folks pretend to approve of the match. They promise to announce a wedding date for MARTÍN and AITANA at a celebration which is to be held in honor of ALCIÓN's departure. Secretly, they intend to delay long enough for youthful passion to run its course and love to turn to hate (Act II). At the last moment AITANA tells ALCIÓN that she will go with him. Upon learning her true feelings, ALCIÓN plans for the two of them to slip off unnoticed from the ceremonies. In the meantime MARTÍN's impatience and irascibility have reached their limit. Unaware of his brother's plans, he threatens to carry AITANA off by force. SILENO and UMBROSA still intend that the two families remain separate. Thus on the day of the festivities, the desires and objectives of all the characters are in conflict. In the heat of the ceremonies, passion drives the celebrants beyond the limits of willful action and determines a tragic outcome (Act III).

In order to transform this action into a cosmic struggle of mythical proportions, Alberti has created a symbolic superstructure. In the text of *El trébol florido*, there are four means of referring us to an allegorical plane. Three of these are direct and established *a priori* ; the fourth, which is more oblique, is elaborated in the course of the first act :

(1)   The occupations of the two families enable us to regard them as archetypes. Alberti had need of a polar opposition between creatures of the earth and creatures of the sea ; therefore he made Góngora's fisherwoman into a miller's daughter.

(2)   The names of the characters are suggestive of archetypal status. SILENO is the god of the fruits of the earth. UMBROSA's name evokes the murky depths of the ocean floor. The names MARTÍN and ALCIÓN are synonyms for the aquatic kingfisher. As María Teresa León tells us, AITANA is the name of a mountain range in the Spanish province of Alicante, «última tierra peninsular que [se ve] antes de salir para la isla de Ibiza...» [2].

---

[2]   Letter to Marrast (4 Aug. 1952). As earlier observed, Aitana is the name of the Albertis' daughter. In our estimation this simply reflects an idiosyncrasy

(3)   A prominent feature of the dialogue of *El trébol florido*
is its highly figurative nature ; the characters frequently refer to
themselves using teluric and aquatic imagery. Thus, MARTÍN
describes his passion for AITANA in the following manner :

> MARTÍN. — Aitana... quema la tierra... El mar nunca se pone
> así. Por eso quiero yo a la tierra, porque es igual que tú... Me
> corre en las venas demasiada agua salada. Necesito que tú la endul-
> ces un poco.
>
> (I, 77.)

AITANA characterizes her feeling for ALCIÓN as «the earth's longing
for that which it lacks» [3]. UMBROSA alludes to earth and sea in
expressing her opposition to the match between AITANA and
MARTÍN :

> UMBROSA. — No quiero nuera molinera ni ser consuegra de un
> borracho. Ni en la familia de tu padre ni en la mía hubo mujeres
> que no fueran del mar. Todas hijas de pescadores.
>
> (I, 75.)

This language encourages us to view the action symbolically, in
terms of an implacable opposition between the two elements. With
its complicated interplay of attraction and hesitation, passion and
hostility, the amorous conflict will not be resolved in favor of any
of the interested parties. Likewise, as when waves break against
the shore, land and sea constantly seek one another out, yet in
the end remain inexorably divided.

(4)   An essential component of Alberti's allegorical superstructure is the *trébol* of the title. Universally prized as a sign of
amorous good fortune, it is traditionally sought by lovers on the
eve of the Feast of Saint John the Baptist. In the first scene of the
play, the author recreates this popular custom. The three lovers
comb the forest floor in search of the coveted object :

> CABRERO. — Hallé el trébol de cuatro hojas. Ya sabes... La
> primera muchacha que se encuentre... Serás mi mujer.
>
> (I, 53.)

The suitors who aspire to possession of the desired woman immediately associate the four-leaf clover with AITANA. The indecisive

---

of the author's and not much more should be made of it. He also likes to name
the different places where he lives after his books (see León, *Memoria*, p. 260).

   [3]   AITANA. — Te quiero, Alción, te quiero como sólo la tierra puede querer lo
que no tiene (I, 99).

maiden uses the image of the less desirable three-leaf clover to allude to the problematical triangle of two suitors and one woman —that is, the lack of good fortune, or the impossibility of possession :

> AITANA.
> ¡Tin ton! ¡Tin tan!
> ¡Juntos los tréboles de San Juan!
> MARTÍN. — Como siempre, Aitana. ¿Y después, cuándo nos casemos?
> AITANA. — ¡Juntos también, mi amor!... ¡Como las hojas del trébol florido!
> MARTÍN. — En cada una, un nombre...
> AITANA. — ¡Martín, Aitana y Alción!... Somos tres, y nos falta una hoja ¡Tres eran tres las hojitas del trébol! ¡Tres eran tres y por una me muero!... Hay que ser dos y dos.

(I, 54-55.)

Throughout the play these two symbols become a means of focusing and commenting upon the action. As the conflict develops, they serve as a barometer on which we can measure changing fortunes, and the ebb and flow of emotion. Used in relation to the land-sea imagery, they help to elevate the struggle between the individual characters to the level of an ongoing cosmic process :

> AITANA. — ¿Qué tienes?
> ALCIÓN. — Mala suerte.
> AITANA. — Es noche de encontrarla buena... Entre los tréboles del bosque.
> ALCIÓN. — Siempre le falta una hoja a los que encuentro... El mío debe encontrarse bajo el agua.

(I, 54.)

ALCIÓN's suggestion is that the four-leaf clover is denied him by the earth *because he is a fisherman*. This is doubly symbolic. On the one hand it is a statement about his unrequited love ; at the same time, it is an allusion to the incompatibility of land and sea.

In Lope's *Peribáñez y el Comendador de Ocaña*, there also occurs a poetic recreation of the St. John's Feast. The classical author provided Alberti with the epigraph for his play :

> ¡Trebolé, ay Jesús, cómo huele!
> ¡Trebolé, ay Jesús, qué olor!

(I, 51.)

Lope's festivities are very different from Alberti's, however. In *El trébol florido*, the picturesque and folkloric festivities of the classical play become a festival of all nature—a Spanish midsummernight's dream whose pagan and supernatural contours evoke the fertility rites of the ancients. To the sensual playfulness of the lovers and their joyful pursuit of good fortune is added the play of the elements—sudden gusts of wind, rays of moonlight that pierce the shadows of the forest, the distant howling of wild beasts, the muffled sound of the sea [4]. A feeling of mysterious approximation between man and nature is conveyed through Alberti's dialogue. As the passions of the characters are cast in images of teluric fecundity, they seem to erupt with the unbridled violence of cosmic forces. Lurching through the forest in search of AITANA, the drunken and lewd SILENO happens upon the equally inebriated UMBROSA:

> SILENO (*prendiéndola por la cintura mientras bebe*). — ¡Ja ji! ¡Como siempre, resiempre! (*a* UMBROSA) Siempre soñé con tu cintura... y me la imaginé abrazada de uvas... de dos en dos, como bolas de vidrio... Y más arriba pensé que había racimos... verdes... duritos todavía... lustrosos...
> UMBROSA (*alejándolo*). — ¡Ja, ja! Pero al despertarte se convirtieron en pasas. (*Ya borracha.*) Si te gustan las pasas, ven por ellas, Sileno.
> SILENO (*buscándola*). — Tengo poder para volvértelas redondas nuevamente, Umbrosita...
> UMBROSA. — Soy también perra de pescador. Te morderé, Sileno, si me buscas. Mira qué dientes: uno, dos, tres, cuatro... Mira qué colmillos: dos, pero como cuchillas.
> SILENO (*dando tumbos*). — Muérdeme, muérdeme, vieja maldita, trébol arrugado... algarroba seca, reseca, cáscara de avellana pelada, pisoteada y estrujada... (*Se da contra otro árbol, cayéndose sentado.*)

(I, 60.)

The traditional disguises worn by the characters echo the metamorphoses of the Olympian gods. This also brings the characters closer to the forces of the earth. ALCIÓN pursues AITANA dressed as a wild boar. The maiden expresses her amorous vacillation in the guise of a tree:

---

[4] María Teresa León tells us that Alberti conceived the first act as «el juego de la fiesta de San Juan. Debe hacerse casi un ballet», she writes, «música y ritmo de fiesta. Un fondo de bosque mágico, de *rama dorada* donde nuestros campesinos vuelven sin darse cuenta al renovarse el solsticio de verano. El espíritu de ese primer acto, de celta, druida. Puede arder al fondo del bosque, quedando éste en contraluz, la hoguera de San Juan haciendo más oscura la busca del amor y del trébol... Todo el bosque es busca y movimiento y juego de *cache cache*» (Letter to Marrast [4 Aug. 1952]).

AITANA.
El árbol cuando se mueve,
vacila en su pensamiento.
Vuelo a un lado, vuelo al otro
sin saber qué quiero...
Las hojas se me consumen
en un fuego y otro fuego.
Sopla, viento, a la derecha;
a la izquierda, viento.
Apaga, viento, este hervor.
Vengo buscando una mata de trébol,
vengo buscando una mata de amor.

(I, 65) [5].

Alberti's treatment of the Saint John's feast is undeniably original, his theatre poetry highly effective. As his images surrender their meaning, they gain in artistic stature. Thus, the creation of an allegorical superstructure is not simply a mechanical process. If this were not so we could not justifiably speak of myth.

By definition, a myth possesses both dramatic force and poetic projection. In *El trébol florido*, the author devotes himself to the task of elaborating his poetic images before undertaking that of dramatic actualization. Although the conflict is announced in the first act, it is scarcely developed until the theatrical illusion is complete and the characters infused with allegorical significance. Then in the second act, Alberti's theatrical language undergoes a three-fold process of intensification. As on numerous other occasions, a multiple set creates increased possibilities for dramatic irony :

> En lo alto de una colina escalonada, por la que suben veredas amarillas, bordeadas de olivos y viñedos, se ve la casa de SILENO, molino velero de grandes aspas. Pozo a uno de los lados, contra el cielo brillante de un celeste marino. Pitas, chumberas, por los terrenos duros, agrios, de sol. Abajo, en primer término izquierda, el comedor de la casa de UMBROSA: ventana al fondo, puerta lateral y puerta al campo.

(I, 70.)

The action shifts back and forth between SILENO's mill and UMBROSA's house. At the same time, the imagery of the dialogue grows increasingly violent and sensual :

---

[5] An allusion to the myth of Myrrha and Adonis. In context, these two disguises function as does the *trébol*, linking plot and symbolic superstructure.

MARTÍN. — Arisca y con agujas, como las pitas y los cardos.
Eso eres tú. Y así te adoro, aunque se me aborrasque la sangre
cuando pinchas. Pero ya les remacharé las puntas a esos clavos.
    AITANA. — No hará falta, Martín. También la tierra tiene
cosas dulces. Mira esas viñas moscateles.
    MARTÍN. — Cuando me veas amargo, apriétame un racimo con-
tra los dientes.
                                                        (I, 77.)

Finally, the author introduces several prominent elements of
augury. The most important of these is the cry of a siren, heard
by ALCIÓN and UMBROSA at the act's conclusion:

    UMBROSA. — Oí como un grito.
    ALCIÓN. — Ya oscuro y de ese lado parece, a veces que se oyen.
    UMBROSA. — Tu padre las oía con frecuencia.
    ALCIÓN. — Y muchos marineros.
    UMBROSA. — En las noches de viento hay quien escucha hasta
palabras. Otros las han visto...
    ALCIÓN. — ¿Gritan, madre?
    UMBROSA. — No, son los pasos de Martín, que baja del moli-
no... (En la oscuridad de la noche estrellada, baja la sombra de
MARTÍN por las veredas.)
                                                        (I, 94-95.)

In the folklore of the Andalusian coast, this ominous sound is
believed to announce an impending storm [6]. Thus, it echoes the
turbulent emotions of the characters and prefigures the explosion
of passions which is soon to occur.
    In the final act of El trébol florido the graduation and inten-
sification of poetic and dramatic elements is carried still further.
The festivities of the first act with their somewhat lyric paganism
give way to another celebration of clearly Dionysian character—a
bacchanale, highlighted by scenographic images of a profuse and
disordered nature:

    (Aparece, tirado por muchachos, el carro donde van SILENO
    y UMBROSA: verdadero altar barroco, pagano y silvestre, agobiado
    desde las ruedas por hojas y racimos, haces de trigo y amapolas,
    prendidos por largas cintas de colores...)
        SILENO (grande y exagerado, vestido con su mejor traje, arro-
    jando pequeñas botas de vino adornadas, que colgarán de las esta-
    cas del carro... Algarabía de voces y músicas). — ¡Bebe, bebe,
    Umbrosita! Sella las paces con un chorro de oro, mi domada con-
    suegra. ¡Que no lo muerdan más entre los dientes los pájaros pre-

6 Marrast, p. 97.

sentes! ¡Que lo vean de una vez y lo crean! ¡Que se les requete-
seque la ponzoña en los labios! ¡Que lo vomiten ya, y sin lengua
y sin habla no puedan volar! ¡Paz pública, mi Umbrosa! ¡Vino,
vino, vino!

(I, 103-4.)

The feeling of a superhuman presence has already been created
by the ironic foreshadowing of Act II. Now it materializes in the
figure of a sacrificial bull, an enigmatic creature who delivers
equivocal responses through the mouth of an old woman:

(*Arrecia la música, cambiándose por un aire de danza, apare-
ciendo, sobre ruedas, y empujado por muchachos del campo y de
la playa, un gran* TORO *de paja, clavado de banderines y flores,
enramadas las astas de pámpanos y olivo. Delante, bailando, dos
parejas de gigantillos. Detrás, severa y enlutada,* UNA VIEJA...)

UNA VOZ (*sonando un clarín*).
    ¡Al toro, al toro, al toro!
    Preguntas de plata,
    respuestas de oro...
MARTÍN (*serio, acercándose al toro*).
    Toro que te han de quemar
    y que has de ser de candela,
    dime si mi corazón
    verá en la mar una estrella.
VIEJA (*cantando*).
    El torito te responde
    que no ve estrella en los mares,
    que sólo mira en la tierra
    una amapola de sangre...
ALCIÓN.
    Toro que te han de quemar,
    di lo que estoy deseando,
    repítemelo en la mar
    cuando vaya navegando.
VIEJA (*cantando*).
    El torito te responde
    con tu mismo pensamiento,
    que lo que no sabe el agua.
    lo empieza a saber el viento...
AITANA.
    Toro que te han de quemar,
    ya tarde, al anochecer,
    si me ves contigo arder,
    dime, ¿quién te ha de salvar?
VIEJA (*cantando*).
    El torito te responde
    como torito de fuego...

(Golpe seco de tambor, interrumpiendo la VIEJA *el canto y mirando a* AITANA *con fijeza.)*
AITANA *(con angustia).* — ¿Por qué se calla, abuela? ¿Qué dice el toro? Siga, siga, que acabe.
VIEJA. — No tiene fin la copla.

(I, 105-9.)

As these prophesies foreshadow more and more explicitly the violent and tragic *dénouement*, the dramatic tension is carried to its climax. The already taut passions of the celebrants have been strained to the utmost by the ascending rhythms of the dance and the increasingly perceptible effects of the wine. Thus, they erupt in a final frenzied outburst:

UMBROSA. — ¡Que se acabe la fiesta, hijos! ¡Huye, Alción, en tu velero, que aquí va a correr sangre! ¡Vámonos!
MARTÍN. — Pero llevándome a mi Aitana, arrancándosela a esa fiera del monte.
AITANA. — Si me tocas, Martín, te dentelleo. Te descuajo una mano.
SILENO. — ¡Venid, familia de pulpos! ¡Acercaos, playeros, aguas turbias! ¿Qué creíais? Aquí tengo a mi Aitana...
ALCIÓN *(queriendo imponerse sobre el tumulto).* — ¡Paz, paz, señor Sileno!... Suelte a su hija...
SILENO. — ¿Que te suelte a mi hija? ¿ A ti, a ti, a ti? ¡Antes al otro! No la tendrás... Es mía. ¡No la tendréis ninguno!

(I, 110-11.)

His reason obscured by lust and alcohol, SILENO can no longer contain himself. Proclaiming the triumph of land over sea, he strangles AITANA before the horrified gaze of all the onlookers:

SILENO. — ¿Por qué calláis ahora? ¿Es que os habéis marchado, cobardes? *(Gritando.)* ¡Eeeeeh! ¿Es que se ha muerto el eco, robándome también mis gritos y mis voces? Hablad. Chillad. Desgañitaos. Que esas lenguas repiquen y me digan que estáis aquí, llenos de júbilo, viendo cómo se acaba una fiesta... *(Enternecido, arrodillándose.)* Aitana, mi niña Aitana, brisa perdida, almendrillo en flor, ramo de olivo: no eran ellos, era la mar quien quería llevarte, robarte, a ti, la única tierra que me sostenía. Pero yo la he vencido... ¡Pronto! ¡Ya! ¡Que le prendan fuego [al toro] ... y que su humo cubra de negro y seque todo ese mar que me mató a mi Aitana!... Y vosotros, gentes del campo y de la playa, preparad ese carro, que quiero con mi Aitana ir por esas veredas y esos montes, para que... comprueben que Sileno fue más fuerte que el mar, fue de tierra, de tierra, de tierra! ¡Vamos! Romped ya

9

ese silencio con un canto capaz de hacer llorar las uvas y despren-
derse las olivas.

*(Entre los últimos fogonazos del sol, empieza a subir, lenta,
la humareda del toro, mientras un canto sordo, sin palabras, va
ascendiendo.)*

(I, 111-12.)

Owing to the convulsive rhythm which propels the celebrants
toward paroxysm, this scene has a peculiarly ritualistic character.
That same rhythm is a central feature of the entire play. In general,
the struggle that culminates in AITANA's death is developed continu-
ously—through a comparatively static first act, a more violent
second, and a frenzied third. Nevertheless, the graduation of
stylistic and thematic elements does not proceed in smooth linear
fashion ; the action of the play involves a series of confrontations,
in which the critical outburst that always seems immanent is
repeatedly avoided. Thus, the tension between the characters is
expressed as a series of pulsations that build through several 'false
cadences' to a final moment of repose. Rhythmically, the last scene
recapitulates and presents in miniature the entire dramatic conflict.
This skillful manipulation of rhythm permits Alberti to complete
the process of mythification undertaken in the first act. As the
rhythmic structure imposes itself upon the consciousness of the
spectator, the events of the plot take on the qualities of ritual. At
the same time, the characters lose their status as free agents.
Increasingly, they appear to be participants in a ceremonial reenactment ; their individual wills seem obliterated by a secret
urgency that drives them toward extreme forms of behavior. When
they annihilate and transcend the normal boundaries of human
experience, they leave behind their lifesized contours, and the
struggle in which they are engaged assumes its full cosmic dimensions. Thus, SILENO's final deed impresses us as a sacrificial act
rather than a crime of passion [7]. At the moment when he strangles
AITANA, the miller is neither a father nor a lover, but the blind
agent of sinister forces ; he is a superhuman creature, whose
reactions cannot be reduced to logic, whose acts lie beyond the
bounds of moral judgment.

In *El trébol florido*, the most glaring defects of *El hombre
deshabitado* have been successfully overcome. In the earlier play
Alberti failed to attempt any sort of dramatic build-up. His theatrical forms were thrown flimsily over a conceptual structure to
which they were unrelated. In this mature work, he has achieved

[7] On this point, see Guerrero Zamora's perceptive comments *(op. cit.*, pp.
109-10).

a superb gradation of dramatic tension. The absence of purely ornamental or stylistically intrusive elements bespeaks an increased capacity to achieve a unified whole. Here, form and content are inseparable from one another. Alberti's island setting contributes to the effectiveness of his artistic statement. Its isolation from the historical world facilitates the creation of symbols in general. Its abundant shores provide a most suitable context for a symbolic confrontation between land and sea. The elemental and traditional life style of the rustic characters is an invaluable source of theatrical language. Without the close proximity of man to nature, the popular and pagan ambiance of the Saint John's Feast, the poetry and forcefulness of the work would be lost. The symbolism that equates human with cosmic events would be dramatically unconvincing, the figurative language of the dialogue meaningless, and the ritualistic quality that transforms allegory into myth nonexistent.

The esthetic hybridism of *De un momento a otro* has also disappeared in *El trébol florido*. Again the caricaturesque aspect of the parents contrasts with the stylized lyricism of the rest of the work. This is especially true of SILENO, whose lewd demeanor and drunken limericks bespeak a kinship with EL BEATO [8]. In this instance, however, the combination of grotesque and non-grotesque elements is justifiable and well-handled. UMBROSA and SILENO are dissonant elements, whose interference with their children's happiness has no claim to legitimacy. The kind of tension to which they give rise is quite unlike that which is generated by AITANA's coquetry or the fraternal rivalry of MARTÍN and ALCIÓN. It is important to call attention to this difference between the two groups of characters. Since one stylization demands another, caricature is an appropriate means of doing so.

With the splendid theatre poetry of *El trébol florido* the playwright initiates a third stage in his career. During this period,

---

[8]   E.g. ¡ Vino, vino
                   del molino !
                   ¡ Vino bueno
                   de Sileno !
                   Por lo galana,
                   para mi Aitana.
                   Por lo delfín,
                   para Martín.
                   Por buen patrón,
                   para Alción.
                   Y por lo hermosa
                   y borrascosa,
                   para la fiesta de mi Umbrosa !
                                                (I, 103-4.)
Marrast also calls attention to this similarity (p. 100).

Alberti returns to the traditional inspiration of his earliest
endeavors. He proves himself to be an impeccable craftsman. For
the first time he exhibits a steadfast refusal to be distracted from
his dramatic task.

El adefesio

El adefesio (1944) has a well-documented origin in Alberti's
childhood experience, his encounter with la encerrada in Rute [9],
and numerous traditions of Andalusian folklore. This work is also
a direct outgrowth of the playwright's earlier experiments with
grotesque stylization. Of the three neo-popular plays, it affords
the most insight into his growth and development.

The action of El adefesio centers about the shenanigans of
three old maids named GORGO, UVA, and AULAGA. These extravagant creatures alternately devote their energies to fawning over
a lice-ridden beggar called BIÓN and torturing their young and
beautiful charge ALTEA. GORGO rules the roost with a despotic
hand in the name of her dead brother Don Dino. She literally
dons his beard and assumes masculine gestures when she feels
her authority to be challenged. For reasons mysteriously related
to the family honor, she has set about preventing the union of
ALTEA with her suitor CASTOR. Repeatedly she attempts to carry
out her resolve over the objections of her two cronies, ALTEA's
maid and confidante ANIMAS, and the maiden herself. In the end
she accomplishes her purpose by falsely perpetrating a rumor that
CASTOR has hanged himself. Believing her lover to be dead, ALTEA
throws herself from a tower. Then at last, GORGO reveals the supposed reasons for her strange behavior: since ALTEA and CASTOR
were half-brother and sister, their marriage would have been incestuous.

The most important formal feature of El adefesio is a pervasive
irony which gives to the 'reality' objectively present on stage an
obviously deficient quality. This alerts the audience to a need for
deciphering literal pronouncements and penetrating surface appearances. As the three old maids pay lip service to concepts of
Christian love and family honor, one suspects that other motives
would better explain their behavior. These are not long in coming
to light. Behind the charitable care bestowed upon BIÓN, there
lies a fierce amorous rivalry—at once a source and a symptom of
sexual frustration; behind the pious declarations that accompany
the torture of ALTEA, there is an ill-concealed and atrocious cruelty.

[9] See our pp. 8-9.

Sadistically, the old maids seek self-appeasement through the martyrdom of another. A peculiar structure which Alberti—or rather the characters themselves—give to the first two acts provides an important clue to the old ladies' true motives. Everything that happens in *El adefesio* must be seen in relation to the twisted psychology of ALTEA's protectors. They create specific appearances because they have certain things to hide ; these appearances—the masks they wear—are placed before the spectator's eyes. But as the characters are to a large extent victims of their own madness, they cannot exercise complete control over the action. Thus, the substitution of appearance for reality is clumsy ; the latter shows through. Each time one mask is abruptly exchanged for another, we are afforded a glimpse of the face that lies beneath.

At times the characters' clumsiness takes the form of abrupt transitions within one scene. In the first act, ALTEA is brought down from the tower where she has been sequestered and placed before a mirror, dressed as a goddess of the fields. GORGO treats her with apparent kindness, praising her beauty in blatantly sensual terms, and suggesting that her long imprisonment will soon be over :

> GORGO. — Mira qué brazos, hija. ¿Crees tú que el cristal miente? Mira qué ojos... qué mejillas... qué boca... qué racimo de pelo... *(Se lo suelta.)* Puedes vanagloriarte de tus hombros... ¡Y qué garganta, niña! ¿Has visto cuello como el tuyo en estos pueblos de la tierra?... Pues ¿y este busto, amigas? Alguna vez leí que las magnolias... Pero aquí, no... Limones luneros... ¡Qué fragancia! Eres toda un jardín.
>
> (I, 125-26.)

Suddenly, GORGO seizes upon an opportune moment to convert the encounter into an inquisitorial trial. She acts as judge ; her two accomplices act as jury :

> ALTEA. — Yo nunca quise hacerte mal, tía Gorgo.
> GORGO. — ¡Hacerme mal! ¿Y por qué piensas eso, hija mía? Me gustaría saberlo. Siéntate. (ALTEA *se sienta. Después de contemplarla un instante)...* Voy a sentarme yo también. ¡Hacerme mal! *(Con ella, se sientan* AULAGA *y* UVA.) Claro que si las celosías no dieran a la calle, seguramente, sobrina, no se te habría ocurrido lo que me has dicho ahora... *(Pausa breve.)* ¿Qué se ve, niña... tras las celosías del salón bajo?
> ALTEA. — La calle...
> GORGO. — ¿La calle nada más? (ALTEA *guarda silencio.* GORGO *se levanta.)* ¿Nada más? Poca cosa, sobrina. ¿Estás segura tú? ¿Nada más que la calle?... Porque la calle se ha hecho para andar-

la... ¿No es verdad, sobrina?... Y las celosías, para ver sin ser
visto... y para hablar también con el que sube y baja por la calle.

(I, 126-28.)

As GORGO fails to discover the identity of ALTEA's suitor admiration turns to scorn, praise gives way to insult, the maiden's finery is exchanged for a «vestido negro de vieja» :

> *(Como tres sombras, como tres rebujos siniestros, riendo, burlonas, hirientes* [*las viejas*], *van y vienen alrededor de* ALTEA *que llora, bajo, cubierta la cara por los cabellos.)*
> GORGO. — Te repito que no me llores, escoba. Destápate la cara, ¿o es que con esas greñas quieres barrer el suelo?
> UVA. — Parece un pejesapo.
> AULAGA. — ¡ La reina de la vendimia !
> GORGO. — ¿ La reina? ¡ Del muladar ! ¡ Del basurero ! ¡ Se acabaron las diosas de la hermosura ! Fuera adornos, colgajos, colorines ! *(Le va arrancando el traje a tirones.)*

(I, 129.)

The reason for this cruel behavior is suggested through the order of episodes which constitute the action. As the play opens, the old maids bicker competitively over BIÓN. They treat the beggar with the same mixture of solicitousness and sadism characteristic of their dealings with ALTEA. As UVA and AULAGA lovingly take charge of his toilette, AULAGA turns on him suddenly and savagely snips off his beard :

> *(*UVA *y* AULAGA *arreglan a* BIÓN... *subido en un taburete al centro de la escena.* UVA, *de rodillas, le remienda un pernil del pantalón.* AULAGA, *en lo alto de una silla, le peina y tijeretea las espesas barbas...)*
> UVA. — Aulaga... cuida no distraerte.
> AULAGA. — ¿ Por qué me lo repites tanto ?
> UVA. — Ahora, por las barbas.
> BIÓN. — ¡ Me clavó usted la aguja, verderol !
> UVA. — ¡ Calla ! ¿ No oyes ?... Mucho tarda Gorgo en volver.
> AULAGA. — Se levantó amarilla, de pronto.
> UVA. — Y yo diría que le rechinaban los dientes.
> AULAGA. — Y que de un ojo iba a escapársele un relámpago.
> BIÓN. — Se le había empingorotado una ceja.
> UVA. — Te he dicho que te calles, o te hilvano la pierna al pantalón.
> BIÓN. — ¡ Una ceja, una ceja !
> AULAGA *(cortándole las barbas de un tijeretazo).* — ¡ Vamos ! Por meticón y charlatán te quedaste sin barbas.

(I, 115.)

This sequence moves directly into the mirror scene. The frustrations accumulated during the contest over BIÓN spill over onto the head of ALTEA, translated into resentment of her youth and beauty.

The second act is constructed along similar lines. First we witness an encounter between GORGO and BIÓN. GORGO discovers that the beggar has brought with him a letter from CASTOR to ALTEA. The youth intends to kidnap the maiden and wrest her from her captors. Learning of this plan, GORGO hysterically enacts the propected crime and decrees that ALTEA is to be re-imprisoned in the tower. Once more the action focuses on BIÓN. GORGO and her accomplices wrap the beggar in a skein of wool. Amidst grunts and animal noises, they snip him loose with the scissors from UVA's sewing basket:

> UVA (*tijereteando los hilos y madejas que lc aprisionan*). —
> ¡Pues a morder, a ladrar libre! ¡Venga! ¡Ladra! ¡Guau, guau!
> ¡Aúlla, Bión, Aúlla largo! ¡Uuuuh! (BIÓN *lanza al par que* UVA
> *aullidos y risotadas grotescas.*) ¡Maldita sea la hora que volviste
> a esta casa!
>
> (I, 144-45.)

As the contest for the possession of the beggar continues, GORGO calls ALTEA down from the tower. The act concludes with a new confrontation between ALTEA and GORGO in the course of which GORGO destroys CASTOR's letter before the maiden's eyes. Again the attack is sudden and launched with obviously sadistic intent:

> ALTEA. — Yo no tengo ya a nadie. Estoy sola, rodeada de es-
> panto...
> GORGO. — ¿Olvidada, sobrina?... ¿Puedes asegurarlo, sin que
> la sangre se te inquiete?... Acércate el oído al corazón... Dudas,
> hija. Lo veo.
> ALTEA. — No me asesines lentamente. Mátame de una vez
> No puedo más.
> GORGO. — Me estás mintiendo, Altea.
> ALTEA. — Déjame. Te he repetido ya lo que deseo.
> GORGO. — Serías injusta. Mira. (*Muestra la carta. Silencio.*)
> ... Te has quedado sin habla, Altea. Y tú, Uva, también. Sí, una
> carta. De Castor.
>
> (I, 151.)

This combination of abrupt transitions and alternating episodes functions ironically to reveal the true reasons for the old ladies' behavior. The seeming arbitrariness of their shifts in attitude lead us to doubt the authenticity of their displays of sweetness. As again

120

and again we are party to similar scenes, we come to trust their cruelty rather than their piety. The sequence of events implies a causal relationship between successive appearances. By deploying his scenes as he does, Alberti further destroys the credibility of his characters. He also causes the real source of their eccentricity to emerge.

In *El adefesio* Alberti returns to three formal devices with which he had experimented during the 1930s. The most explicit of these is the conventional *acotación*. As in *Radio Sevilla*, he continually dictates the attitude of the actor in terms which suggest an exaggeratedly affected delivery : *con aire de hombre... como agonizante... con tono de responsorio... con un gruñidito semiburlón... con mala intención... con fingido cariño.* Again the author has placed a marked stylistic emphasis on artifice, as a result of which the characters appear to be aware of their histrionic nature.

In the action just preceding the mirror scene, there are several tacit allusions to details of theatrical production. The Beggar who has been shorn of his beard—his mask—is categorically pushed off-stage ; he is obviously the character who exits :

> GORGO. — ¡A la basura, Animas! ¡A la calle! ¡Por el balcón o por el hueco de la escalera! ¡Pronto!...
> BIÓN. — ¡Mis barbas! ¡Mis barbas! Bión no saldrá vivo sin sus barbas. ¡Muérdago!
> GORGO. — ¡Largo, largo! *(Empujándolo con* ANIMAS *hacia la puerta lateral izquierda.)* Aquí no hay más barbas que las mías...

> (I, 116-17.)

Subsequently GORGO calls our attention to the matter of role and mask. In a lengthy sequence, she explicitly impersonates Don Dino :

> GORGO *(se pone las barbas nuevamente, iniciando un paseo por la sala).* — A ver, Aulaga. Mírame bien... *(Va y viene ante ella, con aire de hombre.)* Ya no soy Gorgo ahora. Piensa, piensa. *(Levantándole a* UVA *la cara.)* Y tú, Uva, también... *(Se sienta, siempre con aire de hombre, cruzando la pierna, en actitud pensativa.)* «¡El olivar, el olivar! Me saquean estos miserables. Me arruinan. ¡No puedo más, no puedo más! ¡Reviento!» ¿Quién sufría, quién se desesperaba de este modo?

> (I, 117-18.)

Shortly after this performance, GORGO quite literally sets the stage for what is to ensue, attending to details of costume, seating and decor. Finally she sounds the bell which signals the entrance of the *ingénue*. Her peremptory orders resemble those of an actor-director :

GORGO. — ¡Animas! ¡Animas!... Viste a Aitea con su mejor vestido... El espejo. Corredlo acá. Al centro. Y ahora, enfrente, tres sillas. Así. *(Dando unos pasos.)* Uno, dos, tres, cuatro, cinco... A una buena distancia del espejo, que la veamos toda. A ver, siéntate, Aulaga. Y tú, Uva, a mi izquierda. *(Se sienta entre las dos.)* Ya está. ¡Ah, no! *(Yendo a buscarla.)* Falta la campanilla de plata ... Ahora, ya podemos llamar. *(Tocando la campanilla.)* ¡Animas! *(Acompañada por* ANIMAS, *entra* ALTEA.*)*

(I, 123-24.)

In all these passages, the deliberate theatricality of the dialogue and stage business recalls the technique of the *agitprop* plays. Once more, Alberti has used the world-as-a-stage metaphor so that the characters will appear to be acting. By labelling them as 'masqueraders', he reminds us not to mistake appearance for reality.

Throughout *El adefesio* there are abundant examples of parody. ALTEA's suicidal leap from the tower repeats that of Melibea ; this makes of GORGO a kind of anti-Celestina. Alberti repeatedly echoes the botanical imagery traditionally associated with beauty, purity and youth. UVA is accused of planning a secret tryst with BIÓN «en el comedor de los pobres». «¡Soy flor, soy flor! ¡Rosa sin mancha! ¡Nardo limpio!», she exclaims in defense of her withered virginity (I, 121). The characters' names—UVA, AULAGA—and frequent metaphoric references liken them to parasitic plants [10]. There are also parodic allusions to Classical mythology. The old maids are compared to mythological monsters—the Gorgons, the Eumenides [11]. In Act II, as they snip BIÓN free of his bonds, they are likened to the Parcae. As in *Radio Sevilla*, Alberti has used parody as an instrument of irony. That is, parody serves to ridicule the characters *and* to call attention to the falseness of their demeanor.

We can best observe the mechanics of this process in the third act of *El adefesio*. There, parody functions in relation to a number

10 The botanical term *altea* (Eng. 'marsh mallow'), provides a contrast. We differ with Marrast when he dismisses the characters' names as a «caprice poétique» (p. 120). As we shall see, this is an important element of characterization.
11 E.g. UVA. —Gorgo... Gorgoja... Gorgona... (I, 171). N.B. that GORGO's name evokes the Gorgons *and* the Eumenides or Furies, portrayed by Aeschylus as Gorgon-like figures with snakes for hair, bloodshot eyes, etc It also suggests onomatopoeically the Spanish word *gorgojo* (Eng. 'gurgle').

of other technical devices which together give rise to the ironically self-conscious character. As the curtain goes up, we are confronted with the kneeling and 'ecstatic' figure of GORGO. Following the destruction of CASTOR's letter, she has been beaten by her cronies. Now, as she addresses herself to her dead brother, she recounts in hollow tones the atrocities to which she has been subjected:

> GORGO.
> Mírame aquí golpeada,
> por ti, hermano;
> desfallecidas las sienes,
> doloridos los costados.
>
> No fue con varas de lirios,
> hermano.
> Cañas agudas, partidas
> cañas las que me clavaron.
>
> Me viste volcada en tierra,
> hermano.
> Comiendo el polvo, mordiendo
> las losas que tú has pisado.
>
> (I, 155-56.)

The figure of GORGO posing as martyr recalls that of Jesus on the Mount of Olives. As her prayer is superimposed against a background in which ALTEA—the real victim—laments her plight, the inauthenticity of GORGO's behavior is further underlined:

> ALTEA.
> Unas torres dan al campo
> Otras, al mar, a la mar.
> Las torres de mi esperanza,
> ¿adónde dan?
>
> (I, 155.)

Soon the beggars arrive to take part in a charity dinner to which the three spinsters have invited them. In a transparently exaggerated display of humility, GORGO insists on ministering single-handedly to the needs of her guests. Amidst loud protests and exclamations, she washes the hands of all those present. Her gesture alludes to Christ's washing of the feet of the disciples:

> GORGO. — Reíd. Chillad. Mofaos. Mi alma está preparada...
> Vuestros gritos y risas la iluminan, bañándola de gozo y delicias
> sin límites... Venid a mí. Pero no... Soy yo, y de rodillas, la que
> va hacia vosotros... ¡Qué son estas humildes piedras para las grie-

tas y arañazos que reclama mi carne!... Sean tus manos las primeras, sobrina... *(Se las lava.)* Animas...

ANIMAS *(retirando las manos).* — Antes morir, señora...

GORGO *(lavándoselas).* — Te las lavo también. Pueden seguir
ahora con más tino su secreto trabajo...

UVA. — ¿A mí tú? ¡Nunca, nunca! Es mucha humillación,
Gorgo.

GORGO. — No, mi Uvita, al contrario. *(Lavándoselas.)* Es mi
gloria, es la de él, la suya... Van a sentirse santas, a florecer quizás
en ellas el nuevo pensamiento de acariciarme un poco...

AULAGA *(adelantándose).* — Yo sí, yo sí me dejo... *(Mientras
se las lava.)* ¡Oh qué tranquilidad. ¡Qué dulzura! ¡Qué gozo!

GORGO. — Más todavía para mí, Aulaga...

BIÓN. — Bión también, ama mía, aunque no lo merece. *(Incli-
nado, respetuosamente, mientras le lavan las manos.)*

(I, 162-63.)

These extravagances of GORGO's impress AULAGA; but they draw
a skeptical comment from UVA. «Antes yo era la mártir», she
observes, «¡Ahora..., mirad!». Finally, laying aside her towels
and basin, GORGO divests herself of the beard which she had
donned for this last performance. She assumes another pose and
presides over the blessing of the table. In the stage directions, the
author creates a *tableau* which recalls innumerable painted versions
of the Last Supper:

> GORGO. — Y ahora, hijos, yo limpia y ya pura, resplandecien-
> tes todos como la plata, sentaos conmigo a la mesa de la caridad,
> a este festín que es hoy también de la concordia. *(Colocada GORGO
> en el centro de la mesa y cada uno en su sitio, quedan de pie.)*
> Encomendémonos, antes de empezar, a aquél que nos legó esta
> santa y familiar costumbre.

(I, 163.)

At this moment, when the character's affectation is most visible,
a messenger arrives with the news of CASTOR's feigned death.
Suddenly overt appearances break down. With ALTEA's suicide,
pious lie is converted into tragic truth.

GORGO's displays of false piety appear hypocritical largely
because they are so familiar. The spectator perceives them as
topsy-turvy versions of the New Testament events surrounding the
capture of Christ. They strike us as a travesty of Christian ethics,
but not because they are an imitation. The character's behavior
reproduces a common form of provincial religiosity [12]; in the

---

[12] See R. Marrast, «Tradiciones populares en *El adefesio*», *Insula*, 18, No. 198
(1963), 7.

Spanish provinces, the believer frequently reenacts the suffering of his savior as a gesture of extreme humility. Thus, what impresses us is the counterfeit quality of GORGO's acts, rather than their imitative nature. That is, the parodic effect results from the character's affected style and her intention to deceive. Her inauthenticity is all the more obvious in view of the occasion; GORGO consciously and histrionically attempts to convince us of her virtue in an instance where true humility would not endeavor to 'mask its masquerading'. This is a highly original form of parody. Usually the author parodies intentionally; here the ironically self-conscious character does so unknowingly. Normally parody involves denunciation and mockery of the original; here the result is involuntary self-mockery and unwitting self-exposure.

Don Dino's beard is literally a disguise. As we can now understand, the old maids wear many others. In their dealings with ALTEA and BIÓN, they repeatedly masquerade their cruelty as humility, self-sacrifice and charity. The mask changes, but the fact of wearing one does not. Like the *Dos farsas revolucionarias* and *Radio Sevilla*, *El adefesio* is a play about playing. The characters of *El adefesio* outstrip their forbears in complexity and grotesqueness. Nevertheless, they are descended from the imposters of the *agitprop* plays.

Only on one occasion do the three old ladies lay aside their disguises. Immediately following the death of ALTEA, their speech loses its mad quality. What we have here is the classic phenomenon of *dédoublement*. Stylistic variance results because the characters take up a position at some distance from their roles. Each explains her function as a fictional being, the part she has been given and has now ceased to play:

> GORGO. — Lo maté sólo en mí... Lo maté para Aulaga y para Altea, pensando así matar este mal sueño... Llegué a creer que lo que deseaba, que lo que solamente era un pensamiento se había cumplido ya, huyendo de estos muros el aleteo de la deshonra y el escándalo... ¡Que vengan las rameras y los borrachos, los ladrones y los mendigos, que vengan todos y oigan a doña Gorgo, la buena, la misericordiosa, pregonando la lepra y la miseria de su alma!... Yo no... Yo no... Yo no soy más que un monstruo, una pobre furia caída, un adefesio... (*Se tapa toda con un lienzo negro.*)

(I, 171-72.)

This moment can be viewed thematically as exposure and theatrically as 'unmasking'. It is a brilliant culmination to the series of ironically self-conscious impersonations which constitute the action of *El adefesio*. As the characters seek to rid themselves of responsibility for their murderous act, they tacitly confess their complicity in the disaster which has just occurred. Moreover, their attempt at self-acquittal shows them unequivocally to be guilty of the underlying crime of fraudulent and hypocritical behavior. Because GORGO demonstrates her ability to cease to masquerade at will, we know that she has been masquerading all along. Thus in the final moments of *El adefesio*, Alberti destroys the irony which he has built up carefully throughout the play. The mask is removed; the face is revealed in all its grotesque ugliness. The audience is at last given a certain clarity of vision. What has appeared to be appearance is shown to be just that. Paradoxically however, the ending is also an ironic climax. The gap between face and mask is supposedly eliminated, but we discover that the underlying reality is in itself deceptive. Whereas we have assumed the play to be a statement about the stifling effects of spinsterdom on youth, it turns out to be a statement about disguises and the hypocrites who wear them [13]. We find ourselves justified in mistrusting the characters; yet they are the ones who unknowingly lead us to the truth.

Throughout the play, the term *adefesio* can be interpreted as 'extravagance'. In GORGO's final speech, it must be understood as 'ridiculous outfit' or 'disguise'. This suggests a third level of irony. From the standpoint of dramatic technique, the entire play can be regarded as a disguise, a huge exercise in audience deception. Alberti has structured the action very carefully so as to insinuate that which we eventually come to understand; yet the spectator's overt impression throughout is one of cumulative chaos, his final grasp of the theme sudden in its effect. The fact is that through the persistent taking-up and laying-down of masks, there occurs a subtle thematic shift. As the masks, the roles, the fictions are changed but the fact of playing remains constant, our attention is gradually diverted from the announced content—the part, the specific role—, to the total situation—the presence of role, the character as actor. At the end of the play, we suddenly realize what has taken place. Our sudden awareness can itself stand as a statement about playing as deception. Clearly this new experiment with ironic characterization out-strips those of the 1930s in brilliance, scope and tightness of conception. Alberti handles his thematic shift skillfully and imperceptibly, exercising total control over our reactions. He has also effected a perfect wedding of form and content. This new proliferation of masks is a most appropriate means of portraying the hypocrite.

---

[13] For comments regarding other readings of *El adefesio*, see our note 32, pp. 150-51.

The use of irony places us at a distance from the characters. Nevertheless, we are able to take their boisterous antics seriously. That is, we do not simply perceive them rationally as the single cause that determines the course of action ; we experience them histrionically and feel their crushing weight. This is largely because of the irrational nature and extreme density of Alberti's imaginary world. From the moment the curtain rises, the onlooker is plunged into an enigmatic ambiance. The macabre designs of the three old maids materialize in obstreperous declarations, an extreme angularity of gesture, a constant whirling about their prey, a zany hanging on of beards, giving rise to what Pérez Minik has described as a *ritmo delirante* [14]. As images accumulate with accelerating speed, and scenes alternate rapidly sometimes even coinciding with one another, the effect is positively hallucinatory. So as to further remove us from the domain of logic, the characters' behavior is rooted in superstition and alcohol ; GORGO is forever taking a little nip, especially at moments of crisis, and the three old ladies dedicate their afternoons to hunting bats.

The bat hunt is a daily ritual which persists in the household out of deference to the desires of the dead man. In Alberti's portrayal of this custom, we can appreciate the quality of the spectacle and measure its effects. The entire sequence is vaguely allegorical in its thrust and awakens in the spectator associations of unpleasantness and morbidity :

> GORGO. — Animas, trae las cañas. *(Sale* ANIMAS.*)* Es la hora... Vas a distraerte un poquito. Los pájaros... esos, no. Sería como matar a florecillas indefensas. Pero los murciélagos... *(Misteriosa, obsesivamente.)* Mira, mira sobrina... Mirad... Van altos todavía... Acaban de salir... Vuelan enceguecidos, esquivando los quicios de las torres... Anidan en la cabeza del demonio... Y dan vueltas y vueltas y vueltas como el remordimiento... *(Vuelve* ANIMAS, *trayendo cinco largas cañas, con un trapo negro en la punta. Mientras,* ANIMAS *las va dando.)* Matarlos, derribarlos, es como irse limpiando la conciencia de manchas, emblanqueciendo el alma de sus culpas. *(Ya con su caña, en el centro de la azotea.)* Girad, girad despacio esos pañuelos negros y los veréis obsesionados, crujiendo, chirriando como pestillos en la noche... *(Las van girando rítmicamente, mientras suena lejano aún y triste el toque de Oración.)*
>
>   Mensajeros de la muerte,
>   nunca anidéis en mi frente.

[14] Pérez Minik, *op. cit.,* p. 501. The critic adds: «Este ritmo delirante no está reducido en *El adefesio* sólo al automatismo lírico y escenográfico, sino que también brota vehementemente de la acción dramática, del ejercicio del poder dictatorial de Gorgo, del espíritu inquisitorial que lo preside todo, del uso desbordado de las máscaras y de un arrebatado deseo de llegar a las últimas consecuencias».

AULAGA.
    ¡ Caed, volad,
    y dejadme en mi sueño descansar !
GORGO.
    Vuestros designios funestos
    nunca perturben mi pecho.
UVA.
    ¡ Volad, caed,
    y dejadme en mi sueño florecer !
GORGO.
    Nunca vuestras alas ciegas
    se agiten en mi conciencia.
ANIMAS.
    ¡ Huid, girad,
    y dejadla sin miedo volar !
GORGO.
    Vuestro color de desgracia
    nunca enlute esta morada.
ALTEA.
    ¡ Huid, huid,
    y dejadme olvidada morir !

(I, 50-51.)

The bats embody a whole series of imprecise and disagreeable connotations. They are symbolic of the ambiance of madness and sorcery which surrounds ALTEA. One important consequence of this episode is again the emergence of the ironically self-conscious character ; our awareness of role as 'performance' results largely from a highly stylized spectacle. Another is to render the work dramatically convincing as well as technically brilliant. As in *El trébol florido*, Alberti has eluded our intelligence. By means of a skillful wedding of poetic and plastic image, dialogue and scenographic movement, he has addressed himself to our histrionic sensibilities. In this instance, he situates us in a dream world which is the projection of his characters' dismal psychology. The sensorial richness of that world prompts acceptance of the theatrical illusion.

Although the author succeeds in conveying an overwhelming impression of unreality, the theatrical space of *El adefesio* is not isolated from the objectively identifiable world. On the contrary, it has a strong local character :

> *La fábula sucede en cualquier año de estos últimos setenta y en uno de esos pueblos fanáticos caídos entre las serranías del Sur de España, cruzados de reminiscencias musulmanas.*

(I, 144.)

Having specified this in his first stage direction, Alberti takes
great pains to remind us where we are. To this end he employs
a number of scenographic details : the Monte de las Cruces provides
a background for the action ; the *Toque de Oración* calls the faithful to evening prayers.

A myriad of folkloric elements also anchors us in a concrete
setting. The dialogue of *El adefesio* is full of verbal formulas,
rhymes, riddles, idiomatic expressions, turns of phrase still to be
encountered in the oral traditions of Andalusia [15]. The other characters greet the fearsome GORGO with ritual incantations :

> BIÓN *(cayendo del taburete, suplicante).*
> ¡ Toca, moca,
> grillos para tus pies
> y freno para tu boca!
> GORGO. — ¡ Animas, Animas, Animas!
> *(Entra* ANIMAS, *cayendo de rodillas.)*
> ANIMAS.
> ¡ Rata muerta, gato enfermo,
> líbrame, Dios mío, del estafermo!

(I, 116.)

The bat hunt echoes a widespread folk belief ; bats are commonly
thought to embody the wandering souls of Purgatory. The charity
dinner with its accompanying purification by water and GORGO's
Imitation of Christ derive from popular religious practices.
ALTEA's costume in the mirror scene evokes the wine harvest.
Finally, the Andalusian setting is reinforced by representative
characters. We immediately recognize familiar provincial types :
ANIMAS, the beggars, the messenger and especially the three
spinsters. GORGO's displays of righteous indignation, her vicarious
obsession with the imagined sins of others are the hallmarks of the
Spanish *beata.* Thus, what we have in *El adefesio* is a remarkable
balance between the inner world of the characters and their external
milieu, between the subjective and the collective. Alberti has
created a dream world that is midway between that of Quevedo
and that of Freud.

Clearly, this fully grotesque image of Andalusia derives from
the incipiently esperpentic scenes of *De un momento a otro* [16].

---

[15] For a more detailed discussion see Marrast, pp. 111 ff. ; his «Tradiciones
populares» ; his «L'esthétique théâtrale», pp. 70-71.

[16] See Marrast, 109 ff. ; and Guerrero Zamora, *op. cit.,* p. 103. Marrast's
discussion of *El adefesio* is devoted almost entirely to a consideration of traditional
and autobiographical sources and the relationship between the two works in question.
As he has noted elsewhere, *El adefesio* and *De un momento a otro* coincide in their
broad thematic outlines. In each play, Alberti portrays a struggle between purity

GABRIEL's aunts, with their mixture of sexual frustration and hysterical religiosity are the ancestors of GORGO, UVA, and AULAGA. EL BEATO, with his bedraggled entourage and taste for obscene rhymes, prefigures the corrupt and lascivious BIÓN. A number of minor details from the author's life also find their way into the stylized imaginary world of *El adefesio*. There was a church bell that tolled obsessively in the waning hours of his Andalusian afternoons (AP, p. 14). A stifling *ambiente de pesadilla* oftentimes prevailed in the Alberti household (AP, p. 15). The author's mother had a liking for exotic plants with strange-sounding names (AP, p. 118). The bat hunt is also a custom which Alberti encountered in his childhood [17]. This kind of detail recurs in *De un momento a otro*. Thus the brilliantly executed work of 1944 and the clumsier early play have an identical origin in Alberti's experience. This threefold relationship between Alberti's life and his two plays affords important insight into his development as a playwright. With respect to *De un momento a otro*, *El adefesio* represents an inversion of values and an esthetic advance. In the mature work, an ill-advised mixture of literary realism and caricature is supplanted by a uniformly esperpentic vision. The occasional introduction of lyric elements associated with ALTEA's presence is justified as a means of creating irony.

Between one play and the other, Alberti's stylized portrayal of the Andalusian province has undergone a process of intensification. The author has narrowed his field of vision, concentrating on religious fanaticism instead of attempting a more diffuse and general treatment of provincial life. At the same time, he has sharpened and rendered more forbidding the profiles of his characters. In *El adefesio*, GABRIEL's maiden aunts are transformed into hideous esperpentic witches. They retain a deviant psychology which confuses piety and eroticism. Their fanatical attitudes continue to be translated into similar scenographic language—clumsy rigid movements that dehumanize and ridicule. But now the macabre trio is disfigured to a far greater degree. With their angular gesticulation, they share the properties of parasitic plants. With howls and grunts, they enter the ranks of the lower animal world. They assume the attributes of mythological monsters. The old maids of *El adefesio* are no longer merely ridiculous in their

and ugliness which has as its outcome «l'étouffement d'une force vitale sous des préjugés, des superstitions entretenues au nom d'un certain ordre qui démeure étranger a leur victime» («L'esthéthique théâtrale», p. 70).

[17] «También es costumbre en Andalucía cazar murciélagos con cañas y trapos negros. Mis tías de *El adefesio* me enseñaron esta extraña diversión.» (Letter from the author to Marrast [2 March 1952].)

grotesqueness. They are fantastically diabolical creatures, deeply troubling in their horridness.

The scene of the charity breakfast from *De un momento a otro* is reproduced in *El adefesio* down to many specific details. Once more, the guests abscond with the silverware:

> *(Se hace una oscuridad profunda, en la que sólo se oyen los pasos precipitados de todos que corren por el fondo del jardín retirando cada uno su farolito. A continuación, empieza a oírse a lo lejos una musiquilla pordiosera, melancólica... viéndose, bajo una luz que de lo alto ilumina solamente la mesa, a los* CUATRO MENDIGOS *que la roban, guardándose en los zurrones frutas, tenedores, cuchillos, etc. Tarea rítmica, silenciosa, que acabará con unas risas quedas y burlonas, mientras la luz y la musiquilla se extinguen en el jardín.)*

(I, 168.)

In *El adefesio*, however, the artistic statement is more vigorous and more direct. A fairly standard satire of unrealistic and insipid forms of philanthropy has become a grotesque parody of the Last Supper. The dinner of *El adefesio* is an exceedingly pointed denunciation of social evil and religious hypocrisy. Thus, whereas the use of autobiographical material appears to have been constraining to Alberti's imagination in 1938, in 1944 it was seminal. Despite the author's continuing dependence on personal recollections, *El adefesio* is not an autobiographical play; it is an instance of experience transformed into art. Since we have evidence that the author's direct involvement had an adverse effect on his early works, it is likely that the non-confessional nature and esthetic excellence of *El adefesio* are related ocurrences. Both bespeak the clarity of vision and greater artistic integrity of the mature playwright.

The reappearance of the grotesque esthetic, ironic characterization and autobiographical detail of Alberti's ideological period makes *El adefesio* continuous with the works of the 1930s. At the same time this second of the neo-popular plays must be grouped with its companion pieces by virtue of its superior artistic quality and extreme originality. By 1944, Alberti knew that true esthetic quality is only attained when the 'mirror held up to life' interprets as well as reflects our reality. He has learned to exercise his creative talents beyond the bounds of his immediate experience. The exiled playwright exhibits a sophisticated understanding of his art.

La Gallarda

La Gallarda (1944-1945), subtitled «tragedia de vaqueros y toros bravos», is a tale of love and vengeance set among the foothills of the Castilian *meseta central*. Written entirely in verse and traceable in its origin to the *romancero*, it is a return to the formal preoccupations of *Fermín Galán*. It is another mythical play and a work in which scenographic rhythm and psychological conflict are overriding concerns. Thus it can be regarded as a kind of crossroads where many of the author's past and present interests converge.

The principal source for *La Gallarda* is a Salamancan ballad in which a young man named Manuel Sánchez dies in the bullring after his mother has invoked a curse upon him :

> Los mozos de Monleón
> se fueron a arar temprano,
> para ir a la corrida
> y remudar con despacio.
> Al hijo de la Veñuda
> el remudo no le han dado.
> —Al toro tengo de ir
> aunque lo busque prestado.
> —Permita Dios, si lo encuentras,
> que te traigan en un carro,
> las albarcas y el sombrero...
> En el medio del camino
> al vaquero preguntaron
> qué tiempo tiene el toro,
> el toro tiene ocho años.
> —Muchachos, no entréis a él,
> mirar que el toro es muy malo,
> que la leche que mamó
> se la di yo por mi mano.
> Se presentan en la plaza
> cuatro mozos muy gallardos,
> Manuel Sánchez llamó al toro,
> nunca le hubiera llamado...
> Al rico de Monleón
> le piden los buéis y el carro,
> para llevar a Manuel Sánchez
> que el torito le ha matado,
> a la puerta la Veñuda
> arrecularon el carro.
> —Aquí tenéis vuestro hijo
> como lo habéis demandado...

A eso de los nueve meses
salió la madre bramando...
preguntando por el toro;
el toro ya está enterrado[18].

LA GALLARDA, the play's young and beautiful protagonist, leads a
lonely existence in the isolated cabin which she shares with her
husband MANUEL SÁNCHEZ. Far from her beloved herd, the *vaquera*[19] suffers a perpetual nostalgia for Resplandores, a little red
bullock for whom she feels a mysterious affection[20]. One day
LUCAS BARROSO, the driver of the herd, arrives at her cabin and
attempts in vain to conquer her affections. Infuriated by her
resistance, LUCAS vows to avenge himself; he arranges for Resplandores to die in the ring at the hands of MANUEL. When MANUEL
answers this challenge to his virility by acceding to the demands
of the *mayoral*, LA GALLARDA is beside herself. In a frenzy of anger
and grief she invokes a curse upon her husband and wishes for
the victory of the bull (Act I).

The events of Act II take place on two levels. In the *corrida*,
which takes place offstage, LA GALLARDA's wish is fulfilled; MANUEL
dies in the ring. Wounded, Resplandores flees to the mountain
wilderness. Meanwhile, alongside the figure of the fitfully sleeping
protagonist, there occurs a lengthy dream sequence in which LA
GALLARDA is courted by four cowherds—among them LUCAS and

[18] J. M. de Cossío, *Los toros en la poesía* (Buenos Aires: Espasa Calpe [1947]),
p. 23, partially cited in Marrast, p. 132. The probable sources of *La Gallarda* are
multiple and exceedingly complex. The names of most of the characters have their
origin in traditional poetry. That of the protagonist, for example, is taken from an
Asturian ballad («Estándose la Gayarda / en su ventana florida, etc.»). As Marrast
has correctly observed (p. 136), LA GALLARDA is descended from a long line of
Spanish *serranas*. At the same time, she is an original creation. In the French
critic's words, «Gallarda n'est plus une de ces montagnardes solides, à l'aspect viril
que Juan Ruiz rencontrait au cours de ses randonées: elle n'est pas non plus la
serrana aimable de Góngora... elle n'a pas le visage de la Gayarda traditionnelle
du *romance*, qui attirait les hommes, après les avoir séduits de bonnes paroles, et
les tuait». For additional discussion on sources, see our note 20, below and *ibid.*,
pp. 131-36.
[19] The term *vaquera* is virtually impossible to translate. The English 'cowgirl'
fails to capture its poetic connotations.
[20] In connection with the peculiar relationship between LA GALLARDA and the
semi-human Resplandores, Alberti cites in addition to the aforementioned ballad,
another from the region of Avila:
El toro tenía tres meses,
la serrana lo crió,
con la leche de sus pechos
el alimento le dio.
(Letter from the author to Marrast [27 Jan. 1953]). In our opinion, two mythical
figures inevitably come to mind as well—the Celtic bull that appears at the end
of *El trébol florido*, and Pasiphäe. However, we see no reason to conclude as
does Marrast (p. 136) that Alberti's protagonist harbors any of the perverse
sentiments commonly associated with the latter character.

her husband. This is the past event which explains the *mayoral's* behavior and clarifies the situation of the young couple. Lucas' violent reaction is the result of a longstanding resentment brought about by his unsuccessful quest for La gallarda's hand. Earlier he had given expression to this resentment by having the newly-weds banished to their isolated dwelling.

Act III is a prolongation of the events which culminate in the ill-fated *corrida*. Following the death of Manuel and the disappearance of Resplandores, La Gallarda, Lucas, and a crowd of country folk rush off in pursuit of the wounded creature. The protagonist is clearly in the grip of madness, the *mayoral* as determined as ever to possess her or avenge himself. When Lucas' persistence comes to naught and La gallarda rejects his offer of the bull in exchange for her body, he runs ahead of the others and forces Resplandores over a cliff. Thus the play is brought to its tragic conclusion. As the little bullock perishes in the bottom of a ravine, La gallarda falls to the floor exhausted.

As in *El trébol florido*, the setting of *La Gallarda* provides the figurative elements by means of which the dramatic conflict is transformed into a myth. The traditional association of man and beast—the wedding of brute force with human attributes—becomes the nucleus of an allegorical structure in which every event is the expression of a state of mind. The central importance of this association is established in the initial moments of the prologue. A chorus-like personage named Babú appears before an allegorical curtain, recalling similar elements in *Fermín Galán:*

> (*Alegoría de* La gallarda, *abrazada a un torito colorado, sobre la sombra de un toro negro, rodeada de cuatro vaqueros saltando a la garrocha, contra un cielo de grandes nubes.*)
>
> (I, 175.)

Babú will continue to function as omniscient narrator, commentator, and clairvoyant throughout the play. Transcending the limits marked by the proscenium, he addresses the public. In words no less enigmatic than the figures of the backdrop, he underlines his mysterious identification with natural forces:

> Babú.
> ¿Mi nombre? Soy Babú. ¿Lo oís? Que nadie piense,
> que nadie escriba luego que me ignora. Soy todo.
> Todo he venido a ser al subir los cien años.
> ¿Oís el árbol? Soy árbol. ¿Véis el viento? Soy viento,
> la nieve de las sierras y el correr de los ríos,
> el bramar del ganado y el toro que se hunde
> en las estremecidas entrañas de los hombres...

Ninguno se equivoque. Caballo [sic], no te engañes:
soy tú, puedo estar dentro de ti sin que lo sepas;
rumor, eco asombrado de las voces perdidas
y la inmovilidad del canto y de las ramas.

(I, 176.)

Subsequently, the image of the man/beast undergoes a steady
process of materialization. A daily routine which is centered on
the care of the herd facilitates frequent metaphoric comparisons.
In the initial encounter between Lucas and La Gallarda, Babú
attributes to the *mayoral* «la intención caliente de un toro en
primavera» (I, 111). La gallarda insults Lucas with taurine
images. Lucas refers to La gallarda in a similar manner:

La gallarda.
    Tú no eres toro de los que van en frente.
    Tú te arrancas torcido, sin que nadie te incite...
Lucas.
    Tú eras la oscura hembra feroz que desmandabas
    los desasosegados ojos de los vaqueros.

(I, 182-83.)

At the same time the metaphorical language of *La Gallarda* is
rendered visual and plastic. Numerous scenographic details allude
rhythmically to the movements of the *fiesta brava*. Lucas and La
Gallarda confront one another with studied caution, as when
man and bull take the measure of each other's strength. The *ma-
tador* incites the bull to charge:

La gallarda.
    Mayoral, aquí estoy...
Lucas.
                    Vaquera, aquí me tienes...
La gallarda.
    Acércate...
Lucas.
                    Hace tiempo que lo estoy deseando...
La gallarda (*incitándole*).
    ¡Más, Lucas! ¡Y de frente!
Lucas.
                    Sé amansar a las fieras.
La gallarda.
    Pero no a las que embisten con los ojos abiertos.
    Ven ya, Lucas Barroso. ¿No te atreves? ¿Qué aguardas?
    ¿En dónde está la furia del semental que otea
    desde el alcor el aire de las vacas en celo?
    ¡Arráncate!

LUCAS.
                    ¡ Gallarda !
LA GALLARDA.
                    Hiende con la pezuña
la tierra de una alcoba que te quema la sangre.
(Yendo hacia él.)
        Tómame, mayoral, si ya no son dos piedras
        las que te paralizan el fuego en mansedumbre.
(Le escupe, volviéndole la espalda.)
LUCAS.
        Te quiero así, vaquera, entre injurias y gritos,
        entre desmelenadas palabras y temblores.
        Voy a ti con la cara caliente por la espuma
        de tu boca y el ansia de crujir en tus pechos.
(Intentando abrazarla.)
        Gallarda...
LA GALLARDA *(volviéndose y derribándolo).*
                    ¡ Lucas, Lucas !
LUCAS.
                    ¡ Hija de toro malo !

                                        (I, 184-85.)

As we observed earlier, the transformation of metaphor into allegory is a first step in the process of mythification. In *La Gallarda*, this is accomplished through the intervention of a hidden character [21], the little bullock whose invisible presence gravitates over the entire work. Resplandores is a plurivalent and proteic symbol; possessed of a variety of meanings which alternate, coincide and succeed one another in kaleidoscopic fashion, he embodies the frustrations and desires of the protagonist.

As we follow LA GALLARDA from her first youthful illusions to her final madness, Resplandores mirrors the successive stages in her sentimental life [22]. In Act I, the *vaquera* finds herself isolated from the herd and confined to her lonely cabin. Giving expression to her feelings of impotence, she dreams of engendering a creature whose principal attributes are untapped strength and the freedom to roam among the clover :

[21] The second in Alberti's dramatic *opus*. The defunct Don Dino is another such character.
[22] Two of the critics who have written at length on *La Gallarda* disagree with one another and with us on this point. Likening Alberti's protagonist to YERMA, Guerrero Zamora takes Resplandores to be her desired son *(op. cit.,* p. 108). Marrast treats the bull as «le symbole mouvant de la jalousie» (p. 136). In our estimation neither of these readings is incorrect, but both are partial. While tacitly recognizing the existence of a variety of other meanings, neither Guerrero Zamora nor Marrast takes sufficiently into account the proteic and plurivalent nature of Alberti's symbol.

LA GALLARDA.
Ser la madre de un toro pequeñito
que lo acuna caliente entre las pajas
y le ve, por los tréboles, cubrírsele
la piel de clavellinas coloradas;
después, la madre del eral que afila
contra el viento acerado de las ramas
esas puntas de fuego que la muerte
cose en la sangre con furor de ráfaga.
Yo lo soñé, lo tuve, lo tenía;
yo lo sentí batido entre mis ansias
y miré, al descuajárseme una aurora,
que sus ojos de niño me miraban.
¡Quién lo volviera a ver por los arroyos,
recién salido del toril del alba;
quien corriendo en el aire, como el aire
claro y retozador de la mañana!

(I, 188.)

The sense of this passage is reinforced rhythmically through the abrupt, incisive sound of the preterite verbs «lo soñé, lo tuve..., lo sentí». Its meaning is further clarified by the final wishful exclamation.

At the moment of the *corrida*, a similar relationship exists between LA GALLARDA and Resplandores. As MANUEL and Resplandores confront one another in the *plaza*, LA GALLARDA feels trapped by the knowledge that one of them will die. She identifies so strongly with Resplandores, that her entire surroundings take on the configuration of the bullring. Her vision materializes in the appearance of the bullfighters with their capes:

(Suena, lejano, un clarín de corrida de toros.)
BABÚ.
    Gallarda, ya sale el toro.
    Ya está el torito en la plaza...
LA GALLARDA.
    ¿Eres tú, fiero amor, claro amor, quien me mata?
(PEDRO, JUAN, LUCAS y MANUEL, cruzando la alcoba, en forma de aspa. Los tres vaqueros, girando, con las capas rojas abiertas. El mayoral, agitando un pañuelo blanco.)
PEDRO.
    ¡Gallarda!
JUAN.
        ¡Gallarda!
LUCAS.
        ¡Gallarda!

MANUEL.

¡ Gallarda !

(Desaparecen.)

(I, 204-5.)

The bull is here a purely symbolic creature, the projection of LA
GALLARDA's situation. While BABÚ narrates the events of the *corrida*, the *toreros* execute their passes in the direction of the sleeping
woman. As a further sign of the protagonist's acute suffering, the
events of her past take on the character of a bullfight:

BABÚ.
A la Gallarda, en el sueño
su vida se le baraja.
Ve las luces, ve las sombras
presentes y las pasadas:
las distantes, desde cerca,
y las de cerca a distancia.
Ve a lo lejos la corrida
del hijo de sus entrañas;
y el amor entre los toros,
en la alcoba de su casa...
Vaquera ayer perseguida
sin descanso y acosada
por pastizales y montes,
por sendas y por cañadas.

(I, 206-7.)

LA GALLARDA knows the source of LUCAS' rancor and the origin
of her present plight. Thus she envisions her courtship as a *corrida de amor*. In her dream, the *vaquera* is approached by each
of her four suitors:

*(Entra primero JUAN; tras él, PEDRO y LUCAS... Entra MA-
NUEL también...)*
BABÚ *(al colocarse cada uno en una esquina).*
Se plantan, se miran, se esperan, celosos.
Ya está la vaquera con sus cuatro toros.
JUAN *(adelantándose).*
Tu pañuelo rojo te da Juan de Olvega.
Lleno de amor quiero que me lo devuelvas.
LA GALLARDA *(poniéndoselo por los hombros).*
Cuando las estrellas vuelen de mis hombros,
tendrás de amor lleno mi pañuelo rojo.
(JUAN retrocede a su esquina.)
PEDRO *(adelantándose).*
Ten los alhelíes que hurté a tus cabellos.
De tu amor floridos los estoy queriendo

LA GALLARDA *(poniéndoselo en el pelo).*
    Cuando en mis cabellos se duerman los pájaros,
    volverán a abrirse de amor en tus manos.
(PEDRO retrocede a su esquina.)
LUCAS *(adelantándose).*
    Préndete mi vida con tu peinecillo.
    Dame para siempre con él tu cariño.
LA GALLARDA *(prendiéndoselo).*
    Cuando dos agujas crezcan en mi frente,
    peinarán las hebras de mi amor tu peine.
(LUCAS retrocede a su esquina.)
MANUEL *(adelantándose).*
    Tu clavel presida, dichoso, tu pecho.
    Dáselo a mi sangre colorado y fresco.
LA GALLARDA *(colocándoselo).*
    Tú tendrás, vaquero, la flor de las flores
    cuando los claveles se desenamoren.
(MANUEL retrocede a su esquina.)

                                                    (I, 226-28.)

The tortured consciousness that dreams and the maiden who
appears in the dream sequence are one and the same person.
Nevertheless they react to two different sets of circumstances. For
the sleeping woman, the *corrida* is an ill-fated event; for the
young girl it is still a hopeful quest. Thus in the courtship scene,
the bull appears not as a hunted creature, but as a coveted object.
The youthful protagonist identifies Resplandores with MANUEL.
The flower which she offers as a sign of passion and amorous
yielding is tinged with the color red:

LA GALLARDA.
                                        Entre las flores
    se llama rojo clavel;
    en mi corazón, Manuel,
    y en mi sueño Resplandores.

                                                    (I, 224.)

Shortly thereafter, these meanings recur in a sonnet. LA GALLARDA
gives her hand to MANUEL:

LA GALLARDA.
    Toma el clavel, crestado de fulgores,
    el clavel de los toros de candela;
    la flor que clava, entenebrece y cela
    mayorales, vaqueros y pastores.

    Un rojo resplandor de Resplandores
    le encrespa el sueño a su color en vela,

clavado en verde, turbadora espuela,
mortal contra los ciegos lidiadores.

Su flor. Mi flor. Tu flor. Yo te la entrego.
Tres lumbres juntas en un solo fuego:
el toro, la Gallarda, el hombre fuerte.
Arda siempre el clavel enamorado,
y en la sangre del toro colorado
quien a esta flor pretenda dar la muerte.

(I, 228-29.)

When LA GALLARDA first perceives the threat posed to her by
Resplandores' immanent death; she announces: «En las entrañas
siento un nuevo toro/que por matarme sube ya bramando» (I, 201).
In Act III the symbolic identification between the anguished protagonist and the wounded bull echoes this prophecy. As LA GA-
LLARDA pursues Resplandores into the wilderness, the bull is «más
que toro... la braza del toro de la locura» (I, 245). His color, once
a symbol of passion and hope, connotes suffering and violence:

LA GALLARDA.
  Oh sendero de sangre, rojo amor perseguido...

(I, 254.)

Throughout the last act the protagonist withdraws further and
further into the confines of her tortured mind. Accordingly, there
is an increased insistence on the symbolic status of the creature
whose flight represents her journey toward madness. With a
tenuous logic suggestive of delirium, LA GALLARDA exhibits a
growing inability to distinguish her own person from that of the
bull; she repeatedly expresses her fear that Resplandores may be
a purely chimerical being:

LA GALLARDA.
  ¿Es él o soy yo quien gime
  perdida y desconsolada;
  él clavado y yo bañada
  en la sangre que lo [sic] exprime?
  ¿Tu sangre o mi sangre? Dime...
  ¿Dónde estás, que ya no estoy?
  ¿Eres verdad o el bramido
  sólo de un sueño perdido
  tras el que sin sueño voy?

(I, 248.)

As the scene draws to a close, the sapping of vital energy is
expressed through images of physical destruction and dissolution

of form. With Resplandores' death, LA GALLARDA's hope is sustained
solely by a trail of blood on a mountain path. As she makes a last
desperate attempt to salvage her shattered dreams, the little bull
appears—for the only time in the play—as a totally incorporeal
being:

> LA GALLARDA.
>> ¡Resplandores, dolor de mis entrañas!
>> Mirad... ¡Mirad! No ha muerto... Me lastimas...
>> te siento en mí, que alegremente saltas
>> como un nuevo clavel recién nacido,
>> como un amor abierto en la mañana.
>
> *(Se ha ido mientras dibujando extendida sobre el cielo la sombra roja del toro, ante el asombro impasible de todos, que sólo ven su desvarío.)*
>> ¡Vedlo pacer por los azules prados,
>> por los campos del cielo, entre las alas
>> de arcángeles pastores que lo llevan
>> coronado de nubes y guirnaldas...
>> Voy hacia él... Brilla para mí sola...
>
> *(Corre, los brazos alzados, en el momento que la sombra del toro desaparece, quedando dibujada como una constelación de brillantes estrellas.)*
>> ¡Resplandor, Resplandores de mi alma!
>> ¡Espera! ¡Espera! ¡Oh luz resplandeciente!
>> Subo por ti... Ya vuelo... No te vayas...
>
> *(Cae por tierra.)*

                                                        (I, 270-71.)

This pathetic gesture of idealization is a sign of the protagonist's
unceasing struggle [23]. By reducing Resplandores to the shadow
of an illusion, LA GALLARDA shows herself to be a victim of unfulfilled desire—pure anguished consciousness with no possibility of
quarter.

In our opinion, the density of meaning with which Alberti has
infused the figure of Resplandores constitutes a striking example
of esthetic economy. Given his symbolic status, the little red bull
provides a natural focal point for the reactions of all the characters
of *La Gallarda*. For MANUEL, a successful encounter with Resplandores would be proof of the legitimacy of his claim as a husband;
the *corrida* offers him an opportunity to restore his self-esteem.
Since any abuse of Resplandores is an injury to the protagonist,

---

[23] According to our reading, Marrast's interpretation of LA GALLARDA's gesture as a symbol of hope leaves aside important aspects of the text (p. 140). For example, as BABÚ informs us, «Resplandores fue toro de estrellas / *en el llanto sin fin* de la Gallarda (our italics)» (I, 271).

by wounding him the suitors can vent their rage against the woman who has spurned them. In other words, in this work one central symbol determines the entire course of the action. Through the allegorical equation of LA GALLARDA and Resplandores, plot and theme converge.

Throughout the text of *La Gallarda*, there are frequent allusions to a sinister fatality which hangs over the lives of the characters. The narrator presents himself as the victim of some mysterious and tragic suffering:

> BABÚ.
>> Babú de carne y huesos. Babú siempre invisible.
>> Babú de alas y sangre. Babú de llanto y trino.
>> Pobre Babú de llanto... ¡Ah! Pero no lloréis
>> porque no pueda nunca nada contra el destino.
>> Si él se empeña...
>>> Silencio...
>>>> Ya me perdonaréis.

(I, 177.)

When LA GALLARDA flees to the wilderness, BABÚ wonders whether she is not at the mercy of superhuman forces:

> BABÚ.
>> ¿Qué horror, qué extraña violencia,
>> qué castigo o mano inerte,
>> qué nube, qué oscura suerte
>> confabuló la medida
>> de que el toro de la vida
>> fuera el toro de la muerte?

(I, 246.)

On numerous occasions, the protagonist appears to regard herself as a doomed creature. She refers to her life as a «path of blood». Elsewhere she describes herself as «[la] madre de un triste destino / que corriendo ciegamente / mezcla en su sangre inocente / la sangre de su asesino» (I, 260). Early in the first act, there occurs a moment of ironic foreshadowing. LA GALLARDA and BABÚ resume the totality of her existence, and past and future are encompassed as if there were no possibility of eluding a tragedy:

> LA GALLARDA.
>> Vaquera de toros bravos,
>> junto a la montaña.
>> Gallarda entre los vaqueros,
>> entre los toros, gallarda.

BABÚ *(entrando por el portalón y hablando como un eco,
invisible para* LA GALLARDA).
Hoy,
vaquera de vacas mansas.
LA GALLARDA.
Vaquera de toros bravos
por las cumbres blancas.
¡ Cómo pisaban la nieve
y cómo la corneaban!
BABÚ.
Hoy,
Vaquera dentro de casa.
LA GALLARDA.
Siento que me crece un toro
ciego en las entrañas.
Al que ya tengo en el campo
escucho cómo lo llama.
Sé que bramaré en los montes
y mataré entre las ramas.
BABÚ.
Hoy...
Vaquera, es pronto. Mañana.

(I, 186-87.)

Through the symbolic identification of LA GALLARDA with
Resplandores, the sense of these references emerges. According to
a well-established literary tradition, the little bull is a creature
who is born to die or to kill. His existence can be construed as a
projection from the tragic moment of his entrance into the world
toward the inevitable violence of the *corrida:*

BABÚ.
El toro, el toro, el toro, el eral pequeñito
que ya rumia en los tréboles su pasión por la herida ;
el furor de la vaca desmandada en el campo
cuando el pastor le arranca los hijos de las ubres.

(I, 176.)

The fortunes of LA GALLARDA run parallel to those of Resplandores.
As her desires lead invariably to grief, the totality of her hopes
and frustrations partakes increasingly of the sense of destiny
implied by the taurine images. We have no way of determining
which came first—the notion of a life which moves implacably
toward tragedy or the imagery of the *fiesta brava* as a means of
giving dramatic form to a fated existence. In either case, form
and content are bound up in the most intimate of relationships ; it

is impossible to grasp the peculiar significance of the protagonist's spiritual trajectory apart from its symbolic representation.

Alberti's «mundo de vaqueros y toros bravos» affords a rich and complex array of sensory experiences. Its vast quantities of images are multiplied, fragmented and interwoven like the voices in a Baroque orchestration. The author has made brilliant use of polymetrics. A heavy emphasis on visual allegory is counterbalanced in the dialogue by great rhythmic variety. Moreover, the marriage of visual and verbal elements is such that, in this work, verse only attains its maximum expressivity in relation to scenographic movement. The attempted seduction scene of Act I and the courtship scene of Act II have a pronouncedly ballet-like quality. In these two instances the actors' lines must be 'bull-fought' rather than simply recited. For us, the dense polyphonic texture of La Gallarda helps prevent the allegory from becoming too cerebral. Alberti's taurine images have an existence which is primarily musical and kinesthetic. They speak to a sensory modality which has little to do with analytical thought. Thus, they steer us away from those mental processes which might lead to an excessively abstract understanding of the symbolic conflict. This enhances the forcefulness of the dramatic statement. Apparently Alberti realized—as he had not in 1929—that a less intellectual approach often results in a more intense theatrical experience.

In La Gallarda, the author had to convey a feeling of intimacy while at the same time projecting the protagonist's struggle outward into allegorical language of an exceedingly material nature. A truly mythical figure must be unique and individual as well as universal and archetypal. It is thus important that the spectator perceive LA GALLARDA's suffering as a spiritual process. Yet in this instance, the dense and tangible quality of the spectacle almost militates against the notion of subjectivity. Owing to Alberti's skill as a man of the theatre, the creation of this subjective dimension did not entail the sacrifice of sensorial richness. The same spectacle which expresses the dramatic conflict allegorically is suggestive of personal anguish. While all of our senses are called into play, we find ourselves drawn into the arena of the protagonist's consciousness. To this end the author has availed himself of the lesson of the surrealists. In La Gallarda, he abandons the dream of Quevedo in favor of that of Freud.

The jumbled time sequence of the second act is an important means of filtering the action through LA GALLARDA's consciousness. It is possible to conceive of time in two contrasting forms—one objective and historical, the other subjective and anti-historical. Objective time is linear ; the historian—and usually the spectator—

situates himself in the present and directs his gaze backward toward a past which appears remote and somewhat abstract. Interior time, on the other hand, affords no possibility of abstraction. The experiencing subject knows only a series of superimposed presents ; each of these contains the totality of his existence. By introducing a second level of action into *La Gallarda*, Alberti substitutes for our emotionally detached perspective the subjective view of the protagonist. The fragmentary interpolations of Act II impart a heightened sense of immediacy to past events, deemphasizing their meaning as objective reality relative to their significance as intimate reverberation. As the scenes of LA GALLARDA's present and those of her youth alternate and coincide before our eyes, we can experience both as equally vital and painful realities. With our objective vision relegated to a position of secondary importance, we perceive memories as living events and feel the cumulative force of past frustrations.

In order to further impede a logical approach to LA GALLARDA's conflict, Alberti has incorporated into his spectacle many of the sensory distortions most characteristic of dreams. Peculiar light effects and an abnormal use of the actors' voices create an eerie sensation of unreality :

> *(Suena, largo, el segundo toque de clarín de la corrida.* Luz suave rosada. *Entra* BABÚ.)
>
> LA GALLARDA.
>> ¿Qué clarín me pasa el sueño
>> y el alma me desanima?
>> ¿Qué voz me lo sobresalta,
>> qué sombra me lo derriba?
>
> BABÚ (cambiando la voz, como si fuera el toro).
>> Soy Resplandores, el hijo.
>> ¿Por qué, di, no me acaricias
>> y antes que puntas de hierro
>> me pones por banderillas
>> dos manos que en vez de muerte
>> fueran dos flores de vida?...
>
> LA GALLARDA (dolorida, como si la hubieran clavado a ella).
>> Fuiste capaz, Manuel Sánchez,
>> de hincarme las banderillas,
>> de hacer saltar a tus ojos
>> la sangre que te quería.
>
> *(Cayendo de rodillas bajo la cabeza de toro.)*
>> Toro del suplicio, húndeme
>> tus candelas encendidas...
>> Van a matar a tu hijo
>> y es mi amor quien lo asesina...

(Una luz verde clara va sustituyendo a la rosa, *mientras* LA GA-
LLARDA *camina lenta de rodillas como buscando atentamente por el
suelo.)*

BABÚ *(durante el cambio de luz).*
*Cambia la luz del sueño
como un sueño que pasa.
Vuela del rosa triste
de la lidia lejana
al tibio y claro verde
de las praderas claras.*
Allí, los toros libres,
tu torito, Gallarda;
y entre los hombres bravos,
el amor que te asalta,
sin saber quién la lumbre
cortará de tu rama... (our italics and emphasis).

(I, 214-16.)

Spatial relationships are disturbed along with temporal ones as
the *toreros* move back and forth between the bullring, LA GALLAR-
DA's bedroom and the pastures of her youth. Above all, as in *El
adefesio*, images and verses succeed one another with a changing
rapidity reminiscent of delirium. These distortions have such a
marked effect upon the imaginary world of the play that subsequent
to their appearance, they spill over into that which is not dreamed.
When LA GALLARDA's hopes give way to madness, the fragmentary
rhythms of her incoherent utterances suggest her emotional state:

LA GALLARDA *(como hablando consigo).*
Niño desobediente de mi casa...
Niño perdido... Te llamé... Quería
curarte las heridas... Te buscaba...
Estás mordido... Estás sediento... Bebe...
toma en mi mano este poquito de agua...
Eras pequeño... chico todavía
para que Manuel Sánchez te lidiara...
¿Pero qué sabe un toro si le tienden
ante los ojos un capote grana?
¿En dónde estás? Tú vives... Tú estás vivo.

(I, 270.)

Thus, the symbolic action is interiorized at the same time that
the inner struggle of the protagonist is projected outward. The
«mundo de vaqueros y toros bravos» does not just surround LA
GALLARDA; it also lives within her.

In our estimation, the most remarkable feature of Alberti's play is its sustained balance between drama and spectacle, the tormented spirit of the protagonist and the tangible forms of the theatre poetry. The images which take shape on stage have an extraordinarily sensorial quality that corresponds to their status as external reality. But instead of appearing in linear succession—with the coherence and rhythmic regularity of historical flux—they alternate, accumulate and coincide with a chaotic rhythm that corresponds to the ebb and flow of emotion. In other words, in *La Gallarda* the spatial treatment is objective, the temporal treatment subjective; this places the two terms of the conflict —object and subject, action and consciousness of action—simultaneously within the spectator's grasp. The result of our experience is a doubly enhanced sense of concrete struggle. As we witness the confrontation between reality and consciousness, we know the immensity of the adversary, and we share the deep anguish of the victim.

We can now measure the distance that Alberti has travelled since his first experiments with allegory and verse. Like the protagonist of *El hombre deshabitado*, LA GALLARDA is caught between a reality which she perceives and another to which she aspires. But here the disjointed abstractions of the earlier play have disappeared. The dramatic conflict is felt as unceasing and intimate struggle; the protagonist's frustrations are an eternally open wound, a continuing source of dramatic emotion. Like *Fermín Galán*, *La Gallarda* is written in verse and inspired by the *romancero*. However, literal conventions, clumsy versification and loose structures have given way to a brilliant and personal artistic synthesis. Everything in *La Gallarda*—plot and theme, scenographic movement and metric form—springs from the world of the *fiesta brava*, and takes shape around the figure of Resplandores. In this work nothing has any meaning except in relation to the central symbol. Form and content seek each other out, one shaping itself to the other, until it is impossible to distinguish between them.

Alberti's theatre: from a multiplicity of styles to a style of multiplicity

The neo-popular plays of the 1940s are the masterpieces of Alberti's theatre. They are markedly superior to anything the playwright had written during the preceding two decades. All three of these works are examples of dramatic effectiveness and technical skill. Each possesses a notable degree of artistic autonomy—that is, internal coherence, exteme originality, and an existence which is independent of the multiple sources from which it derives. In them we can discern for the first time the contours of a personal style.

During the years of his exile, Alberti continued to experiment with a variety of traditional and contemporary forms. However the experiments of the 1940s were far more successful than any he had previously undertaken. In the trilogy, the playwright's use of source material grows less transparent, and his transposition of literary conventions less direct. He no longer borrows extraneous details from his sources ; that which he does take is carefully and skillfully adapted to his needs. Presumably this bespeaks his increased capacity for esthetic contemplation. As we have said, it is likely that literary composition continued to serve a cathartic function for Alberti in 1944. During the previous decade this kind of involvement had apparently been a source of serious technical flaws in his work. Now even when he is dealing with autobiographical material, his attitude remains markedly detached [24]. In *El adefesio* he demonstrates his ability to distinguish esthetic needs from personal ones. He evidences a greater willingness to serve the demands of his art.

The effectiveness of the neo-popular plays is largely a question of excellent craftsmanship. By this we mean that in all of them the source of the spectator's emotion is to a great extent esthetic. A comparison between Alberti's work and that of Lorca may serve to clarify the matter. There are obvious thematic parallels between our author's masterpieces and those of his friend and contemporary. *El trébol florido* and *Bodas de sangre* depict a complex struggle of passions in a rustic setting. Like *Yerma*, *La Gallarda* deals with an instance of frustrated womanhood. The protagonist of *El adefesio* displays many of the despotic characteristics of BERNARDA ALBA [25]. But whereas Lorca's theatre grew increasingly sober,

[24] Less striking indications of this occur in other works. As earlier observed, *Noche de guerra* is based on a real incident (see our p. 29). With its windmill and its pine-covered cliffs overlooking the sea, the island of *El trébol florido* recalls Ibiza (cf. the descriptive passages in R. Alberti, «Una historia de Ibiza», especially pp. 164, 180 and 197). Note that in the mature works this knowledge is tangential to an understanding of the dramatic texts ; we no longer have to be aware of the origin of autobiographical elements to understand their presence.

[25] This does not neccessarily indicate that Lorca influenced Alberti. Critics have often assumed the reverse, especially in view of the unmistakable parallels which link *El adefesio* to *La casa de Bernarda Alba* (cf. the blindness and hypocrisy of the two protagonists, their use of sticks as symbols of authority, the lies that occasion ADELA's and ALTEA's suicides, the oppressive atmosphere that reigns in both households). However, Alberti explicitly denies that there was any such influence. Claiming that at the time he wrote *El adefesio*, «el manuscrito de *La casa de Bernarda Alba*, el único que existía, lo guardaba, y bien guardado, la

Alberti's became more ornate. More importantly, Alberti's dramatic conflicts are further removed than are Lorca's from the essences which he seeks to portray. That is, the intrigues in which Alberti involves his characters are always more symbolic than real. The substance underlying his plays does not match the density of his theatre poetry; if they were stripped down to the core, one wonders if they might not seem banal [26]. To the extent that this is so, the neo-popular plays reveal an important fact about their creator: even at the height of his career, Alberti's talent was more poetic than dramatic.

The most distinctive feature of the neo-popular plays is probably their 'plural' character [27]. Each of these works differs markedly from the others. In our discussion of *El trébol florido* we had occasion to speak of Lope. The ironic techniques of *El adefesio* are strongly reminiscent of those of Valle Inclán. The profuse baroque ornamentation of *La Gallarda* calls to mind the theatre of Tirso. Undoubtedly this is another result of an artistic temperament which, unlike Lorca's, approached the theatre intellectually [28]. From the beginning Lorca possessed a deep intuitive understanding of the dramatic. Driven by inner impulse,

familia de Lorca», he accuses critics of having overlooked an important difference between the two works: «el clima de mi obra es más tenso y raro que el de la pieza de Federico» (letter to Marrast, 2 May 1954). Note also that GORGO's despotism takes a 'patriarchal', not a 'matriarchal' form (Pérez Minik, *op. cit.*, p. 499); her willfulness and sadistic intent are the fruits of old age and sexual frustration, rather than an obsessive preoccupation with the honor code. It is the author's contention that the striking similarities between *El adefesio* and Lorca's tragedy result from shared experience and common inspiration. «Nuestro honroso parentesco», he has written, «nos lo da el agua de la misma fuente, con toda la diversidad de rumores y cantos que puede arrastrar una misma agua» (*loc. cit.*). Probably this notion can be applied to the other works in the trilogy as well.

   [26] This point was made originally by Mr. David Victoroff with respect to *El adefesio*, in a discussion which took place at one of the Entretiens d'Arras (Marrast, «L'esthétique théâtrale», pp. 78-79). Expanding upon Mr. Victoroff's statement, Ruiz Ramón takes this to be a serious defect in Alberti's theatre *(op. cit.*, pp. 238-39). Our comparison between Alberti and Lorca is not intended to imply any such value judgment; it serves only to point out the difference between two kinds of theatre.

   [27] We have borrowed this term from Guerrero Zamora *(op. cit.*, p. 98).

   [28] The difference in temperament which we find reflected in Alberti's and Lorca's theatre has also been noted by Juan Chabás with respect to their poetry *(op. cit.*, p. 493):

En Lorca, desde sus primeras obras... hay un arranque dramático... Lo popular, en Lorca arranca de una identificación espiritual con la tierra y su canto; es un popularismo folklórico *de origen no aprendido*; pudiera insistirse en que es la voz de la sangre... En Alberti desde el primer momento, su popularismo es culto; no lo respira en el recuerdo de los labradores o marineros de su tierra; lo aprende para transfigurarlo luego, en Gil Vicente, en Encina, en los poetas del xv en general. El popularismo de Alberti tiene algo de preciosidad renacentista; *supone una actitud intelectual* (our italics).

he pursued a single goal. Therefore a striking feature of his theatre is its unity. Viewed in relation to one another, his tragedies form an almost inevitable sequence. Alberti on the other hand is basically a lyric poet. Moreover he has always been extremely susceptible to outside influences. Probably somewhat uncertain of his way, as a playwright he was easily led in a number of directions. All of his creations are responses to external stimuli. Thus, formal variety continues to distinguish his mature works. Paradoxically, the unity of Alberti's opus must be sought in its diversity.

In all of the neo-popular plays there is a unique relationship between dramatic projection, dialogue and scenographic movement. In each instance, rhythm is the integrating factor. *El trébol florido* is constructed around the accelerating rhythm of ritual. In *El adefesio*, the *ritmo delirante* has a collective Quevedesque quality. In *La Gallarda*, the emphasis is more Freudian and subjective. In all of these works, however, visual and verbal rhythms play a significant role. The brilliant syntheses which the author succeeds in effecting are evidence of his technical expertise. His apparent concern for eluding his spectator's reason and facilitating an intuitive grasp of his material is an indication of increased insight into the dramatic process.

Extremely important in these works are diverse and complex techniques which we can designate as 'telescopic' because their effect is always to concentrate and intensify. Some of these are temporal. In the final scene of *El trébol florido*, there occurs a rhythmic recapitulation of the entire dramatic conflict[29]. In *La Gallarda*, the course of the protagonist's fated existence is resumed in a moment of ironic foreshadowing[30]. An alternate form of temporal telescoping involves the accumulation, proliferation or multiplication of images and episodes, frequently accompanied by rhythmic acceleration. This is a frequent occurrence toward the end of *La Gallarda* and throughout *El adefesio*. In the latter work a cumulative structure and scenographic conception becomes quite literally a means of leading us around in circles. The endless confrontations, frenzied activity, constant gesticulation and whirling about that takes place before our eyes all have a dizzying effect. For this reason, life in GORGO's household becomes a hopelessly claustrophobic and static affair. Numerous examples of spatial telescoping also exist in the trilogy. The most rudimentary of these involve a simple juxtaposition of images through the use of the multiple stage. Included in this category too are the complex allegorical and ironic procedures of *El adefesio* and *La Gallarda*.

29   See our p. 114.
30   See our pp. 141-42.

In *El adefesio*, diverse forms of irony make possible a simultaneous perception of face and mask. In *La Gallarda*, a sustained balance between exterior action and inner life is achieved through the use of symbols and a surrealistic dream technique.

The thematic relationship between the neo-popular plays extends well beyond the author's heavy reliance on folkloric material. All three of these works are rationally controlled and disciplined artistic structures which Alberti has built out of the irrational stuff of myth, ritual, dream, augury and superstition. In all of them there exists a strong undercurrent of tragedy—a sense of human impotence and man's inability to gain control over the forces that seek his destruction [31]. At the same time, there is a very basic cleavage among the plays of the trilogy. *El trébol florido* and *La Gallarda* are myths. The victims of these works struggle against supernatural forces. In neither of them is the action local or in any sense historical. In both instances there is a concrete scenographic dimension to the theatrical space ; without this dramatic actualization would be impossible. Conceptually however, the fictional world of each work is divorced from time and space. The popular ambiance of *El trébol florido* is a universal Arcadia in which Alberti never alludes to specifically Spanish elements. While *La Gallarda* is set in a Castile of «vaqueros y toros bravos», it is nevertheless not a play about Spain. Castile is present only as a source of figurative language—a trampoline from which Alberti ascends immediately to an allegorical level and to a poetic exploration of the subconscious.

In *El adefesio* on the other hand, the destructive forces reside in human will [32]. Myth is present as cultural tradition rather than

---

[31]   Traceable through all of Alberti's full-length plays, this use of non-rational material has provided most critics of his theatre with their point of departure. E.g., describing Alberti's allegorical representation of «polos irremediavèlmente oposto... a fase positiva e negativa de um possivel anjo que esteja presente apenas para lutar dentro de cada homen e o vencer», Fernando Guimarães observes that as a result, «os limites da accão humana são... atravessados por uma accão superior» (*op. cit.*, p. 679). Ventura Doreste's study deals with «the inexorable presence of a fatal design running counter to human efforts» as the source of a «sustancial corriente trágica» which keeps Alberti's lyricism from seeming excessive (*op. cit.*, pp. 89-90). Although Marrast's discussion focuses on man's rebellion rather than on his defeat, the French critic too is concerned with Alberti's portrayal of the superior forces which act as corrosive elements in human life.

[32]   Marrast has observed this but merely notes it in passing (p. 41). Because of possible confusion arising from our subsequent choice of terminology, we must here take issue with the French critic's reading of *El adefesio* as «une allégorie de l'Espagne opprimée» (p. 110). This is too broad an interpretation in our opinion, and should be set against Pérez Minik's assertion regarding the difference between Alberti's play and the works of Ghelderode, Ionesco and Genêt. Pérez Minik correctly observes that there exists in *El adefesio* «junto a[l] delirio esencial una voluntad de continencia realista» (*op. cit.*, p. 501). While we agree with Ruiz Ramón that *El adefesio* can be read as a statement about «el significado trágico

genre. That is, myths are frequently alluded to, but only as a means of creating irony. Accordingly, the action of *El adefesio* is solidly anchored in the concrete realities of Andalusia. Although GORGO is a representative character, she is not an archetype. Like her companions she is only understandable in relation to the Spanish provinces[33]. Discounting the plays of the first period, this division pertains in the rest of Alberti's theatre. In the symbolic world of *El hombre deshabitado*, an archetypal protagonist struggles against a superhuman adversary. All the remaining works involve an action of human dimensions which takes place within a concrete Spanish setting. Thus, we can discern two main trends in Alberti's theatre—a lesser allegorical tendency and a larger group of plays, which we shall designate as 'social'. The meaning of the latter term will soon be clear.

The principal sector of Alberti's opus is distinguished by an important structural feature. Each of the social plays possesses an episodic or cumulative structure. In *Fermín Galán*, history is conceived and presented as a series of static and disconnected *tableaux*. In *De un momento a otro*, the action involves a series of confrontations between the protagonist's progressive mentality and different sectors of provincial life. The *agitprop* plays, especially *Bazar de la Providencia* and *Radio Sevilla*, consist largely of a series of gags strung together by a flimsy plot line. Again in *El adefesio* and Alberti's most recent works, single events do not presume any previous or successive action. By way of contrast, the structure of all three allegorical plays is sequential or linear. *El hombre deshabitado* has an underlying conceptual structure ; a certain image of the human condition is advanced, judged to be false and ultimately modified. In *El trébol florido*, the rhythm of ritual drives incessantly toward paroxysm. In *La Gallarda*, there is also a forward thrust to the action ; we experience the protagonist's existence as an implacable journey toward despair and destruction.

Throughout our discussion we have traced the author's development through a series of caricaturesque elements. They appear sporadically in *Fermín Galán* and *De un momento a otro*. They figure consistently in the *agitprop* plays and *El adefesio*. As we shall see, they reappear in the playwright's two most recent works. Except for a few touches in *El trébol florido*, such elements are totally lacking in the allegorical plays. On the other hand they

de todo principio de autoridad...» *(op. cit.,* p. 243), we would observe that this statement by itself fails, as does Marrast's, to take account of elements to which we attempt to call attention here.
[33] See our p. 128.

are always a distinctive feature of the works in which they appear. In these works, caricature is a more persistent trait than didacticism. In fact it is the essential characteristic of the social plays. In Alberti's theatre, the term 'social' is not synonymous with 'tendentious' or 'propagandistic' [34]. Rather it refers to a grotesquely stylized image of Spanish reality.

Alberti's comic style is rooted in the guiñolesque world of *La pájara pinta*. As the author leans increasingly on the traditions of black humor, his vision grows more pronouncedly grotesque. By *El adefesio* it can be regarded as esperpentic by virtue of its highly ironic nature. Nevertheless, GORGO's sharp transitions resemble those of LA CARBONERITA. She and her companions use scissors as a means of inflicting bodily harm. Their noisy squabbles call to mind those of the puppet stage. Don Dino's beard recalls the explicitly allegorical heart which ANTÓN delivers over to LA CARBONERITA. In *Noche de guerra*, guiñolesque elements play an especially prominent role. In *La lozana andaluza* we will still find guiñolesque processions and characters. Thus the slapstick and the naiveté of *La pájara pinta* left a permanent mark on Alberti's comic style. This is a sign of continuity in his theatre.

The cumulative structure of *El adefesio*, *Noche de guerra*, and *La lozana andaluza* contributes importantly to the grotesqueness of the fictional world. The insistence on recurrent behavioral elements and related events generates an atmosphere in which there is feverish activity, yet very little actually happens. In the *agitprop* plays, episodic accumulation serves a similar purpose. Thus, one more prominent feature of the mature style originates early in the playwright's career. The other complex telescopic elements of the trilogy also have their counterparts in Alberti's first plays. Like the esperpentic characters of *El adefesio*, the incipient imposters of the *agitprop* plays juxtapose face and mask. Both LA GALLARDA and the protagonist of Alberti's *auto* exist astride two realities. The multiple stage and the play-within-a-play are two more elements which appear in the early works and recur with great frequency thereafter. In other words, there is present throughout Alberti's dramatic opus a large group of technical resources similarly designed to intensify through multiplication, proliferation, accumulation and juxtaposition. Their number, their crucial importance to an understanding of his dramaturgy and their steadily evolving complexity make them a hallmark of his style.

---

[34] Since for Pérez Minik *(loc. cit.)* and Marrast (p. 107) the term has only this more restricted meaning, both critics are understandably reluctant to regard *El adefesio* as a social play.

The formal variety, telescopic devices, and grotesque comic esthetic to which we have referred signal the unity of Alberti's mature style. These characteristics are an element of continuity in his theatre as a whole. As we have tried to demonstrate, however, before the playwright's eclectic tendency manifested itself as true expertise, there was a period of self-conscious experimentation with literary fads. In the early plays, the author lacked the capacity to articulate diverse esthetic elements into a coherent artistic object. Variety at that point in his career meant diffuseness rather than richness. This means that prior to 1940, we cannot really speak of «a style». Since our study is largely concerned with the author's passage from apprenticeship to mastery, our characterization of his dramatic opus should call attention to the qualitative differences between the early works and the mature plays. We can do this by speaking of a 'multiplicity of styles' which later gives rise to a 'style of multiplicity'. The latter phrase suggests the kind of effect which the playwright repeatedly sought and finally attained in his search for a dramatic form. Both terms highlight the uniqueness of each of Alberti's experiments and take account of the role of his proverbial *fácil versatilidad* in the elaboration of his plays. By referring to an early multiplicity of styles we can address ourselves to the issue of artistic excellence as well. That is, we can reiterate our belief that Alberti's style as it emerged in the 1940s was the result of a long process of exploration and growth.

CHAPTER V

CREATION AND COLLABORATION: THE 1950s AND 1960s

Noche de guerra en el Museo del Prado

Noche de guerra en el Museo del Prado (1956) was composed in commemoration of the twentieth anniversary of the Spanish Civil War and dedicated to the heroic defenders of Madrid. Written in an attempt to apply the didactic theories of Berthold Brecht [1], this work marks a momentary return to the tendentious content and rudimentary comic forms of the *agitprop* plays. Nevertheless, *Noche de guerra* is not simply a belated offshoot of Alberti's 1932 trip. Certain of its stylistic features situate it beyond *El adefesio* and establish its status as a mature work.

In *Noche de guerra*, Alberti again uses interior reduplication. The action takes places during the first aerial bombardment of the Spanish capital. In a prologue, a character-commentator designated as EL AUTOR reminisces nostalgically before a giant movie screen representing the Sala Central of the Prado Museum (frame situation):

> AUTOR. — Casa de la Pintura... La llamo así, casa, porque para mí fue la más bella vivienda que albergara mis años de adolescencia y juventud. A ella llegaba yo cada mañana, quedándome arrobado en sus cuartos más íntimos o en sus grandes salones, por los que oía de pronto el ladrar de los perros de Diana o me encontraba de improviso en el claro de un bosque con las tres diosas de la Gracia... Era yo un inocente pueblerino cuando me atreví a entrar por vez primera en esta casa... *(Aparecen en la pantalla «Las Tres Gracias», de Rúbens.)*

(II, 162.)

As the Author continues to evoke his favorite works, we hear the voice of a militiaman. He and his companions have come to

---

[1] See our note 54, pp. 31-32. We have based our analysis of *Noche de guerra* on the original text as we did not have access to the recently revised version prior to press time. On the nature of Alberti's revisions see our note 3, p. 157. For comments on the Brechtian elements in *Noche de guerra* see our note 7, p. 161.

strip the walls of their treasures, in an effort to protect them from enemy fire. At the same time, the figures contained in the masterpieces come to life, several of them joining in the defense of the beleaguered building:

> MANCO (al FUSILADO y al AMOLADOR, que se mueven con aire de fatiga). — ¡ A ver! Esos sacos. Aquí. Y aquellos otros, a este lado. Que no quede un resquicio. De pared a pared. ¡ Gran barricada va a ser ésta!...
> FUSILADO. — Dicen que ya han ocupado la Pradera.
> AMOLADOR. — Y que se han visto moros por la calle Mayor.
> FUSILADO. — Y que el Emperador está otra vez en Chamartín.
> VIEJA 1 (todavía invisible). — ¡ Ji, ji, ji! ¡ Napoleón! ¡ Qué risa!
>
> (II, 167.)

The major part of the action transpires «on the far side of the picture frame» (interior action). These Goyesque characters for example, do not construe their efforts in relation to those of the soldiers in modern dress. Instead, they behave as if they were engaged in driving back the Napoleonic invaders.

For thematic reasons, the interior action is set principally in the pictorial world of Goya. As the Author reflects upon the situation of the bombardment, he compares the soldiers who are at work in the museum with the popular types immortalized by the Aragonese painter. Thus he establishes a parallel between two significant moments in Spanish history:

> AUTOR. — Milicianos de los primeros días, hombres de nuestro pueblo, como ésos que Goya vio derrumbarse ensangrentados bajo las balas de los fusileros napoleónicos, ayudaron al salvamento de las obras insignes. 1808. 1936. Tenían las mismas caras, hervor idéntico en las venas, iguales oficios.
>
> (II, 162.)

This commentary broadens the meaning of the action and imparts a symbolic dimension to the defense of the museum. What we witness is no longer an attempt to safeguard the national art treasures. In 1936 as in 1808, it is the struggle of humble men for freedom from tyranny [2].

The message which the didactic author conveys is clearly political. Goya's characters are engaged in a popular uprising against a rotten absolutist regime. The play concludes with a

---

[2]   On this point, see Ruiz Ramón's perceptive comments (op. cit., pp. 235-36)

mock trial and execution in which the ruling class is obviously
under attack:

> *(En la barricada aumenta... la señal de alarma, oyéndose... un
> ruido infernal producido por la atroz estridencia de trompetillas,
> matracas, ralladores, cacerolas, guitarras, tambores y pitos, corres-
> pondientes a una gran comparsa—muy semejante a la titulada
> por Goya "El entierro de la sardina»—que avanza del fondo de la
> escena... Es la comparsa de los lisiados... Algunos, además de sus
> musicales cacharros, enarbolan estacas, coronándose otros la cabeza
> con sillas rotas y orinales. Cerrando la comitiva, a lomos de una
> figura toda negra que representa un* BUCO *de grandes y retorcidos
> cuernos, va algo o alguien, tapado totalmente por un trapajo. A
> su lado, sobre un viejo sillón... marcha otro alguien, también todo
> cubierto...* EL MANCO, *bajando de un salto de la barricada, arranca
> el trapo que cubre [la primera] figura, dejando al descubierto un
> viejo pelele de cara amarillenta, desgreñados cabellos y largo traje
> negro de encajería.)*
>
> MANCO *(con estupor).* — La señora de D. Carlos IV. ¡La rei-
> na María Luisa!
>
> TODOS *(como un susurro).* — ¡La gran puta!... *(EL* MANCO
> *destapa luego la [otra] figura... apareciendo un enorme* SAPO *de
> ojos saltones y rasgos humanos en traje militar: espada al cinto,
> gran banda al pecho y condecoraciones.)*
>
> MANCO. — ¡Anda! Pero si no es Napoleón Bonaparte... ¡Si
> es don Manuel Godoy!... ¡El Generalísimo! ¡El Príncipe de la
> Paz! ¡El Choricero!
>
> TODOS *(en sordina).* — ¡La gran bragueta de la Reina!
> UNA VOZ. — ¡Mueran los traidores!
> OTRA. — ¡A la horca con ellos!

(II, 190-93.)

The real traitor, repeatedly referred to as *el sapo* and assumed
to be the foreign invader, turns out instead to be an enemy that
has arisen within Spain itself. While we are apparently in 1808,
this general is obviously to be compared with another. Thus the
theme of *Noche de guerra* is at once broad and narrowly topical
—pro-Marxist and anti-Franquist.

As is indicated by the subtitle «*aguafuerte* en un prólogo y
un acto» (our italics), Alberti intented for the interior action
clearly to take place in a world of painted figures. Thus, there
appear a number of characters representative of widely divergent
periods and artistic styles. In the first of three episodes which
interrupt the efforts of the Goyesque characters, the figures from
Titian's «Venus and Adonis» reenact their tragedy. They interpret

the sounds of modern warfare as a punishment visited upon them by the angry god Mars:

(Se oyen ruidos confusos, entre cristales rotos que caen y aullidos lastimeros.)
ESTUDIANTE. — ¡Se están viniendo abajo los muros!
MANCO. — ¡Animo, ánimo! ¡Las luces! ¡Los faroles! ¡A encender los faroles! ¡Sólo tengo una mano! ¡Luz, luz! *(En vez de la de los faroles, cae de lo alto... un opaco rayo de luz que deja en una total penumbra a la barricada. El cañoneo se va alejando. Volcados en el suelo, medio desnudos, están VENUS y ADONIS.)*
ADONIS. — ¡Oh, Venus, niña blanca de la espuma! No tiembles. Levántate. Y huyamos a lo más hondo del bosque. Se me han ido los perros. Han roto las traíllas. He perdido las flechas. Estamos indefensos. La ira roja de Marte nos persigue. Oye el estruendo de sus armas. Va a matarnos.

(II, 172-73.)

In a subsequent episode, Velázquez's Philip IV and the dwarf Don Sebastián de Morra react with abject terror to the sound of the bombardment. This occasions a rather scatological bit of anti-Monarquist satire:

ENANO. — La verdad es que no sé dónde estoy. He perdido a mi rey. *(Como buscando con la mirada.)* ¡Eh, tú, narizotas! ¿Estás ahí? Buenos cuescos andas tirándote esta noche. Atruenas el palacio. ¡Pobre de mi señora la reina! *(Gritando.)* ¡Felipe! ¡Felipe! ¿Dónde diablos te has metido? Guarda esa caja de los truenos, que voy a desmayarme, Felipe!

(II, 178.)

In a third instance two archangels—one of them by Fra Angelico and the other by the anonymous master of Arguís—reflect upon the hostilities as a violation of the precepts of Christian love:

GABRIEL. — Estoy caído para siempre. Tengo un ala quebrada en su raíz. En mi vuelo bajaba la alegría y se me cruzó el odio. No sé qué ha sucedido esta noche.
MIGUEL. — Las legiones del mal andan de nuevo sueltas por el mundo.

(II, 190) [3].

[3] The principal difference between the original and the newer revised text is apparently that the latter contains an additional exchange between Goya and Picasso—in the words of the author, «un encuentro... en el que ambos, en aquella eterna noche del 36 dialogan, se animan mutuamente y padecen la tragedia amarga de nuestra tierra, España... Picasso con su Guernica y Goya con el llanto de la gracia y la sonrisa del horror» («Rafael Alberti hace dialogar a Goya y Picasso», *La Opinión* [Buenos Aires, 20 April 1974], p. 19).

Desirous of keeping the painters' signatures before our eyes,
Alberti often borrows quite literally from the graphic works. In
his instructions regarding costuming, his attempt to approximate
the originals extends even to color and tonality. Goya's characters
*han de vestir como a comienzos del siglo XIX—unos, en colores
vivos, pero opacos, y otros en grises, sepia, blancos y negros,
buscando el claroscuro de los dibujos y aguafuertes*; Titian's
Venus *ha de ir casi desnuda, con un color blanquecino de esta-
tua* (II, 159).

On numerous occasions, the dialogue of *Noche de guerra* reproduces *verbatim* the captions of Goya's etchings and engravings.
Thus, in a final summarizing speech, EL MANCO uses one of the
titles from *Los desastres de la guerra* [4]:

> MANCO. — ¿Quién era ése que pretendía ceñirse la corona de
> nuestros reyes y se colgó a sí mismo los nobles rótulos de Genera-
> lísimo y Príncipe de la Paz? Un violador de esa misma paz, un
> ambicioso cómplice del más odiado destructor de pueblos, derrama-
> dor de infinita sangre... ¿Y qué sucede ahora? Pues que otra vez
> tenemos a su hipócrita amigo, a su insaciable dueño, el verdadero
> sapo—*ese buitre carnívoro*—llamado con la muerte a los heroicos
> muros de nuestra capital española... (our italics).

(II, 196.)

As a further means of extending the analogy between life and
art, the author has assimilated into the scenography of his play
numerous iconographic details drawn directly from the originals.
These are used principally as props or elements of transition. An
incident is needed to give rise to a verbal attack upon the «malditos franchutes». It is supplied by a bit of stage business in
which two characters attempt to extract a knife from the breast
of another:

> AMOLADOR *(intenta andar, pero cae de rodillas)*. — Sacadme...
> esta navaja de los huesos. No puedo casi respirar. *(Rueda por el
> entarimado.)*
> MANCO *(intentando sacarle la navaja que hasta la empuñadura
> lleva clavada en la mitad del pecho)*. — ¡A ver! *(al* FUSILADO.)
> ¡Tú! Está demasiado honda para una sola mano.
> FUSILADO *(logrando sacársela)*. — ¡Fuerte cosa! ¿Y por qué?
> AMOLADOR. — Por eso. Por una navaja. Yo era amolador. Afi-
> laba cuchillos por las calles. Registraron la choza. Y me encontra-

---

[4] No. 76, similarly entitled «El buitre carnívoro» (E. Lafuente Ferrari, *Los
desastres de la guerra* [Barcelona: Inst. Amattler de Arte Hispánico, 1907]).

ron ésa... Me dieron garrote... Después me la clavaron... Y se
fueron.
   VOZ DE LA VIEJA 1. — ¡ Malditos franchutes! ¡ Malditos franchutes!
                                                    (II, 168.)

In another instance, a decapitated figure of Goya's hurls his head,
rather than a stone, at the enemy. The interpolated episodes are
introduced in a similarly conventional manner. The barking of
hunting dogs precedes the appearance of Venus and Adonis ; the
dogs appear in Titian's painting.
   The stylized imaginary world of *Noche de guerra* resembles
doubly that of Alberti's other social plays. On the one hand, we
recognize the incessant scurrying about, lewd rimes and macabre
semi-human figures of *El adefesio*, the dance effects, multiple
focal points of action, cumulative structures and other 'proliferating' devices of the mature comic style. Like Goya's images,
these elements derive from the tradition of black humor [5]. Thus
they afford an appropriate means of rendering the Aragonese
painter's vision in theatrical terms. In *El adefesio* however,
esperpentic elements predominate over the guiñolesque. In this
newly didactic work on the other hand, Alberti had need of the
clarity and explicitness which he had earlier achieved using the
conventions of puppet theatre. Therefore, certain of the more
rudimentary comic forms of the early plays briefly take on
renewed importance. The result is a sophisticated mixture of
esperpentic nuance and childlike directness. The naively sadistic
violence, lilting musicality and obstreperous hilarity of the short
plays are easily spotted in *Noche de guerra*, even when the visual
images are most diabolical and disquieting and the dialogue most
obscene.
   This balance between guiñolesque and esperpentic elements is
most evident in two sequences whose antecedents can be identified
with precision in the early works. The trial scene is strongly
reminiscent of several moments in the *Dos farsas revolucionarias;*
the scenographic emphasis on processions and dummy figures,
the surprise unmasking of the traitors, the mayhem which
accompanies their final denunciation all hark back to Alberti's
experiments with *agitprop* theatre. At the same time, the mutil-
ated figures and the cacophony and confusion surrounding the

   [5] Even more specifically, Alberti's emphasis on scatology has led Guerrero
Zamora to observe that *Noche de guerra* harks back to the medieval *juego de
escarnio* and the Quevedesque tradition of obscene satire *(op. cit.,* p. 104). The
same can be said of the *agitprop* plays, some scenes of *El adefesio* and *La lozana
andaluza.*

crowd of rebels call to mind the more grotesque stylization of
El adefesio.
Our second example is an episode inspired by Goya's Capricho
No. 51 [6]. For reasons of military expediency, a witch named
HUBILIBRORDA resolutely attempts to cut the toenails of her companion GENUFLEXA:

> VIEJA 2. — ¡Bravo, bravo, Hubilibrorda! ¡Qué bien te zaran
> deas todavía!
> VIEJA 1 *(burlonamente).* — No tan bien como tú, Genuflexa.
> ¡Quién diría que me llevas sólo un año!...
> VIEJA 2. — Ya he cumplido los cien. *(Como en secreto.)* Lo
> que pasa, Hubilibrorda, lo que debe pasar es que en los pies no
> tengo tantos juanetes y callos como tú.
> VIEJA 1. — No mientas, Genuflexa. ¿Piensas acaso que no he
> visto los tuyos? ¿Olvidas que las uñas te dan vuelta y se te hincan
> en las plantas? Tú siempre has rengueado... Y en estos tiempos
> de espantos y ruidos, garfios tan largos no son buenos. Siéntate
> aquí conmigo. Tú llevas siempre unas tijeras...
> VIEJA 2. — Sí... Pero son para otras cosas...
> VIEJA 1. — ¡Dámelas! *(La* VIEJA 2 *saca unas grandes tijeras
> como de esquilar).* — ¿Para qué diantre pueden servirte ahora?
> Suponte tú que el sapo gordo apareciera...
> VIEJA 2. — Volaría. Para eso tengo también mi escoba.
> VIEJA 1. — Sí, sí... Pero a veces hay que correr antes de
> echar el vuelo... y no podrías. No es lo mismo bailar que darse
> una carrera... Dámelas.
> VIEJA 2. — ¡No, no! ¡Cualquier cosa, menos perder mis uñas!
> ¿Has empinado el codo, Hubilibrorda? ¿Verías tú con agrado que
> yo te cortara los bigotes o los pelos de esa verruga?...
> VIEJA 1 *(agitando las manos, como alas).* — No te me vayas
> por otro lado, taimada, y dame pronto esas tijeras. *(Se tira sobre
> ella para quitárselas.)*
> VIEJA 2 *(forcejeando).* — ¡No! ¡No!
> VIEJA 1. — Te cortaré las uñas, o te las arrancaré de cuajo
> como lo hace el Santo Oficio... *(Del fondo del salón vienen unos
> largos rebuznos.)*
> VIEJA 2 *(gritando).* — ¡Perico! ¡Perico! ¡Llegas a tiempo!
> ¡Sálvame!
> VIEJO 1 *(derribándola y golpeándola en el suelo).* — ¡Las tije
> ras! ¡Las tijeras! ¡Te mato! ¡Te destripo! ¡Te arranco los ojos!

(II, 186-88.)

---

[6] Entitled «Se repulen». The caption reads «Esto de tener las uñas largas es
tan perjudicial que aun en la Brujería está prohivido» (J. López Rey, *Goya's
«Caprichos»* [Princeton: Princeton Univ. Press, 1953], I, 2028).

In this instance GENUFLEXA's repeated refusals, HUBILIBRORDA's attempts to use coercion, the half-playful struggle between the two characters, and the use of scissors as an instrument of aggression all bring to mind ANTÓN PERULERO's pursuit of DON DIEGO in *La pájara pinta*. On the other hand, the noisy nervousness of the witchlike characters is a part of the mature comic style. Finally, the preponderance of theatrical over tendentious elements in *Noche de guerra* is another indication that we are closer to *El adefesio* than to the *agitprop* plays. It matters little that the dialogue is punctuated with allusions to EL SAPO, the Queen, the war, or that GENUFLEXA wants to keep her toenails intact «para matar al francés / con las uñas de los pies» ; what impresses itself upon the spectator's awareness is above all the extravagance of the situation and what there is of pure *juego teatral*. This is the opposite of what occurs in the *Dos farsas revolucionarias* and *Radio Sevilla*. In those earlier plays, the propagandistic content remains in the foreground.

Even more than that of the *Dos farsas revolucionarias* and *Radio Sevilla*, the stylized theatrical language of *Noche de guerra* is an effective didactic instrument. It transmits the author's political views without need of overt discourse. The clumsy effigies of the degenerate María Luisa and her paramour Godoy are a vivid reminder of the decadence and rottenness of the ruling class. The lively antics of HUBILIBRORDA and GENUFLEXA convey their message even when the characters are not engaged in fighting off the enemy. The attitude of obscene mockery with which the *pueblo* enters the fray bespeaks their courage, their love of freedom and justice and their capacity for survival. Alberti's 'frame-within-a-picture-frame' device successfully approximates Brecht's *verfremdungseffeckt*. The literal use of conventions, the repeated anachronisms and the intervention of painted characters of markedly contrasting periods and artistic styles make it impossible for us to accept the theatrical illusion. This guarantees that our critical capacities will remain intact, and permits the didactic author to deliver his tendentious message [7].

Had Alberti been consistent in his use of caricature and willing

---

[7] The narrator-commentator and movie screen of the prologue, and Alberti's insistent use of *coplas* and ballads in the dialogue also echo the Brecht-Piscator tradition of Epic theatre. However, the appearance of comparable elements in *Fermín Galán*, a work which Alberti wrote at a time when he was presumably unfamiliar with Brecht's work, makes it impossible to determine whether or not this simply reflects a continuing natural affinity with the German playwright. For Ruiz Ramón, the Brechtian element lies principally in Alberti's use of historical parallelism *(loc. cit.)*.

to rely exclusively on ironic commentary, *Noche de guerra* would be an unqualifiedly successful didactic play. However, his old tendency to be overly explicit reappears in this play. The strident tones and pedestrian slogans of the early plays occasionally intrude themselves into the dialogue, causing momentary disruptions in stylistic unity. The interpolated episodes involving the non-Goyesque characters result in a fragmentation of the action. While they are stylistically consistent with the purposes of Epic theatre, we find it difficult to justify their presence on thematic grounds. The episode involving Velázquez's characters presents less of a problem in this connection. However the Venus and Adonis episode and the one involving the two archangels are insufficiently related to the tendentious thematic material of the rest of the play[8]. During the 1940s Alberti had successfully demonstrated his command of dramatic tecnique. Yet his return to the didactic emphasis of the 1930s brings with it some of the stylistic and structural diffuseness characteristic of his second period. Thus, this late work seems to confirm our suspicions regarding the inverse relationship between ideological content and esthetic quality in Alberti's theatre. Again commitment appears to have had an adverse effect on the playwright's critical judgement.

Inasmuch as the presence of intrusive elements echoes the clumsy self-consciousness of the inexperienced playwright, *Noche de guerra* points backward toward an earlier moment in Alberti's career. At the same time, it is a transitional piece which joins *El adefesio* to Alberti's most recent work. An important feature of this play is the organic relationship between Alberti's creative imagination and that of Goya. Goya's works are of crucial importance in determining the course of the action. The playwright makes extensive use of details drawn directly from his sources. He insists on depicting the characters in strictest conformity with the vision of their creator. This gives rise to a phenomenon akin to dual authorship whose origin does not seem difficult to explain. Alberti was undoubtedly aware of the documentary value of Goya's opus; such an awareness may have been germane to the conception of *Noche de guerra*. If so, an overt manifestation of his own lack of autonomy would be a logical way for the author to recognize his debt. The painter Alberti may also have desired to

---

[8] Our judgment on this point differs from that of Ruiz Ramón, who justifies the presence of the non-Goyesque characters as an attempt to «ampliar semánticamente el contenido del drama, bien [presentándolos] como víctima[s] de la agresión—Venus y Adonis o el amor y la paz asesinados por el nuevo Marte; el arcángel de la Anunciación a quien la agresión !e ha impedido terminar su mensaje a María—; bien [teniéndolos por] culpables irresponsables—el rey Felipe IV...» *(ibid.*, p. 237).

render homage to Goya; the autobiographical references of the
prologue make it likely that *Noche de guerra* was conceived as a
personal tribute as well as a didactic work. For whatever reason,
the presence of the Aragonese painter as 'co-author' in *Noche de
guerra* anticipates something Alberti would do in his most recent
dramatic work. The playwright here seems to construe his role as
something less than autonomous; he thinks of himself as 'col-
laborator' rather than independent creator [9].

In *El adefesio*, negative social elements are presented as caricature, while positive elements are accorded a contrasting treatment.
In *Noche de guerra* all of the characters undergo an identical process of stylization. This suggests that, as such, caricature has lost
some of its didactic function; in and of itself it no longer implies
a value judgement. We can trace this shift in emphasis throughout
the social plays. As Alberti's grotesque vision grows more complex,
it also grows more detached. Evidently, as the author gained
control of his theatrical language, he also gained a clearer perception of his task. He became increasingly aware of the primary
importance of artistic over doctrinal concerns. Accordingly, he was
able to conceive of caricature less and less as a form of social
commentary; more and more, it became a means of giving shape
and substance to an imaginary world. Thus, in *Fermín Galán* and
De un momento a otro caricature is exclusively an instrument of
aggression. The grotesque theatre poetry of *El adefesio* always
retains a satirical function. In *Noche de guerra* on the other hand,
a grotesque vision encompasses both vice and virtue, repression
and freedom, tyranny and justice, decadence and vitality. In *La
lozana andaluza*, such would also be the case.

In this sense we must regard *Noche de guerra* as the most
advanced of the social plays written prior to 1963. Here for the
first time, Alberti uses caricature fundamentally as a means of
breathing life into his characters. Only secondarily is it a means
of commenting on their relative worth.

La lozana andaluza

The last of Alberti's social plays (1963) is a stage version of
La lozana andaluza (1563), a dialogued novel by the Renaissance
cleric Francisco Delicado. It is extremely faithful to the spirit of

---

[9] We have chosen the term 'collaboration' because it alone seems to imply
the kind of balance to which we are here referring. Goya's work is not a source
upon which Alberti has drawn in the course of an essentially independent creative
act. On the other hand, since *Noche de guerra* clearly bears the stamp of Alberti's
personal style, it is not an adaptation as are the two versions of *Numancia*.

the original at the same time that it bears the stamp of Alberti's personal style. Thus, it is neither an adaptation in the normal sense of the word nor a wholly original composition. Rather it is a kind of joint undertaking—a result of the unique creative process which we have designated as 'collaboration'.

Like Delicado, Alberti paints a picture of life in the Spanish quarter of Rome just prior to the arrival of the plundering armies of the Emperor Charles. A comparison of the two texts reveals important similarities of structure, action, setting, language and characterization. A long critical preface which accompanies the dramatic text helps us to measure Alberti's debt to Delicado.

(1) *Structure and Action.*—Using as his focal point the career and fortunes of a lusty young Andalusian whore, Delicado built his novel around «diálogos esquemáticos como saltarinas secuencias cinematográficas» (II, 10). These are designated as *mamotretos* rather than chapters. *Mamotreto*—literally 'memorandum book'— figuratively connotes 'a bulky and disorganized bundle of papers'. While also reflecting his predilection for cumulative and seemingly chaotic structures, Alberti's choice of the subtitle «*mamotreto* en un prólogo y tres actos» (our italics) bespeaks an intention to follow the example of his illustrious forbear. Like Delicado, Alberti adheres to a biographical and chronological format: beginning with Lozana's arrival in the papal city, he traces her ascent to fame and fortune among the corrupt and libertine elements of Roman society. Most of the principal episodes in the play have been taken from the novel.

(2) *Setting.*—Though broad and impressionistic in scope, the imaginary world of both authors is portrayed in exceedingly concrete detail. References to elements of dress, gastronomy, occupation, social organization and such abound in both texts. The *costumbrista* elements function in conjunction with the rhythms and dialect forms of popular speech, imparting considerable density to the atmosphere of remorseless license and abandon which surrounds the protagonist. In its own way, each work is a vast *cuadro de costumbres*—«[la imagen de] una Roma no muy moralmente regida por un Papa de la familia de los Médicis... pozo de corrupción, abismo de iniquidades, antesala de los vicios del infierno... 'teatro del mundo' con gran reparto de personajes... colorido escenario del placer de la vida corporal y de la eterna» (II, 10).

(3) *Language.*—Delicado's dialogue is already eminently theatrical in that it conveys an overwhelming impression of torrential

vitality and unbridled sensuality without the aid of a narrative voice [10]. Undoubtedly appreciative of this fact, Alberti leaves intact entire sections of the original; he simply transfers them to his play. On occasion he modernizes the Renaissance text, especially in those instances where the faithful reproduction of dialect forms or thieves' language would present difficulties for a contemporary audience.

(4) *Characterization.*—Above all, Alberti has taken pains to respect the integrity of Delicado's characters. «Al entrar en esta selva de gracia [y] fescura popular», he writes, «abigarrado mundo y submundo de las mil maneras de ganarse la vida los españoles instalados en la ciudad papal, me sobrecogió el miedo de hacer perder a la Lozana su lozanía y que el retrato de la andaluza, al levantarse en una escena, no respondiese a la calidad que reclamaba de mí la antigüedad y prestigio de su talento» (II, 9). Like her Renaissance prototype, Alberti's LOZANA is a cross between CELESTINA and the Baroque *pícara*. She is neither as demoniacal as the one, nor as devoid of moral fibre as the other. A beautiful and sharpwitted creature, she demonstrates a marked concern for her customers' welfare—«preocupación... por unir a sus servicios de amor su deseo de ser útil curandera para quienes se acercan a pedirle consejos... [y] también medicina de palabras, de agudezas, de halagos propios de su gran labia andaluza» (II, 11). She also possesses a great capacity for feeling, which she exhibits through the passion she shares with her lover and servant RAMPÍN. The image of the young ruffian who accompanies LOZANA in her pursuit of profit and pleasure is similarly based on the character of his prototype. Finally, Alberti has leaned heavily on the original in his portrayal of minor characters. In the course of her daily existence, LOZANA mingles with an army of clerics, thieves, artisans and whores of all nationalities, ages, appearances, and social stations; these characters are largely a creation of Delicado's.

As Alberti indicates in his critical preface, the transformation of novel into dramatic work required a good deal of innovation as well as borowing. «No ha sido tarea fácil para mí someter a tres actos de teatro este... retrato hecho tan a lo real y vivo», he observes. «Muchas fueron las libertades que yo me tomé, quitando tanto como añadí» (II, 12). In fact, there are many points of divergence between Alberti's text and Delicado's. The principal of these will serve both to suggest the full range of possibilities and to facilitate a grasp of the balanced relationship involved in

---

10 Though occasionally the author-narrator speaks as witness.

'collaboration'. For reasons of critical expediency, we have grouped our examples under the three categories of selection and omission, reorganization, and additions and innovation.

(1) *Selection and Omission.*—Alberti has eliminated much of the detail surrounding LOZANA's life prior to her arrival in Rome, retaining only enough to convey the feeling of her *lozanía* and explain her presence in the Holy City. Many elements relative to her life in Rome are also missing from the dramatic text. For example, in Delicado's work, many unfortunate victims of the famous *mal francorum* come to LOZANA in search of a cure. In the play, there remains only a certain ill-fated cleric who acts as their spokesman:

> CANÓNIGO. — ¡Por vida de Santa Nefixa, que aquí me duele algo que no puedo decir, y si esa señora no me lo sana pronto, tendré yo mismo que arrancármelo!

(II, 54.)

Such omissions are a frequent occurrence in Alberti's work, especially in instances involving redundancy. When several episodes or details serve in the novel to highlight similar facets of the protagonist's personality and talents, Alberti's usual procedure was to retain only what struck him as most vivid.

(2) *Reorganization.*—In several instances Alberti has retained elements originally present in the novel, but incorporated them in somewhat different fashion into his play. The most important of these are concentrated in a long sequence in which LOZANA obtains payment from three of her prospective customers without rendering the services sought. In Delicado's work, these episodes are exclusively the result of her astuteness. Alberti has them come about also through the intervention of a jealous RAMPÍN. In the play, the rogue repeatedly appears just at the right moment to impede the logical outcome of events:

> MACERO *(en la oscuridad).* — Señora mía, están llamando.
> LOZANA. — Será mi criado, señor.
> MACERO. — Muy pronto vuelve el muy tunante.
> LOZANA. — Preparaos a salir.

(II, 47.)

The motive for RAMPÍN's behavior is made clear following the last such interruption. Sneaking about in the dark, he stumbles into a latrine and emerges all covered with filth:

LOZANA. — ¿Y cómo te caíste, bragazas?

RAMPÍN. — Señora, que dormía con el gato en aquel mueble que me dijisteis. Y se me fue de pronto, maullando. Y yo, para que no os despertara, corrí tras él por la escalera y caí...

LOZANA. — Mira lo que te digo, Rampín: que todo eso del gato es mentira, que tú has pasado la noche al pie de la escalera y por curioso y mal criado has ido a dar en la letrina. (RAMPÍN *sigue en silencio.*) ¿Qué respondes, muchacho?

RAMPÍN. — Señora, que no podía dormir solo en aquel mueble mientras que vos lo hacíais cómodamente con el de la valija.

(II, 57-58.)

In the novel, this mishap occurs independently of LOZANA's encounters with the MAESTRESALA, MACERO, and VALIJERO. Thus in Delicado's work, the first series of incidents serves exclusively to point up the protagonist's talent for exploiting her clientele, and RAMPÍN's fall is merely a means of poking fun at the character. Alberti's restructuring of these episodes adds to the complexity of RAMPÍN's psychology.

(3) *Additions and Innovation.*—Of course, Alberti had to supply the scenography of his play [11]. He has also replaced Delicado's ending and radically altered the meaning of the work. At the conclusion of the novel, LOZANA retires to the Isle of Lipari without witnessing the sack of Rome. Later the author comments rhetorically on the cataclysmic events, interpreting them as a punishment visited by Divine Providence upon the new Babylon. All that remains of this didactic conclusion in the dramatic version are the cries of a passing friar whose intervention is merely an element of local color:

> *(Aparece un* FRAILE *rudo y harapiento, alzando una cruz de palo.)*
> FRAILE *(pregonando a gritos).* — ¡Ay, Papa Clemente! ¡Hijo de Sodoma! ¡Por tus muchos pecados, Roma será destruida! ¡Arrepiéntete, Roma! ¡Arrepiéntete Roma! ¡Ay, Papa Clemente!...

(II, 70.)

In Alberti's play, the onset of hostilities becomes a tragicomic event in which LOZANA participates as victim and victor. At the instigation of the syphilitic CANÓNIGO, who sees his only hope for

---

11 Discussion of this point follows on pp. 171-73.

survival in LOZANA and her kind, she becomes instrumental in an
ingenious plan to forestall the impending attack :

> *(Entra, presuroso, en casa de la* LOZANA, *el* CANÓNIGO. *Viene
> disfrazado de mujer.)*
> LOZANA. — ¡Vaya vestimenta, señor!
> CANÓNIGO. — Por lo que veo, señora Lozana, como la de vues-
> tro criado. Soy canónigo, sí... y vengo en esta fecha porque ya no
> hay en toda Roma quien se atreva a salir en hábito de clérigo...
> que el Papa ha huido a Sant' Angelo y que un inmenso ejército
> de hambrientos y ladrones está invadiendo la ciudad por todas
> partes, y que por los clavos de Cristo, vos, señora Lozana, y miles
> de mujeres lindas y generosas como vos, podéis hacer que Roma...
> llave del cielo, cabeza de santidad... no sea del todo destruida por
> esos renegados.
> LOZANA. — ¿Qué nos queréis decir, señor canónigo?
> CANÓNIGO. — Señoras, son hombres los que vienen... Pienso
> que me entendéis... ¿Qué más bellos escudos que vuestras señorías?
> Me atrevo a aseguraros que es el alma de Roma la que os suplica
> ayuda en este trance. ¿Qué respondéis, señoras?
>
> (II, 75.)

As she successfully importunes her contingent of whores to rush
out and meet the invading armies, LOZANA soars to new heights
of fame and glory :

> LOZANA. — ¡Hermanas mías, sí...! ¡La que más y la que me-
> nos tenemos lo nuestro, ya sabéis, y todo lo demás...! Yo seré la
> primera, con estas damas que aquí véis, en distraer por nada a esos
> soldados, echándome con ellos si fuera menester, y vosotras debéis
> hacer lo mismo... Y ganaremos más salvando a Roma que murién-
> donos todas entre hedores y escombros...
>
> (II, 77.)

Then, as the protagonist reaches the *apogée* of her career, Alberti
inserts an element of tragic adversity into the sequence of events.
In a triumphal scene which recalls the guiñolesque processions of
the early farces, LOZANA is proclaimed victorious leader. At the
same time, we hear her calling plaintively for RAMPÍN, from whom
she has become separated in the confusion :

> CAPITÁN. — ¡Viva la reina de Roma!... ¡En procesión por toda
> la ciudad! ¡Vamos! ¡La Lozana primero!... ¡Y todo el mujerío
> con la tropa! *(Gran confusión y más algarabía. De la casa, sacan
> a* LOZANA... *levantándo[la] sobre unas andas formadas por los ar-
> cabuces. Los demás soldados alzan a las otras mujeres y hombres
> disfrazados...)*

LOZANA (*en medio del estruendo de los tambores, gritando, desgarrada*). — ¡Rampín! ¡Rampín! ¡Rampín!
CAPITÁN. — ¿Quién es ése, señora? ¡Adelante! ¡Adelante! ¡Adelante! ¡Viva la Lozana Andaluza!
SIETECÓÑICOS (*también llevado en alto, agitando su pandero*).
                    ¡Lozana, Lozana!
                    ¡Lozana, paloma!
                    ¡Dios te salve, reina!
                    ¡Dios te salve, Roma!

                                                (II, 81-82.)

As LOZANA's cries are heard mingling with the voices of the drunken revelers, the pathetic figure of the rogue appears amid the flames and crumbling towers of the besieged city:

> (*Aparece* RAMPÍN, *desgarrado y herido, rota la espada, colgándole algunos jirones de su disfraz... Trata de subir a la casa desierta y con todo derribado.*)
> RAMPÍN (*gritando, cayendo, levantándose*). — ¡Lozana! ¡Lozana! ¡Señora mía! ¡Señora mía!... (*Silencio. El cielo de Roma sigue ardiendo.*)

                                                (II, 82.)

Thus the lovers' journey finds its unfortunate issue at the same time that love is enshrined alongside its most illustrious advocate as the sole force capable of saving the universe. This ironic insistence on man's suffering and his capacity for regeneration enhances considerably the meaning of Delicado's text. LOZANA becomes «el símbolo de la intervención de lo inesperado en la solución de los conflictos» (II, 12). In the pathetic figure of the rogue, we have a familiar vision of man struggling vainly in opposition to superior forces. RAMPÍN's cries, the author tells us, «puede[n] corresponder a esa final y necesaria sed inextinguible del hombre de salvarse en el lucero de Venus» (II, 12).

The playwright's departures from Delicado's text can be understood largely in terms of the generic differences between theatre and the novel; they are a series of responses to the restrictions imposed by the nature of dramatic composition. The diffuse character of the novel and the lack of direct contact between narrator and reading public make a good deal of repetition permissible and often desirable in that genre. On the other hand, the relative brevity of drama and the immediacy of the theatrical experience militate in favor of a tighter structure, and render repetition unnecessary. This provides a justification for the omission of redundant material in Alberti's text. The novelist conveys a sensa-

tion of frenetic vitality through the helter-skelter accumulation of
a vast number of episodes ; the playwright had to condense before
he could attempt anything comparable. Nevertheless, the diverse
components of Delicado's work often fulfill several functions
simultaneously. Moreover, without a certain profusion of incidents
and occurrences, the 'proliferating effect' of any cumulative
technique is lost ; the elimination of some episodes from the novel
would have entailed the sacrifice of a desirable impression of
boisterousness and hilarity. Thus, Alberti wisely chose an alternate
means of pursuing his ideal of artistic unity. He modified the
meaning of several incidents so as to better accomodate them
within his more limited framework. A judicious sense of just how
far he could go without violating the integrity of the original
ensures Delicado's continuing role in the elaboration of the dramatic
text. At the same time, our author's reorganization of the
novelistic material accounts for the originality of his play.

We can best measure the pervasive effect of Alberti's modifi-
cations in the sequence involving the encounters with the MAESTRE-
SALA, MACERO and VALIJERO, and RAMPÍN's fall into the privy. As
we have observed, Delicado's rogue is a mere *pícaro* who earns
his livelihood by exploiting the amorous sentiments of whores.
Alberti transforms him into an enamoured adolescent whose
jealousy interferes with his desire for material gain. This added
dimension complicates the psychology of the character and renders
him more convincing. It also makes possible a more complex
relationship between the two lovers. First, RAMPÍN's jealous
behavior gives us reason to suspect that LOZANA's astuteness with
her three victims may not correspond wholly to a desire for profit ;
later, his unfortunate predicament provides her with the opportunity to confirm our suspicions. Following his misadventure, LOZANA
upbraids the bedraggled and infatuated youth, overtly sympathiz-
ing with him as well :

> RAMPÍN. — ¿Os pagó [el de la valija]?
> LOZANA *(haciendo sonar una bolsa que saca de la mesa)*. — La
> casa por seis meses y esa valija llena de ricos paños y algunas joyas.
> RAMPÍN. — Muy poco es, señora, para lo que valéis.
> LOZANA. — ¿Poco dices, Rampín?
> RAMPÍN. — Señora, sí, que una noche con vos no se paga ni
> con todo el oro del mundo. *(Llora disimuladamente.)*
> LOZANA. — ¿No estás contento, hijo?
> RAMPÍN. — Señora, sí.
> LOZANA. — ¿Lágrimas tienes?
> RAMPÍN. — Señora no...
> LOZANA. — Algo será, hijo. *(RAMPÍN calla.)* Dime. *(RAMPÍN*

calla. Enternecida.) Mira, ven acá, dolorido, que de aquí en adelante, pues sé cómo se baten las calderas, no quiero que de noche
duerma ninguno conmigo sino tú.

(II, 58.)

Ultimately this deeper and more subtle relationship makes possible
a dramatic climax. Alberti replaces the original portrait of LOZA-
NA with the more balanced image of two lovers gone abroad
together in search of good fortune. Thus he makes the threat of
separation into a potential source of dramaticity. In the final scene,
LOZANA appears as the agent who triumphantly sends her «escua-
drón de putas»—the forces of life and love—into battle against
the forces of destruction. By setting the poignant reality of the
lovers' plight against this humorous image, Alberti appeals
simultaneously to our sense of the comic and the tragic. In this
way he is able to fill a gap which presents no problems in the
novel, but would surely have been felt as such in the brief and
intense experience of a theatre audience.

The Renaissance cleric shared our author's liking for grotesque
caricature, scatological detail and cumulative techniques. Therefore, Alberti's favorite comic devices afforded a natural means of
rendering the imaginary world of the novel in theatrical terms. The
exuberant vitality of Delicado's characters materializes in abundant
movement, guiñolesque processions, exaggeratedly histrionic displays. The theatrical space of *La lozana andaluza* bears a marked
stylistic resemblance to that of Alberti's other social plays. This
stylistic continuity is especially apparent in the stage directions
of the dramatic text. On the one hand Alberti dictates a broad
scenographic emphasis on crowding and strident noises—*griterío,
estruendo de tambores, rebuznos, risotadas.* At the same time
the individual figures are distinguished by a preponderance of
clumsy staggering movements, disfiguring grimaces and wooden
gestures. An old whore named DIVICIA is successively envisioned
by the author as *derrengada y hecha una botarga... desplomán-
dose sobre la mesa... [dormida] como un pelele muerto y pinta-
rrajeado* (II, 64-65). This rag-doll like figure is typical of a host
of minor characters. A familiar function is likewise served by two
«farsantones rufianescos» who repeatedly cavort about the stage,
gesturing obscenely and reciting crude rhymes. Clearly they are
descended from the beggars of *De un momento a otro* and *El
adefesio:*

BADAJO.
¿Adónde va, señor Marzoco?

MARZOCO.
    ¿Adónde va, señor Badajo?
BADAJO.
    ¿Qué me cuenta?
MARZOCO.
    Que me desmoco.
BADAJO.
    Pues yo, señor, que me descuajo.
MARZOCO.
    Dicen que Roma está cercada
    y se avecina una gran guerra.
BADAJO.
    Por eso llevo aquí esta espada
    para metérsela a esa perra.
MARZOCO (*haciendo con la mano ademán de robar*).
    Pues yo, señor, voy de paseo
    por ver si encuentro algún trabajo...
BADAJO (*alzando la pata*).
    ¡Señor Marzoco, que me meo!
MARZOCO (*lo mismo*).
    ¡Que me meo, señor Badajo!
    (*Se van, cada uno por un lado.*)

                                            (II, 71-72.)

The presence of these popular types is intended primarily to create
an impression of boisterous hilarity. Like many of Alberti's
grotesque characters, they contribute to the density of the theatrical space rather than furthering the action.

    Another familiar feature of *La lozana andaluza* is the multiple
stage. Most of Alberti's sets for his work consist of several levels,
and afford a simultaneous view of one or more interiors and the
street:

> *Al fondo, panorama de Roma. En primer término, a la dere-*
> *cha, puerta lateral de la casa de las camiseras andaluzas. Al frente,*
> *sala, modesta, de la misma. A la izquierda, en diferente plano,*
> *puerta y habitación cerrada o a oscuras, de la TÍA de RAMPÍN. Más*
> *arriba, también cerrada, la tiendecilla de TRIGO, el prestamista. A*
> *ambos lados de la escena y a distintas alturas, ventanas. Escaleras*
> *o rampas, a modo de calles, que unan los diferentes planos de esta*
> *decoración.*

                                            (II, 20.)

This spatial arrangement results in a highly plastic image of
profuse activity and boundless energy. One can imagine a kind of
swarming effect as the characters scurry back and forth between
diverse planes and focal points of action, filling the stage with

their garbled language, raucous laughter and endless stream of activity. The crowding of *Noche de guerra* is combined with the sense of perpetual motion leading nowhere which distinguishes the scenography of *El adefesio*.

The creation of a theatrical space analogous to the imaginary world of a dialogued novel is difficult under any circumstances, since a dialogued novel lacks the narrative and descriptive passages on which the scenographer could otherwise rely. For Alberti in this instance, there existed an additional difficulty. All of the exuberance of Renaissance Rome is present in the speech of Delicado's characters. This had to be matched by a rich and vivid scenographic conception; otherwise, a serious imbalance between spectacle and spoken word would have resulted [12]. Alberti's success in approximating Delicado's vision is two-fold. His teeming and multifaceted world equals in density and dynamism the image which is projected through Delicado's dialogue. He has worked with the most familiar elements of his own comic technique. Yet he never exceeds the limits imposed by his desire to remain faithful to the original. The theatrical space of *La lozana andaluza* markedly resembles that of *El adefesio* and *Noche de guerra* in plasticity, tangibility and boisterousness. Nevertheless, its winsome vitality is more the product of Delicado's imagination than of Alberti's own.

Formally and thematically, *La lozana andaluza* bears a close relationship to *Noche de guerra*. The two works are joined by the apparently collaborative nature of the playwright's efforts. Moreover, they form a unit as the last of Alberti's social plays. In them, the author evidences a growing ability to dissociate caricature from ideological commentary. In 1956, his grotesque vision encompassed both degeneracy and vitality; by 1963, caricature bespeaks no negative judgement whatsoever. In Alberti's colorful and lively evocation of Renaissance Rome, grotesqueness connotes only vital impulse and never corruption. At this point in Alberti's career, caricature has become a form of pure esthetic contemplation. Thus, *La lozana andaluza* represents another step along the road which led him toward artistic independence.

* * *

In *Noche de guerra en el Museo del Prado* and *La lozana andaluza*, Alberti continues and carries to a logical conclusion the

12 This danger does not exist for example in the *Celestina*. Fernando de Rojas' imaginary world is broad and impressionistic in scope, but not as busy as Delicado's.

principal stylistic and thematic trends characteristic of his social plays. In both of these works there is a discernible shift away from the tendentious focus of the 1930s. The author's interests and concerns lead him towards a dramatically purer form of theatre, in which caricature is divested of its satirical function, and an esperpentic vision comes to dominate the fictional world. This change reflects a greater degree of critical detachment on Alberti's part ; it signals his apparent willingness to relegate ideological elements to a position of secondary importance. An analogous phenomenon can be observed in the allegorical sector of his opus when he abandons the didactic *auto sacramental* and turns his attention to the creation of myths. In both instances, we can construe a shift in emphasis as evidence that Alberti has gained a superior understanding of his role as dramatist.

Noche de guerra and *La lozana andaluza* are also unique among the social plays in that both are the results of 'collaboration'. Both works bear the unmistakeable stamp of Alberti's genius ; both are strongly rooted in the creative imagination of others. A certain painstaking attention to detail which is involved in the process of collaboration points to Alberti's artistic past—to his proverbial versatility as an imitator of styles, and his first clumsy attempts to make use of non-dramatic conventions in the theatre. However, the skillful syntheses which have resulted from his most recent efforts represent a new and significant development in his dramatic technique. Collaboration can be viewed within the conceptual framework of the 'style of multiplicity'. In these two plays as in the trilogy, the more expert craftsman appears to have abandoned a former tendency to flirt with a 'multiplicity of styles'. He has achieved a more careful integration of diverse esthetic components. Thus, the newest trend in Alberti's dramaturgy is not pure novelty ; it too is an outgrowth of the playwright's long years of experimentation with dramatic form.

CONCLUSION

ALBERTI'S THEATRE: ITS RELEVANCE AND REPERCUSSIONS

Scholars have barely begun to take cognizance of the dramatic works of several exiled writers. Alejandro Casona is commonly included in historical accounts of Spanish theatre. However, Fernando Arrabal is usually thought of only within the framework of the French Theatre of the Absurd. Pedro Salinas and Alberti continue to be regarded almost exclusively as poets. Max Aub is known primarily as a novelist. We hope it is clear that in at least one instance the generally accepted views are myopic.

In a letter to Marrast, Alberti spoke of «un teatro visto, y mi acercamiento a ese ser ideal que sería a la vez autor, director de escena, decorador y—¡oh sueño!—actor» [1]. His plays represent diverse attempts to attain this goal. In his mature works, he is clearly a man of the theatre. Though his early efforts are less successful, they are never frivolous or lacking in potential. All of Alberti's plays are original, varied, rich in poetic and dramatic elements. Without a doubt Pérez de Ayala would have considered them «serious theatre» [2]. This in itself is a sign of the playwright's significance. As we know, the Spanish stage has not had a surplus of 'serious authors'.

As we have noted, Alberti's plays and Lorca's reflect their respective modes of composition. While Lorca's genius flowed naturally and passionately toward the theatre, our author searched self-consciously and falteringly for a dramatic form. Even in his best works, Alberti was primarily a poet. Formal variety is a hallmark of his style. Thus, another important aspect of his theatre is its exemplary quality. Its evolution sheds light on some of the mysteries of the creative process.

The works with which we have been concerned span four decades

---

[1] Dated 2 May 1954.
[2] See Ramón Pérez de Ayala, *Las máscaras* (Madrid: Imprenta clásica española [c 1919]), I, 35-44.

of one of the most brilliant literary careers of the twentieth century. They partake of the playful and experimental tenor of the 1920s, echo the political and social consciousness of the 1930s and arise out of the anguished feeling of isolation that came with the exile. They are a meeting point of past and present, popular and learned elements, Spanish and European modes, *tradición y originalidad*. As a faithful representation of the author's circumstances, they are invaluable historical documents. They embody the preoccupations of a whole generation of Spanish artists and intellectuals. They exemplify the eclectic attitude of the poets of '27.

Throughout his career Alberti has carried on time-honored traditions of Spanish theatre. He has sought his inspiration in the *guiñol*, the *romancero*, the Classic authors. He has breathed new life into the *auto sacramental*. He has learned from Cervantes and the *prelopistas*. As early as 1931, his social theatre contains esperpentic elements. The local character and critical focus of *De un momento a otro* recall the longer works of Arniches. More recently he has translated into scenographic terms the works of Goya and Delicado.

Alberti's experiments antedate or coincide with those of his most illustrious contemporaries. At roughly the same time that Lorca wrote *Los títeres de cachiporra* and *Mariana Pineda* (1925), Alberti also became interested in balladry and puppet theatre. He was one of the first to profit from the lesson of Valle Inclán; the caricaturesque *militares* of his *Fermín Galán* may even have been inspired by those of *Los cuernos de Don Friolera* (1921). He revived the *sainete trágico* almost a decade before Buero Vallejo composed *Historia de una escalera* (1947). Combining Brecht's influence with the vision of Goya, he again anticipated Buero; *Noche de guerra* prefigures by fourteen years *El sueño de la razón* (1970). Alberti's role as innovator and reformer has not been recognized. He joins company with the leading figures of the modern Spanish stage. Like them, he has found the future in the past.

It is held by many literary historians that with the outbreak of the Civil War, Spanish cultural life came virtually to a halt. Supposedly Spain did not have a theatre between 1936 and 1947; the *première* of *Historia de una escalera* marked the end of a long hiatus. Yet in 1938-39, Alberti composed a play of markedly Spanish character and concerns. Between 1940 and 1945, he wrote two works which clearly derive from the poetic theatre of the Golden Age. His *El adefesio* (1944) has been described as «la única obra que en el teatro español pueda parangonarse en cuanto estética de la irrisión con el teatro de Valle Inclán» [3]. In other words, certain of Alberti's works provide a continuity which has thus far gone unnoticed. Thanks to his efforts' the traditions of Spanish theatre lived on uninterrupted.

Most chroniclers of the Spanish stage persist wrongly in regarding Alberti as a rebel—a mere *valor de escándalo*. As a youth he contributed significantly to its revitalization; in his maturity he has helped to sustain it from afar. Unfortunately his case is similar to that of a number of distinguished Spaniards. The theatre of most of the exiled writers has for too long been overlooked. By according Alberti the credit due him as a playwright, we should like also to have benefited these others. Perhaps now more scholars will extend their gaze beyond the geographic confines of the Iberian peninsula. We look forward to the time when our study will be one among many. In our estimation, an entire chapter in the history of contemporary Spanish letters needs to be revised.

---

[3] Guerrero Zamora, *op. cit.*, p. 103.

SELECTED LIST OF WORKS CONSULTED

1. Primary Sources

Alberti, Rafael. *Abierto a todas horas (1960-1963)*. [Madrid]: Aguado, [1964].

—. *La arboleda perdida: libros I y II de memorias*. Buenos Aires: Fabril, [c 1959].

—. *La arboleda perdida y otras prosas*. Mexico: Ed. Séneca, [1942]. Contains «Una historia de Ibiza», «La miliciana del Tajo», «Las palmeras se hielan».

—. «Autocrítica: *El hombre deshabitado*». *ABC*, 19 Feb. 1931.

—. *Bazar de la Providencia (negocio); dos farsas revolucionarias*. Madrid: Ed. Octubre, 1934. Contains *Farsa de los Reyes Magos*.

—. *Canciones del Alto Valle del Aniene y otros versos y prosas (1967-1972)*. Buenos Aires: Losada, [c 1972].

—. *De un momento a otro; Cantata de los héroes y la fraternidad de los pueblos; Vida bilingüe de un refugiado español en Francia*. [Buenos Aires]: Bajel, [1942].

—. *El enamorado y la muerte (escenificación de un viejo romance)*. Contained in «Una obra escénica inédita de Rafael Alberti». Introduction by Manuel Bayo. *Revista de Occidente*, 128 (Nov. 1973), 151-58.

—. *Fermín Galán*. [Madrid]: [Chulilla y Angel], 1931.

—. *El hombre deshabitado*. Madrid: Gama, 1930.

—. «Jóvenes itinerarios de España: Rafael Alberti». *La Gaceta Literaria*, 1 Jan. 1929.

—. «*Lope de Vega y la poesía contemporánea*» seguido de «*La Pájara Pinta*». Prologue by Robert Marrast. Paris: Centre de Recherches de l'Institute d'Etudes Hispaniques, [c 1964].

—. *Los ocho nombres de Picasso y no digo más que lo que no digo*. Barcelona: Kairos, 1970.

—. *Poemas escénicos: 1.ª serie (1961-1962)*. [Buenos Aires]: Losada, 1962.

—. *La poesía popular en la lírica española contemporánea*. Leipzig: Wilhelm Gronau, 1933.

—. *Poesías completas*. Edited by Horacio Becco. Buenos Aires: Losada, [1961].

—. *El poeta en la calle: poesía civil (1931-1965)*. Paris: [Ed. de la Librairie du Globe], 1966.

—. *El poeta en la España de 1931 seguido del Romancero de Fermín Galán y los sublevados de Jaca*. Buenos Aires: P.H.A.C., [1942].

—. *Primera imagen de...* *(1940-1944)*. Buenos Aires: Losada, [c 1945].
—. *Prosas encontradas (1924-1925)*. Edited by Robert Marrast. [Madrid] · Ed. Ayuso, [1970].
—. *Radio Sevilla*. *El Mono Azul*, No. 45 (May 1938), pp. 6-8
—. *Roma, peligro para caminantes*. Mexico. Mortiz, [1968].
—. *Teatro*. 2 vols. Buenos Aires: Losada, [c 1950-1964]. Vol. I contains: *El hombre deshabitado, El trébol florido, El adefesio, La Gallarda*. Vol. II contains: *La lozana andaluza, De un momento a otro, Noche de guerra en el Museo del Prado*.
—. «Teatro de urgencia», *Boletín de Orientación Teatral*, 15 Feb. 1938, p. 5.
— and Pérez Domenech, José. «Rafael Alberti dice que la burguesía tiene el teatro que se merece», *El Imparcial*, 23 April 1933.
Cervantes Saavedra, Miguel de. *Numancia*. Adaptación de Rafael Alberti. Madrid: Signo, 1937.
—. *Numancia*. Versión modernizada por Rafael Alberti. [Buenos Aires]: Losada, 1943.
Farsa del licenciado Pathelin. Translated by Rafael Alberti. *Sur*, 10 (March, April, May 1941).

2. *Secondary Sources*

Altolaguirre, Manuel. «Nuestro teatro». *Hora de España*, 9 Sept. 1937, pp. 29-34.
Aparicio, Antonio. «El teatro en nuestro ejército». *Comisario*, No. 4, Dec. 1937, pp. 42-50.
Aub, Max. «Acerca del teatro: carta a un actor viejo». *Boletín de Orientación Teatral*, 1 June 1938, pp. 5-6.
—. «Prólogo acerca del teatro español de los años '20 de este siglo». *Cuadernos Americanos*, 24, No. 140, 194-210.
Bowra, C. M. *The Creative Experiment*. London: Macmillan, 1949.
Bravo Villasante, Carmen. *Historia de la literatura infantil española*. 2 vols. [Madrid]: Doncel, 1963.
Calderón de la Barca, Pedro. *Autos sacramentales*. Vol. III of *Obras completas*. Edited by Angel Valbuena Prat. Madrid: Aguilar, 1952.
Cardwell, Richard A. «Rafael Alberti's *El hombre deshabitado*». *Iberoromansch* (München) 2, 122-33.
Cernuda, Luis. *Estudios sobre poesía española contemporánea*. Madrid: Guadarrama, [1957].
Cervantes Saavedra, Miguel de. *Entremeses*. Clásicos Castellanos. Madrid: Espasa-Calpe, [1962].
Chabás, Juan. *Literatura española contemporánea: 1898-1950*. La Habana: Cultural, 1952.
Cipliauskaité, Biruté. *La soledad y la poesía española contemporánea*. Madrid: Insula, 1962.
Connell, Geoffrey W. «The Autobiographical Element in *Sobre los ángeles*». *Bulletin of Hispanic Studies*, 40 (July 1963), 160-73.

—. «The End of a Quest: Alberti's *Sermones y moradas* and Three Uncollected Poems». *Hispanic Review*, 33 (July 1965), 290-309.

—, trans. «Introduction» to *Concerning the Angels*, by Rafael Alberti. London: Rapp & Carroll, [c 1967].

—. «A Recurring Theme in the Poetry of Rafael Alberti». *Renaissance and Modern Studies*, 3 (1959), 95-110.

Corrales Egea, José. «Notas sobre la temporada teatral». *Insula*, 19 (July-Aug. 1964), 6.

Cossío, José María de. *Los toros en la poesía*. Buenos Aires: Espasa-Calpe, [1944].

Couffon, Claude, ed. *Rafael Alberti*. Collection «Poètes d'aujourd'hui». [Paris]: Seghers, [c 1966].

Cueva, Jorge de la. «En el Español: *Fermín Galán*». Review of *Fermín Galán*. *Informaciones*, 2 June 1931.

—. «[Review of] *El hombre deshabitado*». *El Debate*, 27 Feb. 1931.

Debicki, Andrew P. *Estudios sobre poesía española contemporánea*. Madrid: Gredos, [1968].

Déhennin, Elsa. *La résurgence de Góngora et la génération poétique de 1927*. Paris: Didier, 1962.

Delicado, Francisco. *La lozana andaluza*. Edition and prologue by Antonio Vilanova. Barcelona: Selecciones Bibliófilas, 1952.

Díez-Canedo, Enrique. «[Review of] *Fermín Galán* de Rafael Alberti». *El Sol*, 2 June 1931.

—. «[Review of] *El hombre deshabitado* por Rafael Alberti». *El Sol*, 27 Feb. 1931.

—. *El teatro español de 1941 a 1963: artículos de crítica teatral*. 4 vols. Mexico: Mortiz, [1968].

Domenech, Ricardo. «Introducción al teatro de Rafael Alberti», *Cuadernos Hispanoamericanos*, 259 (January 1972), pp. 96-126.

Doreste, Ventura. «Sobre el teatro de Alberti». *Papeles de Son Armandans*, 30, 80-90.

Durán, Agustín. *Romancero general*. Biblioteca de Autores Españoles. Vols. 10, 16. Madrid: Imprenta de los Sucesores de Hernando, 1924.

Durán, Manuel. «El surrealismo en el teatro de Lorca y Alberti». *Hispanófila*, 1 (1957), 61-66.

Eichelbaum, Samuel. «[Review of] *El adefesio*». *Sur*, 14 (July 1944), 100-102.

Espina, Antonio. «[Review of] *Fermín Galán*». *Crisol*, 1 June 1931, p. 5.

Esslin, Martin. *Brecht: the Man and his Work*. New York: Doubleday, [1961].

Fernández Almagro, Melchor. «Estreno de *El hombre deshabitado*, en la Zarzuela». Review of *El hombre deshabitado*. *La Voz*, 27 Feb. 1931.

—. «[Review of] *Fermín Galán*, en el teatro Español». *La Voz*, 2 June 1931.

Fevralski, A. «Farsy Rafael Alberti». («The Farces of Rafael Alberti».) *Literaturnaya Gazeta*, No. 122 (12 Sept. 1934), p. 3.

Fuente, Pablo de la. «Alberti en su rincón». *Insula*, 18 (May 1963), 15.

—. «Rafael Alberti en Roma». *Seara Nova*, 44 (June 1965), 180-81.

García Lorca, Federico. *Obras completas*. 4th ed. Madrid: Aguilar, 1960.

Gómez de la Serna, Ramón. *Ismos*. Buenos Aires: Poseidon, [c. 1943].

González López, Emilio. «[On] *El adefesio*». *Revista Hispánica Moderna*, 11 (1945), 71-72.

González Martín, Jerónimo Pablo. «Alberti y la pintura». *Insula*, 28 (April 1972), 1+.

—. «Rafael Alberti en Antícoli». *Insula*, 25 (May 1970), 3.

Gourfinkel, Nina. «La politique théâtrale russe et le réalisme». *Le théâtre moderne: hommes et tendances*. Edited by Jean Jacquot. 2nd ed. Paris: C. N. R. S., 1965.

Gravier, Maurice. «Les héros du drame expressioniste». *Le théâtre moderne: hommes et tendances*. Edited by Jean Jacquot. 2nd ed. Paris: C.N.R.S., 1965.

Guerrero Zamora, Juan. *Historia del teatro contemporáneo*. 4 vols. Barcelona: Juan Flors, 1962.

Guimarães, Fernando. «Alguns aspectos do teatro de Rafael Alberti ou o homen sustituido pelos mitos». *Estrada Larga* (Porto), 1962, pp. 679-83.

Gullón, Ricardo. «Alegrías y sombras de Rafael Alberti: primer momento». *Insula*, 18 (May 1963), 1+.

—. «Alegrías y sombras de Rafael Alberti: segundo momento». *Asomante*, 21, No. 1, 27-36 and No. 2, 22-35.

—. «Realidad del esperpento». *Insula*, 23 (April 1968), 1+.

Hernández-Catá, A. «El chaleco de Gauthier y el 'jersey' de Alberti». Review of *El hombre deshabitado*. *Ahora*, 6 May 1931, p. 10.

Ilie, Paul. *The Surrealist Mode in Spanish Literature*. Ann Arbor: Univ. of Mich. Press, [c 1968].

Jiménez, Juan Ramón. *Españoles de tres mundos*. Madrid: Aguado, [1960].

Junqueiro, Guerra. *A velhice do padre eterno*. Porto: Livraria Chardron, [n.d.].

Lafuente Ferrari, Enrique. *Los desastres de la guerra*. Barcelona: Inst Amatller de Arte Hispánico, 1907.

León, María Teresa. «La guerra, el teatro, la revolución y la industria». *Boletín de Orientación Teatral*, 1 March 1938, pp. 2-5.

—. *Juego limpio*. Buenos Aires: Goyanarte, [1959].

—. *Memoria de la melancolía*. Buenos Aires: Losada, [1970].

Lima, Robert. *The Theatre of García Lorca*. New York: Las Américas, 1963.

Lope de Vega Carpio, Félix. *Santa Casilda. Obras de Lope de Vega*. Vol. II. Madrid: Real Academia, 1916.

López-Rey, José. *Goya's Caprichos*. Princeton: Princeton Univ. Press, 1953.

Marrast, Robert. *Aspects du théâtre de Rafael Alberti*. Paris: Société d'Editions d'Enseignement Supérieure, 1967.

—. «Essai de bibliographie de Rafael Alberti». *Bulletin Hispanique*, 57 (1955), 147-77.

—. «Essai de bibliographie de Rafael Alberti (addenda et corrigenda)». *Bulletin Hispanique*, 59 (1957), 430-35.

—. «L'esthétique théâtrale de Rafael Alberti». *La mise en scène des oeuvres du passé.* Edited by Jean Jacquot and André Veinstein. Paris: C.N.R.S,. 1957.

—. *Miguel de Cervantès: dramaturge.* [Paris]: L'arche, [c 1957].

—. «Situation du théâtre espagnol contemporain». *Théâtre Populaire,* No. 13 (1955), pp. 15-23.

—. «Le théâtre à Madrid pendant la guerre civile». *Le théâtre moderne: hommes et tendances.* Edited by Jean Jacquot. 2nd ed. Paris: C.N.R.S., 1965.

—. *Le théâtre de Rafael Alberti.* Unpublished Mémoire de Diplome d'Etudes Supérieures, University of Bordeaux, 1954.

—. «Théâtres nationaux: l'Espagne. Les grands dramaturges de la république». *Histoire des spectacles.* [Paris]: [Gallimard], [c 1965].

—. «Tradiciones populares en *El adefesio».* *Insula,* 18 (May 1963), 7.

Menéndez Pidal, Ramón de. *Flor nueva de romances viejos.* Madrid: Espasa-Calpe, 1959.

Monterde, Alberto. «Inquietudes y medievalismo en la poesía de Rafael Alberti». *Revista de la Universidad de México,* 9 (Sept.-Oct. 1964), 8-11.

Moreno Villa, José. *Vida en claro.* [Mexico]: Colegio de México, [1944].

Morris, Cyril B. *A Generation of Spanish Poets (1920-1936).* London: Cambridge Univ. Press, 1969.

—. «Las imágenes claves de *Sobre los ángeles».* *Insula,* 18 (May 1963), 12

—. «Parallel Imagery in Quevedo and Alberti». *Bulletin of Hispanic Studies,* 36 (July 1959), 135-45.

—. *Rafael Alberti's «Sobre los ángeles»: Four major Themes.* [Hull]: Univ. of Hull, 1966.

—. «*Sobre los ángeles:* A Poet's Apostasy». *Bulletin of Hispanic Studies,* 37 (Oct. 1960), 222-31.

Murcia, Juan Ignacio. «Aboutissants du grand guignol dans le théâtre d'essai en Espagne». *Le théâtre moderne: hommes et tendances.* Edited by Jean Jacquot. 2nd ed. Paris: C.N.R.S., 1965.

Palacios, Leopoldo E. «Anotaciones a *El hombre deshabitado».* *La Gaceta Literaria,* 15 March 1931, p. 5.

Pérez, Carlos A. «Rafael Alberti: sobre los tontos». *Revista Hispánica Moderna,* 32 (1966), 206-16.

Pérez de Ayala, Ramón. *Las máscaras,* 2 vols. Madrid: [Imprenta clásica española], [c 1919].

Pérez Minik, Domingo. «Itinerario patético de una generación de dramaturgos españoles». *Insula,* 20 (July-Aug. 1965), 3 +.

—. *Teatro contemporáneo europeo: su libertad y compromiso.* Madrid: [Guadarrama], 1961.

Prieto, Gregorio. «Arboleda encontrada de una adolescencia perdida». *Papeles de Son Armadans,* 30, 129-42.

Proll, Eric. «'Popularismo' and 'Barroquismo' in the Poetry of Rafael Alberti». *Bulletin of Spanish Studies,* 19 (Jan.-April 1942), 59-86.

—. «The Surrealist Element in Rafael Alberti». *Bulletin of Spanish Studies,* 18 (April 1941), 70-82.

Puccini, Darío, ed. *Le Romancero de la résistance espagnole: anthologie poétique bilingue.* Paris: Maspero, 1962.

Puchy de Morales, Carlos. «Rafael Alberti y *El adefesio*». *Quaderni Ibero-Americani*, 2 (June 1953), 366-67.
Rodríguez Marín, Francisco. *Cantos populares españoles*. 5 vols. Sevilla: F. Alvarez, 1882-1883.
Rodríguez Richart, J. «Entre renovación y tradición: direcciones principales del teatro español actual». *Boletín de la Biblioteca de Menéndez y Pelayo*, 41 (1965), 383-418.
Rouanet, Léo, ed. *Colección de autos, farsas y coloquios del siglo XVI*. 4 vols. Madrid: Biblioteca Hispánica, 1901.
Ruiz Ramón, Francisco. *Historia del teatro español siglo XX*. Madrid: Alianza, [1971].
Salinas, Pedro. *Literatura española siglo veinte*. Mexico. Séneca, [1944].
Salinas de Marichal, Solita. *El mundo poético de Rafael Alberti*. Madrid: Gredos, [1968].
—. «Los paraísos perdidos de Rafael Alberti». *Insula*, 18 (May 1963), 4+.
Sánchez, Roberto G. *García Lorca: estudio sobre su teatro*. Madrid: [Jura], 1950.
S[ánchez] B[arbudo], A[ntonio]. «[Review of] *Los salvadores de España* de Rafael Alberti». *El Mono Azul*, 22 Oct. 1936.
—. «[Review of] la *Santa Casilda* de Rafael Alberti». *ABC*, 27 Jan. 1931, p. 36.
Sassone, Felipe. «La opinión de ...¿un podrido?» Review of *El hombre deshabitado*. *ABC*, 12 March 1931, pp. 23-24.
Soldevila Durante, Ignacio. «Sobre el teatro español de los últimos veinticinco años». *Cuadernos Americanos*, 22 (1963), 256-89.
Ter Horst, R. «The Angelic Prehistory of *Sobre los ángeles*». *Modern Language Notes*, 81 (1966), 174-94.
Tirso de Molina. *Los lagos de San Vicente. Obras dramáticas completas*. Edited by Blanca de los Ríos. Vol. II. Madrid: Aguilar, 1952.
—. *La venganza de Tamar. Obras dramáticas completas*. Edited by Blanca de los Ríos. Vol. III. Madrid: Aguilar, 1958.
Torre, Guillermo de. *Historia de las literaturas de vanguardia*. Madrid: Guadarrama, [c 1965].
—. *¿Qué es el superrealismo?* [Buenos Aires]: Columba, [1955].
Torrente Ballester, Gonzalo. *Literatura española contemporánea*, 2 vols. Madrid: Guadarrama, [1963].
—. *Teatro español contemporáneo*. 2nd ed. Madrid: Guadarrama, 1968.
Valbuena Prat, Angel. *Historia del teatro español*. Barcelona: Noguer, [c 1956].
Vivanco, Luis Felipe. *Introducción a la poesía española contemporánea*. Madrid: Guadarrama, [1957].
Wardropper, Bruce. *Introducción al teatro religioso del Siglo de Oro*. Madrid: Revista de Occidente, [1953].
Zardoya, Concha. *Poesía española contemporánea*. Madrid: Guadarrama, [1961].

Colección Támesis

SERIE A — MONOGRAFÍAS

III.   *Teatros y comedias en Madrid: 1600-1650.* Estudio y documentos. By
        J. E. Varey and N. D. Shergold, pp. 195.
IV.   *Teatros y comedias en Madrid: 1651-1665.* Estudio y documentos. By
        J. E. Varey and N. D. Shergold, pp. 258.
V.   *Teatros y comedias en Madrid: 1666-1687.* Estudio y documentos. By
        J. E. Varey and N. D. Shergold, pp. 206.
VI.   *Teatros y comedias en Madrid: 1688-1699.* Estudio y documentos. By
        J. E. Varey and N. D. Shergold, *Forthcoming.*
VII. *Los títeres y otras diversiones populares de Madrid: 1758-1840.* Estudio
        y documentos. By J. E. Varey, with 17 illustrations.

SERIE D — REPRODUCCIONES EN FACSÍMIL

I.   CAYETANO ALBERTO DE LA BARRERA Y LEIRADO: *Catálogo bibliográfico
        y biográfico del teatro antiguo español, desde sus orígenes hasta me-
        diados del siglo XVIII* (Madrid, 1860), pp. xi+727.